Forecasting Oracle Performance

Craig Shallahamer

⟨**IOUG**⟩
Independent oracle users group

Apress®

Forecasting Oracle Performance

ISBN 978-1-59059-802-3 [*Originally published as a hardcover first edition on April 20, 2007.*]

ISBN 978-1-4302-4293-2

ISBN 978-1-4302-4294-9 (eBook)

President and Publisher: Paul Manning
Lead Editor: Jonathan Gennick
Technical Reviewers: Jody Alkema, Tim Gorman, and Jared Still
Editorial Board: Steve Anglin, Mark Beckner, Ewan Buckingham, Gary Cornell, Morgan Ertel, Jonathan Gennick, Jonathan Hassell, Robert Hutchinson, Michelle Lowman, James Markham, Matthew Moodie, Jeff Olson, Jeffrey Pepper, Douglas Pundick, Ben Renow-Clarke, Dominic Shakeshaft, Gwenan Spearing, Matt Wade, Tom Welsh
Coordinating Editor: Richard Dal Porto
Copy Editor: Marilyn Smith
Compositor: Kinetic Publishing Services, LLC
Indexer: John Collin
Cover Designer: Anna Ishchenko

Distributed to the book trade worldwide by Springer Science+Business Media New York, 233 Spring Street, 6th Floor, New York, NY 10013. Phone 1-800-SPRINGER, fax (201) 348-4505, e-mail orders-ny@springer-sbm.com, or visit www.springeronline.com.

For information on translations, please e-mail rights@apress.com, or visit www.apress.com.

Apress and friends of ED books may be purchased in bulk for academic, corporate, or promotional use. eBook versions and licenses are also available for most titles. For more information, reference our Special Bulk Sales–eBook Licensing web page at www.apress.com/bulk-sales.

Any source code or other supplementary materials referenced by the author in this text is available to readers at www.apress.com. For detailed information about how to locate your book's source code, go to www.apress.com/source-code/.

Sometimes the wind blows
the majestic across my face.
And when I open my eyes,
I see wonders
of truth, of depth,
and mysteries
unveiled.

About IOUG Press

IOUG Press is a joint effort by the **Independent Oracle Users Group (the IOUG)** and **Apress** to deliver some of the highest-quality content possible on Oracle Database and related topics. The IOUG is the world's leading, independent organization for professional users of Oracle products. Apress is a leading, independent technical publisher known for developing high-quality, no-fluff content for serious technology professionals. The IOUG and Apress have joined forces in IOUG Press to provide the best content and publishing opportunities to working professionals who use Oracle products.

Our shared goals include:

- Developing content with excellence
- Helping working professionals to succeed
- Providing authoring and reviewing opportunities
- Networking and raising the profiles of authors and readers

To learn more about Apress, visit our website at **www.apress.com**. Follow the link for IOUG Press to see the great content that is now available on a wide range of topics that matter to those in Oracle's technology sphere.

Visit **www.ioug.org** to learn more about the Independent Oracle Users Group and its mission. Consider joining if you haven't already. Review the many benefits at www.ioug.org/join. Become a member. Get involved with peers. Boost your career.

www.ioug.org/join

Apress

Contents at a Glance

Contents

About the Author

CRAIG SHALLAHAMER has more than 18 years of experience working in Oracle, empowering others to maximize their Oracle investment, efficiencies, and performance. In addition to being a consultant, researcher, writer, and keynote speaker at Oracle conferences, he is the designer and developer of OraPub's Advanced Reactive Performance Management and Forecasting Oracle Performance classes. He is also the architect of Hori-Zone, OraPub's service-level management product.

Prior to founding OraPub in 1998, Craig served for nine years at Oracle Corporation as one of the company's leading system performance experts. At Oracle, he cofounded a number of leading performance groups, including the Core Technologies Group and the System Performance Group. His love for teaching has allowed him to personally train thousands of DBAs in fifteen countries on five continents.

When not maximizing efficiency, Craig is fly fishing, praying, backpacking, playing guitar, or just relaxing around a fire.

About the Technical Reviewers

With a passion for emerging technology and smart software, **JODY ALKEMA** is a software developer who specializes in network and database programming. As Technical Lead for the development of OraPub's HoriZone, Jody lends his expertise to this book as technical editor. He currently works as a programmer analyst for Raymond James Ltd., a full-service investment dealer. Jody lives near Vancouver, B.C., with his wife and two daughters.

TIM GORMAN has worked with relational databases since 1984, as an Oracle application developer since 1990, and as an Oracle DBA since 1993. He is an independent contractor (www.EvDBT.com) specializing in performance tuning, database administration (particularly high availability), PL/SQL development, and data warehousing. Tim has been an active member of the Rocky Mountain Oracle Users Group (www.rmoug.org) since 1992. He has coauthored three books: *Oracle8 Data Warehousing*, *Essential Oracle8i Data Warehousing* (both published by Wiley) and *Oracle Insights: Tales of the Oak Table* (Apress). Additionally, Tim has taught classes in the Americas and Europe, and has presented at conferences in the Americas, Europe, and Australia.

JARED STILL is a senior DBA at RadiSys Corporation, with several years of experience as both a production and development Oracle DBA. He has successfully used Craig Shallahamer's performance forecasting methods on past projects, and has keenly anticipated the publication of this book. While Jared enjoys exploring the world of databases and the process of turning data into information, he sometimes takes time to pursue other endeavors that get him away from the computer monitor, such as auto racing.

Introduction

Contained in this book are, dare I say, secrets—really. There is a mystery surrounding topics like forecasting, performance management, capacity planning, performance modeling, performance prediction, and managing service levels. Add into the mix a dynamic Oracle system, and you have realities that bring professional capacity planners to their knees. In the pages of this book are the secrets I've uncovered and discovered through more than 20 years of working with literally thousands of IT professionals around the world. My goal is to expose these secrets as plainly and completely as I possibly can.

One of these secrets is unraveling the relationship between service-level management and forecasting Oracle performance. The difficulty lies in the breadth and depth of each of these topics. They are both massive and fork off in a variety of directions. If you are able to bring the two together, you will be able to architect, build, use, and explain to others how they can better manage the delivery of IT services. I will, as clearly as I can throughout this book, present both these areas of IT and then weave them together. The result will leave you with a confident understanding so you can deal with the realities of IT.

At some level, every IT professional (DBA, IT manager, capacity planner, system integrator, and developer) must understand forecasting concepts. Have you ever talked with someone about weather forecasting who does not understand barometric pressure? Just last week, I was talking with a prospective customer (a technical manager) and he asked, "How can you know when performance is going to get bad?" He had no understanding of basic queuing theory, modeling, or the capabilities and limitations of performance forecasting. Before I could answer his question, I had to step way, way back and quickly teach him about fundamental performance management. What compounds my frustration with conversations like these is that someone in his position (technical management) should have a solid understanding of performance management. Reading this book will prevent you from being on the "no understanding" side of that conversation.

Performance forecasting is just plain fun. Seeing into the future is amazing and touches on something very deep in each one of us. Whether forecasting the weather, a company's performance, our work, or response time, we just can't stop trying to predict what is going to happen. So don't fight it. Learn how to forecast performance in a way that adds value to your company and to your career.

Why Buy This Book?

Every capacity planning book I have read leaves me with an uncomfortable feeling. They do not leave me prepared, equipped, and trained to deal with reality. I feel like the authors are in love with mathematics,[1] want to convince me that they are a genius, have to publish a book to keep their professorship, live in a laboratory with little or no responsibilities dealing with Oracle, do not have even a basic understanding of Oracle architecture, certainly do not have to deal with the realities of a complex Oracle environment, and truly believe that management is pleased with statements like, "Our models indicate average CPU utilization will hit 75% in about three months." If you have felt the same way, then buy this book now! My goal is to teach you about real-world Oracle performance forecasting—period. There is no hidden agenda.

Oracle systems are dynamic and contain a wide variety of transactions types. This makes Oracle forecasting notoriously difficult. In fact, if you read books or listen to people speaking about forecasting, it doesn't take long to figure out that Oracle makes their life very difficult. In the past, transactions were clearly defined and forecasting statistics were a part of the operating system. Traditional capacity planners never had it so good. There was little or no caching, delayed block cleanouts, or simultaneous writing of multiple transactions to disk. The idea of writing uncommitted data to disk would send shivers up spines. While times have changed, performance must still be forecasted.

This book is obviously Oracle-focused. I will teach you how to flourish with the complexities of forecasting performance in a dynamic and highly complex Oracle environment. But be warned, this book is not about laboratory or academic forecasting. The solutions to real problems are sometimes kind of gritty and may seem like you're compromising academic purity. If you want to responsibly deal with reality, then this book is for you.

What makes seasoned IT professionals run for cover? Forecasting Oracle performance! While this is a complex topic, it can be very satisfying, very practical, and very valuable to both you and your company. As you read this book, I hope you discover a newfound enthusiasm while forecasting Oracle performance.

What Is the Value to Me?

Within 60 minutes, you will be able to forecast performance and identify risk on you production Oracle database server. I kid you not. Just jump to Chapter 3 and scan the chapter, and you'll be ready to go! Obviously, there is more—a lot more. But value does not suddenly appear after spending hours reading, studying, and practicing. This book is structured so you get value fast, and then get increased value as you study the material.

Forecasting Oracle performance can be incredibly complex. The topics covered in this book and how they are presented are completely focused on making this complex topic as simple as possible to understand and apply. It's all about making the complex simple.

---

1. Latin *mathematica* was a plural noun, which is why mathematics has an "s" at the end, even though we use it as a singular noun. Latin had taken the word from Greek *mathematikos*, which in turn was based on *mathesis*. That word, which was also borrowed into English but is now archaic, meant "mental discipline" or "learning," especially mathematical learning. The Indo-European root is *mendh*, "to learn." Plato believed no one could be considered educated without learning mathematics. A *polymath* is a person who has learned many things, not just mathematics.

This book will lead you and teach you. While my company does sell Oracle-oriented service-level management products, they are not the focus of this book. That gives me tremendous freedom to focus on you, the reader. By focusing on you, I can provide the information you need. There is no need for mathematical derivations and ruminations. What you need is field-tested, Oracle-focused, and practical. And that's exactly what you'll get.

This book is a kind of training course. After reading, studying, and practicing the material covered in this book, you will be able to confidently, responsibly, and professionally forecast performance and system capacity in a wide variety of real-life situations. You will learn how to use a variety of forecasting models, which will enable you to methodically:

- Help manage service levels from a business value perspective.

- Identify the risk of overutilized resources.

- Predict which component of the architecture is at risk.

- Predict when the system will be at risk.

- Develop multiple risk mitigation strategies to ensure service levels are maintained.

If you are more management-minded (or want to be), you will be delighted with the material about service-level management. Forecasting performance is just one aspect of service-level management. Separating the two is absolutely absurd. The reason we forecast is to help manage service levels. Understanding service-level management helps you understand how forecasting-related work can provide company value.

This book is about equipping. Without a doubt, you will be equipped to deal with the realities of forecasting Oracle performance. But this book gives you more. Not only will you receive a technical and mathematical perspective, but also a communication, a presentation, and a management perspective. This is career-building stuff and immensely satisfying!

Who Will Benefit?

So many people from a variety of backgrounds need to know about this information, it's difficult to pinpoint just who will benefit. But when pressed for a list of those who will most likely benefit, I would have to say DBAs, IT managers, capacity planners, systems integrators, and developers.

If you're a DBA, you know what it's like to be asked on Friday at 4:30 p.m., "On Monday, we're adding those employees from that acquisition to our system. That's not going to be a problem, is it?" This book will allow you confidently and responsibly answer this question and many like it.

If you're an IT manager who absolutely must manage service levels, you know how difficult it is to determine if significant risk exists, what the risk is, when the risk will occur, and what can be done to mitigate the risk. This book will provide you and your employees with the knowledge, the methods, and the skills to effectively manage risk. What you'll receive is a group of excited employees who will build a service-level management system.

If you're a full-time capacity planner, you know that database optimization features are great for Oracle users, but they're also your worst nightmare. Characterizing even the simplest Oracle workload can be daunting and leave you with an uncomfortable feeling in your gut. This book will teach you just enough about Oracle internals and how to pull from Oracle what you need to develop responsible forecast models.

If you're a systems integrator, you need to work with the DBA, IT manager, capacity planner, and developer. You need to help them understand how their systems work together, how to manage performance, and how to optimize performance while minimizing risk and downtime. You are their service-level counselor. This book will give you the hands-on practical insight that truly provides value to your customers.

Most people don't think that developers care about forecasting performance, not to mention performance optimization. But I think the problem is more of a result of management's focus and the pressure managers apply. Developers want to write good code. And good code means code that delivers service amazingly well. But when management heaps on specifications, the release schedule tightens, and only data from emp, dept, and bonus tables is available, service levels will undoubtedly be breached. Deep down, everyone knows this. If you are a developer, the information contained in this book will allow you to better communicate with your management and give you a new perspective into the world of IT. I promise you, your management will take notice.

How This Book Is Organized

I think you get the idea that I want to teach and equip. This book is structured to this end. We'll start at a high level, focusing on service-level management and the essentials for forecasting, and then work our way deeper into using specific forecasting models.

Here is a quick summary of each chapter:

Chapter 1, "Introduction to Performance Forecasting," sets the stage for the entire book. We will focus on the nontechnical areas of forecasting, such as service-level management, risk, and the broad model types. You'll find out why forecasting Oracle performance haunts the seasoned capacity planner. In this chapter, you'll learn what your company needs from forecasting and where the value resides. If you want to be a techno-forecasting-freak, then you might want to skip this chapter. But if you want to truly add value to your company and enhance your career, this chapter will be invaluable.

Chapter 2, "Essential Performance Forecasting," focuses on the key concepts, how they fit together, how they are modeled, and how this works in an Oracle environment. This chapter is the transition from thinking *management* to thinking *technical*. It begins linking Oracle into traditional forecasting techniques.

Chapter 3, "Increasing Forecast Precision," takes the essentials and brings into the mix some of the complexities of forecasting. Fortunately, there are ways to address these complexities. This chapter is important because, many times, a low-precision forecast will not meet your requirements. I'll present ways to increase forecast precision by selecting the appropriate forecast model, choosing the right workload activity, and calculating the deceptively simple term *average*. Along the way, you'll learn some additional technical tidbits.

Chapter 4, "Basic Forecasting Statistics," will protect you and free you. After reading this chapter, you will never casually say, "It will take 3 seconds." You will be able to communicate both the specifics and the meaning of statements like these, without your head coming to a point.

Chapter 5, "Practical Queuing Theory," covers one very important component of forecasting. Because performance is not linear, you must have a good, basic grasp of queuing theory. If you have been bored to death, felt overwhelmed, or just don't see what all the fuss is about, I think you'll appreciate this chapter. Leaving math derivations behind, we focus on the meaning and how to use queuing theory.

Chapter 6, "Methodically Forecasting Performance," is important for successful and consistent forecasting. I present a six-step process that will embrace the natural scientific nature of forecasting, validate the precision of your forecast models, and allow you to explain to others how you structure your work—all without suffocating your creativeness.

Chapter 7, "Characterizing the Workload," is about transforming raw workload data into something we can understand, is useful to us, and is also appropriate for forecast model input. Oracle workloads are notoriously complicated. As a result, the task of grouping—that is, characterizing the workload—can be very difficult. The trick is to create a workload model that embraces the application, Oracle, and the operating system, while respecting their uniqueness, and considers their interaction. When done well, it allows for amazing forecasting flexibility and precision. In this chapter, I will lead you through the process of characterizing a complex Oracle workload.

Chapter 8, "Ratio Modeling," allows you to perform very quick low-precision forecasts. Ratio modeling is absolutely brilliant for architectural discussions, vendor recommendation sanity checks, and sizing of packaged applications. For the laboratory scientist, ratio modeling can be uncomfortable, but for the hands-on Oracle forecasting practitioner, it's beautiful.

Chapter 9, "Linear Regression Modeling," is one of my favorite forecasting techniques. Modeling systems using regression analysis is easy to do and can be automated without much effort. It is statistically sound and incredibly precise. However, this technique can be easily misused, leading to disastrous results. To mitigate this risk, I'll present a rigorous method to ensure regression analysis is being used appropriately.

Chapter 10, "Scalability" is one of those things we wish we didn't have to deal with. Most forecasting modeling techniques do not internally address scalability issues. This means we must do some additional work to ensure a robust forecast. In this chapter, I will present four proven scalability techniques, how to pick the best scalability model for your situation, and how to integrate scalability limitations in your forecasting.

What Notations Are Used?

Table 1 shows the notation used in this book for numbers. Decimal, scientific, and floating-point notation are all used where appropriate.

Table 1. *Numeric Notations Used in This Book*

Decimal	Scientific	Floating Point
1,000,000	1.0×10^6	$1.000E + 06$
0.000001	1.0×10^{-6}	$1.000E - 06$

Units of time are abbreviated as shown in Table 2.

Table 2. *Abbreviations for Units of Time*

Abbreviation	Unit	Scientific Notation
hr	Hour	3600 s
min	Minute	60 s
sec	Second	1.0 s
ms	Millisecond	1.0×10^{-3} s
μs	Microsecond	1.0×10^{-6} s
ns	Nanosecond	1.0×10^{-9} s

The units of digital (binary) capacity are as shown in Table 3. The corresponding units of throughput are, for example, KB/s, MB/s, GB/s, and TB/s.

Table 3. *Abbreviations for Units of Binary Capacity*

Symbol	Unit	Decimal Equivalent	Power of 2 Equivalent
B	Byte	8 bits	2^3 bits
KB	Kilobyte	1,024 bytes	2^{10} bits
MB	Megabyte	1,048,576 bytes	2^{20} bytes
GB	Gigabyte	1,073,741,824 bytes	2^{30} bytes
TB	Terabyte	1.0995116×10^{12} bytes	2^{40} bytes

Table 4 gives an alphabetized list of symbols used in this book. A word of caution: For most symbols, there is no formal standard. This makes relating formulas from one book to another sometimes very confusing. I have tried to keep the symbols straightforward, in line with the standard when there appears to be a standard, and consistent throughout the book.

Table 4. *Mathematical Symbols Summary*

Symbol	Represents	Example
trx	Transaction	10 trx
λ	Arrival rate	10 trx/s
S_t	Service time	1 s/trx
Q_t	Queue time or wait time	0.120 se/trx
R_t	Response time	1.12 s/trx
Q	Queue length	0.24 trx
U	Utilization or percent busy	0.833 or 83.3%
M	Number of servers	12 CPUs or 450 IO devices
m	Number of servers per queue	12 CPUs, or 1 for IO subsystems

What Is Not Covered?

The more work I do, the more respect I have for scope. There are many topics that are "out of scope," and therefore are not covered or are not covered in depth in this book.

Performance optimization (tuning) is not covered. This includes the many areas of Oracle performance optimization such as instance tuning, wait event analysis, latching, locking, concurrency, and so on. When these areas relate to modeling and scalability, they will be mentioned, but they certainly are not our focus. Oracle response time analysis (which includes a focused analysis of Oracle's *wait times*) relates to forecasting, but is a more reactive, performance management-focused topic. When I mention *response time* in this book, as you will quickly learn, I am not referring to *Oracle* response time analysis.

Some people would like nothing else than to get a nice hot cup of coffee, sit in a cozy chair next to a fire, and study mathematics. Even a phrase like "the mathematical treatments of probability and queuing theory" brings a level of deep satisfaction. This book is not written for these people. This book is about facing and conquering the brutal realities of managing service levels through Oracle forecasting. While mathematics is a significant part of this, mathematical derivations will only distract, defuse, and distance you from your objectives.

Operating system-level memory forecasting is not covered. Low-precision memory forecasts are very straightforward, and high-precision memory forecasts are so packed full of risk I don't go near them. Individual physical disk-level forecasting is not covered. The complexities of modern-day IO subsystems make drilling down to the physical disk with any degree of responsible precision nearly impossible. Fortunately for us, it is extremely unusual that forecasting performance of specific physical devices would be practical and worth anyone's time (in our area of work). However, we will cover how to model and forecast groups of physical disks (think of RAID arrays, volumes, filers, and so on) with a very satisfactory degree of precision.

While I will contrast the differences between benchmarks (stress tests of any kind) and mathematical modeling, benchmarks are not our focus. Keep in mind that when benchmarking, the workload must still be characterized. So if you are benchmark-focused, in addition to the foundational chapters, the chapter about workload characterization (Chapter 7) will be valuable.

This book focuses squarely on the Oracle database server. When mathematical references are made to response time, they specifically refer to the time from/to the Oracle database server machine to/from the Oracle client process. This book does not attempt for forecast true end-to-end response time—that is, from the database server to the end user's experience. However, all the topics presented in this book can be applied to the other computers in your computing environment, not just the Oracle database server. There will surely need to be some modifications, but you should not have any problems making those adjustments.

CHAPTER 1

■ ■ ■

Introduction to Performance Forecasting

It's not just about numbers, and it certainly is not just for geeks. While forecasting is attractive to the more technically minded, the consequences of forecasting impact nearly every human being. All of our friends and all of our families step out into the world each day equipped with the results of multiple forecasts. The classic is the weather forecast. Don't we all look outside when we wake up? Don't we take a quick look at the weather page (online or offline)? It's something we do without thinking, and it would seem strange—even unnatural—not to have a clue about the day's weather.

Just like a weather forecast, the most valuable forecasts seem natural, normal, and in a way, hidden or unnoticed. We don't expect to be impressed by some big mathematical marvel. Rather, it's just part of our existence. When forecasting becomes embedded in our lives, you can be sure that forecasting is adding real value. Why? Because the focus is not on the forecast but on the forecast result: the weather, the stock market, interest rates, political elections, service-level management, and so on.

What is so fascinating to me is that every person loves to forecast. Now they won't tell you that, but they do . . . nearly every minute of every day. Before you step outside in the morning, you take a quick look up into the sky and at the trees to make a quick weather forecast. If you are driving, you make millions of predictions! You predict the person next to you is not going to merge into your lane, but just in case they do, you plan how you would react. When you approach an intersection and the light is green, you predict that no one will run the red light and crash into you. But you may also quickly perform some risk mitigating permutations, just in case someone does run the light. I could go on and on, but as you can see, forecasting is deeply entrenched into each one of us. In fact, it's just not us who needs forecasting. It's broader than that. The world needs forecasting, and it needs people who can do forecasting.

Forecasting and risk assessment go hand in hand. If you want to assess risk and all the information is not before you, you must forecast. Anticipating risk through forecasting provides yourself, your family, your company, your country, and our world with information to avoid disasters.

The bigger the impact of something bad happening, the more value forecasting provides. For example, what's the impact of a Windows PC locking up on you? Well, it's inconvenient, but you've learned to live with it. But what's the impact of a Category Five hurricane? People can die. Because people can die, the forecast value dramatically increases, and people suddenly care strongly about forecasting. In fact, they care so much that governments invest heavily in developing and using forecasting to avert massive disasters.

Is there a significant risk impact when implementing a new business application on a 64 CPU HP Superdome using Oracle Database 10g Enterprise Edition with a combined cost in the multiple millions? You bet! This is when forecasting's value skyrockets. It would be foolish to implement a system like this without forecasting to ensure (at some level of comfort) service levels will be met. Not forecasting in situations like these is what I like to call a "career decision."

With IT-related forecasting, our focus tends to be related to answering these questions:

- Does significant risk exist?

- What is at risk?

- When will the risk occur?

- What can we do to mitigate the risk?

Short-term risk assessment is relatively straightforward. It's like looking into the sky to forecast the weather for the next few hours. But don't expect a reliable ten-day forecast without some additional complexity! When systems are dynamic and we forecast far out into the future, forecast complexity will undoubtedly increase. To keep risk to an acceptable minimum, various forecast methods and models will be needed to suit the wide variety of situations in which we find ourselves.

Hurricanes, tornadoes, earthquakes, and Oracle-based systems are full of risk. And because people's lives are intertwined with these potential disasters, forecasting absolutely must occur. With the exception of Oracle-based systems, I think most people would say forecasting has come a long way over the past couple of decades. My hope is that the application of what is contained in this book will help bring a little more respect to forecasting Oracle performance. But that will not happen until forecasting becomes commonplace and something people don't consciously think about . . . like looking up into the sky.

Risk: A Four-Letter Word

Question: What is equally unsettling to a manager who hears someone yell, "Fire!" It's someone who says, "We've got some risk here, and it's significant." A manager doesn't need an exclamation point to start feeling like it's going to be a long day. Managers are trained to identify (hopefully early) and mitigate risk. A good manager knows what risk looks like and knows how to deal with it. A bad manager thinks risk is a board game by Parker Brothers.

I was involved in a capacity-planning project where usage of the word *risk* was closely guarded. We found out early on in the project that the word *risk* carried so much baggage and fear that we should only use terms like *significant risk*, *no significant risk*, or my favorite, *poses no significant risk to the project's success*. Notice the word *risk* was always qualified so managers could better frame the risk situation. Equally entertaining to me was that the word *failure* was never, under any circumstances, to be used. It was acceptable to say, "There exists significant risk to the project's success" but never "There exists significant risk the project may fail." As you can see, management lives and dies by appropriately identifying and artfully dealing with risk.

Risk management implies identification and mitigation. If you cannot identify risk, then you cannot mitigate risk. Initially, forecasting is focused on exposing and identifying where risk resides, how significant the risk is, and when it will likely occur. Not addressing the identified risk is like telling someone there is a small fire in their house, but not telling them where it is—criminal. Mitigating something you have not identified is futile. Once the risk is understood, your effort shifts to focusing on developing strategies to mitigate the identified risk. Identification and mitigation are two separate terms and operations, yet must harmoniously exist for forecasting to bring value to your company.

Much of your forecasting time will be focused on gaining a clear understanding of risk and what to do about it. This may sound simple, but it's not. It can take quite a while to develop strategies to mitigate risk that are politically, financially, and responsibly sound. Risk management is vital; it is an integral part of and a central theme in service-level management.

Service-Level Management

The worldwide IT infrastructure market is in the billions of US dollars.[1] It is that important. A significant part of managing an IT infrastructure is managing the level of service it provides.

Service-level management (SLM) is a very broad and powerful term. It encompasses just about everything we do in IT. SLM is the primary management of IT services, ensuring the agreed-upon services are delivered when and where they are supposed to be delivered. If the services are not delivered as agreed, it can be like a hurricane—devastating.

More than ever, companies live and die by how well IT delivers. It is not uncommon to meet people working for a company whose entire existence is based on IT. If their systems are down, so is the company. So crucial is SLM that companies will spend billions of dollars ensuring IT delivers on its promises.

If you are a developer or a database administrator, SLM is probably not something you think about often. Sure, you are thinking about performance, writing optimal SQL, and tuning Oracle, but the concept of managing "services" seems somewhat abstract and not quite precise enough. It is important for your company and for your career to widen your thinking and the way you speak about performance. Start thinking about how what you are doing affects the service your users will experience. And start thinking about how this service can be measured, monitored, and improved.

SLM focuses on value. *Value* is one of the words that seem somewhat intangible and not precise enough. But if you focus on the return on your investment (ROI), or what your business gains from the service you are providing, you will be thinking in value terms. Here are some examples to contrast the differences between thinking technically versus thinking in value terms:

---

1. According to the IDC study, "Worldwide Distributed System Management Software 2005–2009 Forecast and 2004 Vendor Shares," the worldwide distributed system management software market achieved revenue of $5.54 billion in 2004 and is forecast to grow to $8.99 billion in 2009, an increase of 62.3% for the period. IDC defines the worldwide system management software market as "including those software tools that are routinely used in IT operations or by end users to manage system and application resources." IDC defines the distributed system management software as the portion of system management software used to manage systems and applications for distributed operating environments, principally Unix, Windows, and Linux.

Technical	Value
This query completes in less then two seconds! I'm a flipping genius!	We can now process 500 more customer calls each hour. As a result, we can reduce our call center head count by 50%, saving us $500,000 each year.
Our upgraded order-entry system is incredible!	We can enter orders twice as fast, saving our company 200 hours each day in order-entry-related costs.
We can now do hot backups!	Now our business can operate 24 hours each day. This allows us to bring on an additional shift, which will increase our manufacturing capacity by 15%, resulting in a 10% revenue increase.

SLM focuses on processes such as reviewing existing services, negotiating with customers, producing and monitoring the service-level agreements (SLAs), implementing service improvement policies and processes, establishing priorities, planning for growth, and the involvement in the accounting process. This stuff bores a technician to death. But to those responsible for IT operations and its future existence, it is life everlasting.

The processes of SLM can be grouped into four management areas:

Capacity management: Ensures the infrastructure is adequate to provide services at the right time, at the right volume, and at the right price. There is a definite focus on efficiency; that is, minimizing cost while maximizing service. As you might imagine, capacity management relies on performance and workload monitoring, application sizing, forecasting, and performance modeling. Forecasting Oracle performance is most closely aligned with capacity management.

Continuity management: Focuses on ensuring IT can recover and continue operations should a fault occur. This is not simply about backup and recovery. The focus is the process, the plans, and their implementation. For example, continuity management involves prioritizing the processes to be recovered and performing a risk assessment for each IT service to identify the risks, threats, vulnerabilities, and countermeasures. Also included are evaluating recovery options, producing a contingency plan, and ensuring the plan actually works and is kept up-to-date.

Availability management: Focuses on identifying availability requirements and mapping those to service levels. The objective is to leave no service level unmeasured and undefined to enable SLA measurement and compliance. Areas to focus on are reliability, recoverability, maintainability, resilience, and security. For example, the production database availability SLA may require the database to be available 24 hours a day, Monday through Friday. The availability manager says we must devise a method to measure the database availability to ensure it operates within the defined service levels.

IT financial management: Focuses on ensuring the IT infrastructure is obtained at the most cost-effective price while meeting service levels. Those involved or contributing to this management area will be very familiar with cost benefit analysis (CBA) and ROI analysis. All of IT is included: equipment, software (operating system, database, tools, business applications, and infrastructure software), organization (staff labor), facilities, and outsourced operations (such as human resources activities). Capacity, continuity, and availability management all feed into IT financial management.

Personally, growing up in IT focusing on Oracle database management, the whole concept, process, and implementation of SLM has been overwhelming. I simply could not get my hands around it. I was not trained to be a manager of people and organizations. I was trained to be a manager of data and to effectively communicate. Over the years, and in particular as the result of bringing an SLM product to the market, I have learned (more like had forced down my throat) to view value in terms of service to a company—not to myself or even to my users, but to the company. You and I might not like what all this may imply, but the reality is that companies employ us because they must provide their customers with certain specific values and their hope is we can help in this process. In exchange for our services, they compensate us in a variety of ways that we must deem acceptable.

Our forecasting work must feed directly into the management of service levels. In fact, SLM should drive and provide focus for our forecasting-related projects. If you are a hard-core technology person, this can be difficult. I suspect that most of you reading this book have this kind of background, so throughout this book, I have taken extra care in helping you demonstrate the value of what you are doing and how that can support SLM-related initiatives. If our forecasting work does not support the management of service levels, then eventually its shrouded value will be unveiled to show a pure technical exercise, and our efforts will be put to an uncomfortable halt. Performance forecasting provides an opportunity for technologists to provide a significant value to their company—much more value than just simply performing a technical exercise and forwarding the answer to someone.

Modeling: Making the Complex Simple

The world is much too complex for us to understand. To compensate, we create models to simplify the world around us, turning it into something we can comprehend. Models help us understand our world. When focused on a specific area in which the scope is very limited, a model can teach, expose, describe, reveal, and draw out the understanding we may desperately need. Modeling is all about making the complex simple.

Models are designed to be very focused and limited. This allows them to reveal to us what we need to know, while at the same time not address the other areas of complexity. For example, consider a paper airplane. Although it's extremely simple to construct and examine, it can help teach us about basic aerodynamics. But like all models, it has a very focused and limited use. That same paper airplane will not teach us about landing gear or traveling at supersonic speeds. To learn about these things, a different model is required. In our work, we may choose a ratio model to forecast batch processing load, while choosing queuing theory to forecast online transaction processing (OLTP) load. The trick is to match the requirements with the model.

SLM requires models in many different areas. IT financial management will have, at a minimum, cost benefit and ROI models. Capacity management will have resource forecasting models (like the ones I will present in this book). Any time a forecast (financial, CPU utilization, workload activity, or stock price) is made, it is based on a model. Modeling is central for all forms of forecasting.

I like to say that models are an abstraction of reality. From paper airplanes to supermodels, they are not real but an abstraction. One of the dangers to those of us deeply involved with modeling is believing that our models are real. This may seem strange, but after spending weeks developing a forecasting system, you can start to get a little strange. People who suggest or hint that your model is not perfect will rub you the wrong way. So please, remember that models are not reality. They are not perfect, cannot be expected to be perfect, and are not designed to be perfect. It would be foolish to think what a model says will absolutely 100% occur. Even proprietary forecast models are not perfect—close, but not perfect.

Have you ever seen hurricane path forecasts? They usually contain many different forecast models, all created for the sole purpose of forecasting where a hurricane will travel. But notice that no two models forecast the exact same path! That's because each path is based on a forecasting model. Even the best models are not perfect, because nature, life, and computer systems are so very complex.

Don't be impressed by seemingly complex models. Just because a model is complex does not mean it produces more value. For example, adding independent values to a regression formula typically reduces the forecast precision. On the flip side, a simple model may not have the wherewithal to provide the insight you need and to grapple with real system complexities. A model car is not going to show you how fast your real car can take a turn without sliding off the road. The perfect model is one that allows you to understand something you need to understand with minimal cost and effort.

Models are central to managing service levels and to forecasting Oracle performance. Contained in this book are some very simple to some fairly complex models. As you'll come to understand, picking the right model for the right job is crucial.

Model Types

Models come in all shapes and sizes. When forecasting Oracle performance, you need to be comfortable using a wide variety of mathematical models. Each model has a natural affinity to certain types of forecasting. For example, regression analysis may work wonderfully when you want to determine the maximum number of orders your system can handle. But add to that question a hardware configuration change, and you'll need a different model.

Most of us tend to gravitate toward certain models. Some people really like to use ratio modeling; some are dangerously fanatical about queuing theory. Don't be like the new Oracle DBA who goes to a conference, listens to a presentation on latch contention, and then upon return, proclaims that Oracle is suffering from significant latch contention. Take the time to understand, appreciate, and use a wide variety of models. Knowing which model to use in a variety of circumstances greatly increases your forecasting prowess.

There are three fundamental model types; mathematical, benchmark, and simulation. For sure, there are other forecasting models available. But these broad model categories will cover our work nicely, not leave gaping holes, and prepare us to assimilate other models when necessary.

Mathematical Models

Mathematical models are fast, flexible, portable, and therefore extremely useful. They are also the focus of this book! While the underlying math can be complicated (but as you'll see in upcoming chapters, it does not have to be), once developed, the models typically run in under a second. Flexibility is important when forecasting Oracle performance. It seems like no two projects are the same, and you'll need the flexibility and portability to modify an existing model. Most mathematical models can be implemented in a spreadsheet or in a third-generation programming language.

In this book, I'll present many mathematical forecasting models. We'll cover basic forecasting math, how to improve on the basics, ratio modeling, queuing theory, and regression analysis. This will equip you to forecast in a wide variety of situations.

Someone once asked me to forecast the performance improvement if he upgraded his Oracle database. Another person asked me which Oracle latch would raise its ugly head first. I told them both the same thing: "The closer you get to Oracle's internal and proprietary algorithms, the less useful a mathematical model becomes." While a mathematical model can forecast a variety of things, implementing algorithmic details is usually beyond the scope of our knowledge, time, money, and sanity. In fact, many algorithmic details are proprietary and simply not meant for us to know. When you need to see what specifically will break, you need to benchmark.

Benchmark Models

Benchmarking gets a lot of good press because that's what MBAs and project managers are taught. At the same time, these folks tend to loathe mathematical models, even though they use them heavily in financial analyses . . . go figure. Many implementation processes require some type of performance assurance test to be performed. When project schedules and budgets get tight, the project manager will retreat to what is the most comfortable and seemingly the lowest risk.

A benchmark is a model because it simplifies something complex, highlighting areas we want to study. As explained in the "Differences Between Benchmarks and Simulations" section, a benchmark is not a true simulation because it runs the system it is studying.

The beauty of a benchmark is it is a copy of the real system and therefore will behave exactly like the real system. This is true until the benchmark deviates from the real system, which is nearly always the case. When this occurs, all sorts of problems can occur. If a benchmark fails (and many do), it is probably due to the workload. You must spend a great deal of time, energy, and money to get the workload correct for a benchmark to be meaningful. The scary thing about a bogus benchmark is that most people don't know it's bogus until the real system is placed into production. By then, it's too late.

The other problem is benchmarks contain physical computing components. Depending on the benchmark scope and architectural complexity, it can take a prohibitive amount of time to physically construct the system, load the initial data, warm up the benchmark, finally run the benchmark, and then repeat this for each scenario. Doing this many times can take what seems like forever.

While there are many negatives surrounding benchmarks, a benchmark has the potential to provide the most precise forecast of any model.

Simulation Models

I like to say a simulation is a *living* forecast model. Simulations are very different from mathematical equation-based models like regression analysis or queuing theory. With simulations, the solution is not solved or evaluated. With simulation, we create a controlled environment where artificial transactions are placed into the system. The transactions work their way through the system just like real transactions in a real system. The beauty of simulation is that the model is instrumented to closely observe and record transaction activity. To find out how the real system would react to certain changes, we can introduce these changes into our model and run the simulation. When the simulation is complete, the data is analyzed, and we can learn a lot about the real or proposed system.

Nearly every scientific discipline embraces simulation: manufacturing floor layout, managerial staffing decisions, chemical engineering, civil engineering, nuclear physics, mathematical research, computer games (think SimCity)—the list goes on and on. Simulation is fascinating. It can include eye-popping graphics, produce a plethora of statistical data, and be incredibly precise. However, it can also take a long time to complete a single forecast and, in many cases, be practically impossible to construct.

Usually when forecasting computer system activity, mathematical equations and benchmarks work just fine. But sometimes a mathematical solution is impossible given the current state of mathematics and the complexities of what we are trying to model. In these situations, simulation may offer a reasonable alternative. If we insist that all forecasts must be solved mathematically, we may find ourselves oversimplifying or overabstracting the system so that it can be mathematically solved in order to come up with a mathematical solution. This can sacrifice precision and result in bogus forecasts. Simulation enables us to forecast what may be mathematically impossible or mathematically inappropriate.

Not too long ago, simulation had to be performed by hand or using handheld calculators. This made running even a single simulation very time-consuming and expensive. This, combined with the model callibration process, prohibited the use of many simulation models. However, the world is not as it was. The introduction of grid computing (by BigBlueRiver, www.bigblueriver.com) provides massive computing power at a relatively low cost. As a result, I suspect we will see a rise in simulation modeling in the coming years.

What prohibits Oracle forecasting using simulation is model construction time and the time required to run a single simulation. Callibration of a simulation model requires thousands of iterations, and when identifying risk, we typically run hundreds of forecasts. Even a single simulation can take a few minutes to complete on a standard office PC. And, of course, there is the cost of the simulation software. Unless you are creating a professional forecasting product or have access to a lot of computing power, using simulation for forecasting Oracle performance just doesn't make good sense.

Differences Between Benchmarks and Simulations

There are significant differences between a simulation and a benchmark. And calling a benchmark a simulation will cause communication confusion with both IT and just about every scientific community.

A simulation program does not run on what is being studied. For example, during a nuclear physics simulation, actual atoms are not split. Traffic simulations are not run on the highway, but rather inside a computer. This is in stark contrast to a benchmark, where the benchmark is actually running Oracle, the software application, and the operating system on particular hardware.

When I started creating Oracle load generators, I used to say I was simulating an Oracle load. I had a rude awakening when I begin looking for *simulation* books. I quickly discovered there is a massive industry and field of study whose focus is squarely on true simulation. And it had absolutely nothing to do with my *Oracle simulations*. In fact, I felt a little embarrassed at being so presumptions by calling my load generator a simulation. As I begin to learn, study, and actually write simulation programs,[2] it became clear that Oracle benchmarks and simulations

---

2. OraPub's SLM product, HoriZone (www.horizone.orapub.com), sometimes uses simulation models to forecast Oracle performance. Creating the simulation program to specifically forecast Oracle performance brought about a whole new level of respect for the simulation community. Simulation programs can be incredibly complex. Calling an Oracle benchmark a simulation is like calling a bicycle an automobile.

where two distinct industries and topics. While they have a common goal, how they are constructed, run, and analyzed are very different.

To avoid confusion and not offend those in the simulation industry, I started using the words *synthetically loaded system* to describe a benchmark. While I admit it sounds strange, especially when talking to a group of Oracle-centric folks, it certainly differentiates the two models and eliminates any confusion.

NEURAL NETWORK MODELS

To me, neural networks are the most fascinating models of all. However, I have yet to find an appropriate Oracle-centric application of neural networks.

Just what is a neural network? A *neuron* is a relatively simple biological cell, and we have a lot of them in our brains. An artificial neuron is the simple mathematical equivalent. Each neuron can be connected to many other neurons. When a neuron receives energy, it holds the energy until it reaches a threshold, and then releases the energy to all the neurons to which it's connected. The same thing happens to all the neurons in the network, resulting in a type of cascade reaction. By specifically manipulating and controlling a neuron's threshold activity in conjunction with the network architecture, a neural network can hold an amazing amount of information.

Neural networks are terrific at recognizing patterns. They will beat any other model in recognizing a known pattern. However, if the neural network has never seen the pattern, then it essentially guesses. And guessing is not good when forecasting Oracle performance. I have spent untold hours working with neural networks, heard academics speak on the subject, and conversed with an author on the subject. I have yet to hear of a neural network that can forecast Oracle performance. However, proprietary forecasting models do sometimes incorporate aspects of neural network technology.

Challenges in Forecasting Oracle Performance

No one knows better how difficult it is to do a good job forecasting Oracle performance than traditional mainframe capacity planners. A few years ago, I attended a major capacity planning conference. During one of the presentations, the speaker was describing an architecture. When he mentioned the word "database," there was a slight grumbling in the room, and you could feel the angst. Being an Oracle person, I was starting to feel a little uncomfortable. The speaker continued and all was well. But later, he mentioned the word "Oracle." Even the speaker grumbled, and the entire room joined in. At this point, I quickly located the nearest exit. I am not exaggerating, and I was perplexed.

After my escape, I spent some time ruminating as to why people whose lives are dedicated to capacity planning did not embrace the elegance of an Oracle database. Then it occurred to me: capacity planners like transactions and their characteristics very well organized and well defined. (That's why I had never got much out of capacity planning books: they didn't address the complexities of an Oracle system.) Oracle transactions and their resulting workloads are very difficult to characterize, enumerate, and understand.

One of the Oracle database's selling points is its speed. This incredible speed is the result of years of research and development focused on *optimization*. Optimization makes Oracle fast, but blurs resource usage responsibility and accountability. For example, Oracle uses caching to reduce physical input/output (IO) for future transactions, utilizes complex transaction concurrency algorithms, and groups multiple data-block changes into a single physical write.

When caching and batch-writing algorithms are used, Oracle is faced with a daunting resource assignment challenge. For example, suppose three sessions change a single cached database block and a fourth session reads the cached block. (Which triggers the cached block to be physically written to disk.) How should the resource usage be assigned? Oracle could divide the IO activity equally between the four sessions, or it could simply assign the IO to the last session. And consider this unfortunate fact: the more perfect resource assignment becomes, the more resources are consumed to determine the resource assignment.

Ultimately, a resource assignment decision must be made. Oracle typically assigns resources to sessions for the code they run and operating system resources they consume, regardless of whether the session is also doing work caused by other sessions. The hope is, with a little abstraction, the error will not be significant. So while resource-sharing strategies can yield improved performance and high concurrency, perfectly assigning responsibility for every activity is impossible.

The job of measuring, understanding, and developing mathematical representations of something that is constantly changing is just plain difficult, if not impossible. For an Oracle system, application activity constantly changes. In fact, computer software application usage changes by the second. Computer hardware components (such as CPU and memory) are frequently upgraded and therefore change. Change also makes a perfect (even a near perfect) workload measurement impossible. To represent these complexities, we must abstract.

Oracle transaction resource requirements fluctuate wildly. You must be very careful in determining, for example, the average CPU time it takes to service a transaction. For example, querying a customer may consume between 500 to 5,000 milliseconds of CPU time. This average is, you guessed it, a method of abstraction.

We talk a lot about the "transaction." This word is probably on just about every page in this book, and nearly every forecast model uses the word *transaction*. But what is a transaction? Unfortunately, there are many accepted definitions for this word. The definition of an Oracle database transaction is different from the definition of a business transaction. An aspect of forecasting is communicating a workload in ways that a person can easily grasp. A person can easily understand a business transaction. For example, the entry of a single order may be considered a business transaction. However, an Oracle transaction is a well-defined technical term.[3] Oracle transactional information, which must be queried from the Oracle database, may have no meaningful relationship to the business. So once again, we must generalize—that is, abstract to better communicate.

Database optimization, transaction resource variance, change of all kinds, and basic word definition challenges all contribute to make typical Oracle workloads very complex and difficult to enumerate. Some people will tell you that the required abstraction is far too great to enable any reasonable forecast. But those of us who are responsible for service levels can't simply say, "It's too hard. Let's buy tons more hardware!"

Reasonable forecasts can be made and are made all the time. In fact, an entire industry is dedicated to forecasting performance. If reasonable forecasts are not possible, then these companies are surely liable and operating with an unethical intent. Every responsible forecast contains steps to validate precision. If the precision is not acceptable, then the model is not used. My personal experiences have shown that forecasting can produce very reasonable forecasts. A reasonable forecast does not imply a high-precision forecast (less then 5% error),

---

3. An Oracle transaction begins when data changes and ends with either a `commit` or a `rollback`. There is no implied relationship with the business.

although sometimes this is required. The bottom line is this: if validated forecasts are within the acceptable precision tolerance, then forecasting is fulfilling a vital IT service.

These challenges are some of the reasons you don't see many good Oracle forecasting products on the market. What most people typically do is significantly abstract the workload while retaining the relevant aspects of the workload. This process is called *workload character-ization*, and I've devoted an entire chapter (Chapter 7) to the subject.

With these challenges, it's no wonder that the conference speaker grumbled when he uttered the word "Oracle." Forecasting can be very frustrating sometimes. But challenges also present opportunity! Sure, you have to be creative and a little gutsy, but it can be done. No matter what people say, it is possible for you to responsibly forecast Oracle performance in a wide variety of real-word situations using a variety of forecasting models. I'll lead you through this process over the remaining chapters of this book. We'll take it a step a time, starting with the essentials and then building some very powerful forecasting techniques.

## CHAPTER 2

Essential Performance Forecasting

Forecasting is like walking. You need to learn, and the sooner the better. Everyone in IT needs to know the essentials of forecasting performance, and the sooner the better. I would wager that at least once every day, you get asked a forecasting-related question. It may not be in the traditional form, or the question may be rhetorical, but it is still a forecasting question. How many times has your manager walked by your office late Friday afternoon and sheepishly asked you something like, "Well, ah . . . all those users from that company we acquired are going to start using our applications next week. That's not going to be a problem is it? OK. See ya." You're left with this knot in your stomach, and your weekend just got a lot shorter. We all need the ability to quickly forecast performance. Identifying future performance problems and developing risk mitigation strategies are an essential IT professional skill.

As you'll discover, you don't have to be a math whiz to forecast Oracle performance. All it takes is some basic knowledge and a little time. This chapter will provide you with enough information to immediately begin forecasting performance. The forecasts won't be very precise and may not be all that useful (but they may be). However, the process you go through, the mathematics you use, and the skills you'll learn, when appropriately applied, will provide value to your career and your company.

The Computing System Is Alive

It may seem strange at first, almost eerie, but a computing system is, in a way, alive. Its dynamic nature, its need for energy, and its need for guidelines are all characteristics of the living. We have these same characteristics, as does the Earth's water cycle or a honeybee colony. When we view a computing system as dynamic, in flux, and constantly changing, we begin to see past the equations. Sure, equations help us forecast, but equations can never fully capture the complexities of a computing system, just as equations can never fully capture the complexities of a living system. But we can abstract and model these complexities.

Let's take a closer look at a honeybee colony. Honeybee colonies are fascinating. If you stand back and watch a colony, you would swear there is a master honeybee quietly governing the colony. The master honeybee would be assigning and coordinating tasks to ensure the hive lives long and prospers. The other bees are all living for the survival of the colony, each dedicated to performing specific tasks, and each willing to sacrifice for the good of the community. How else could the colony exhibit such complex behavior? You would not only think there is a master bee controlling everything, but that the bees have a deep desire for community, communication, and relationship.

But on closer inspection, this is not the case—not even close. Each bee is bred for specific tasks and reacts predictably based on a number of stimuli. There are drone bees, worker bees, and the queen bees. For example, the worker bee is tasked with cleaning comb cells for future eggs, attending the queen, feeding brood, capping cells, packing pollen, secreting wax, general hive cleaning, receiving and processing nectar, guarding the hive, and foraging. Only the worker bee does these things. So while the system as a whole seems very well organized and the needs of the few outweigh the needs of the many, each bee is highly predisposed to behave in very specific ways.

The amazing thing to me is, as with most complex systems, while the system looks and behaves with complexity, the underlying elements can be very simple and working under very simple rules. But when you stand back and look at what's going on, you say, "Wow, look at how complex the behavior is."

When we view computing systems in this light, it helps us understand we are not just dealing with ones and zeros. It's more than that. Just as with a honeybee colony, we are dealing with more than just a worker bee and a queen bee. There is complexity in hive behavior, just as there is complexity in computing system behavior.

Every living system needs energy and guidelines. Bees need honey for energy, and we need food as well. Bees need guidelines (I previously outlined some of the worker bee guidelines), and so do we. If bees did not operate under their guidelines, there would be chaos and the hive would die. When people behave without guidelines, lawlessness and chaos ensue, people die, and eventually so does society. Computing systems take energy in the form of electricity. Their guidelines are the programs, which they dutifully run and obey. Without good electricity and good programs, the computing system cannot survive and will eventually shut down.

So when thinking, working with, and forecasting Oracle performance, remember that computing systems are very dynamic, always shifting and changing, like you and I.

Every complex system is made up of multiple smaller pieces, each working under very simple rules. Computing systems perform units of work, and this work arrives in special ways. There are work processors, and when there is too much work, the system backs up and can get bogged down. Each of the characteristics is essential to understanding and forecasting performance. Each of these characteristics is involved in our mathematical formulas and commonly used when discussing forecasting.

Transactions Are Units of Work

When forecasting performance, we need a fundamental unit of work to communicate and to calculate. We call this basic unit of work a *transaction*. The beauty (and the beast) is we can define a transaction however we wish, as long as we can communicate and calculate that definition (that is, forecast).

This is not as simple as it sounds. Not only people in general, but also IT professionals, have various definitions for a transaction. And most of these definitions are accepted by the industry! So which one is right? Is a transaction when a user saves an order, when the Oracle database receives a commit or rollback command, or when customer information is queried? Yes, all of these can be legitimate transactions.

You must be flexible or needless arguments will arise. The solution is to clearly define what you mean by a transaction when communicating with others. Just as important is to consistently use these definitions through all aspects of a forecasting project. Shifting definitions will cause not only hard feelings, but also meaningless forecasts.

For most forecasting projects, the definition of a transaction becomes fairly obvious. It just seems to work well for most everyone involved. But regardless of your specific definition, a transaction will always represent and define the fundamental unit of work.

The Arrival Rate

Transactions are more than a static definition; they are in motion or wanting to be in motion. Transactions arrive into a computing system like people arrive into an office building elevator (or if you prefer, lift). Transactions represent work. The more work occurring in a system, the more transactional activity.

There are times of heavy arrivals (that is, work) in a computing system, just as there are times of heavy elevator activity. Traditionally, in the office elevator, heavy transaction arrival times are early morning, lunch, and early evening. Computing transactions not only arrive into a system at repeatable patterns, but also specifically into the CPU subsystem and the IO subsystem.

How often transactions arrive is one of their key characteristics. For example, there could be five people entering an office within a one-minute period. Perhaps 5,000 transactions arrive into an Oracle system every hour. Whatever your transaction definition, the transaction arrival rate is always the number of transactions arriving within a given period of time.

In our Oracle performance forecasting work, a transaction and the resulting arrival rate can be defined in many ways. Common transaction definitions are related to orders, invoices, or some key business process. In addition, common definitions arise from the Oracle performance view v$sysstat statistic names, such as logical reads, block changes, physical writes, user calls, logons, executes, user commits, and user rollbacks. All of these can be defined as a transaction, be measured, and therefore have a calculatable arrival rate.

If you are familiar with Oracle's Statspack reports, you will know that the first page enumerates and summarizes the workload in a variety of ways. Some of these are the statistics I just mentioned. Using certain statistics will result in better predictions than others, but each can be used as a legitimate transaction definition and result in a subsequent arrival rate.

Every forecasting-related publication always uses the Greek letter lambda (λ) to represent the arrival rate. The units are always work per time, such as 50 transactions per second, written as 50 trx/s. Be very careful that you do not flip trx/s to s/trx, as this will cause errors, frustration, and serious miscommunication.

The Transaction Processor

People don't enter a restaurant without a reason. They want to be served! When a transaction arrives into a computing system, it expects to be served. The architectural component providing the service is called the *transaction processor*, or commonly the *server*. From a forecasting perspective, a server processes transactions.

CPUs service transactions, so they are called servers when forecasting. IO subsystem devices service transactions, and they are also called servers when forecasting.

Please note the use of the word *server*. When communicating about forecasting, the server is not a computer host, node, or a computer server. Just this past year, I was teaching an all-day session on forecasting Oracle performance. At the first break, a student came up to me and asked if I was talking about Oracle's clustered environment (Real Application Clusters, or RAC) when referring to multiple servers working together to service transactions. After a minute, it occurred to me that his definition of a server was a *computer*, not a *transaction processor*. Once we were both working from the same definition, it became clear how multiple servers can work together.

Each transaction consumes a certain amount of server time. For example, a transaction may consume 5 milliseconds (ms) of CPU time. This is commonly called the *service time* and is labeled as time per unit of work. For example, if a transaction consumes 150 ms of CPU time, the service time is 150 ms/trx.

It is important that the arrival rate and service time are correctly labeled. By *labeled*, I mean, for example, transactions per second versus seconds per transaction. Service time is usually shown as time per unit of work, but the arrival rate is shown as unit of work per time. An arrival rate will be labeled something like transactions per millisecond, such as 145 trx/ms. In contrast, the service time will be labeled something like milliseconds per transaction, such as 10 ms/trx.

Be aware that it is common to receive arrival rates and service times with their labels flipped. For example, you may be given the service time in transactions per millisecond, which is more correctly called the *service rate*. When you are given the arrival rate and the service time, double-check and ensure the labels are in the correct format. If not, use the number's reciprocal.

Sometimes when people speak about arrival rates or service times, or when they speak of the tools we use to collect such information, they will naturally use the reciprocal. For example, a person may say something like, "The CPUs can service 150 transactions each second." The service time label format in this example is communicated as transactions per second. We may need to take the reciprocal to get the number in seconds per transaction. Table 2-1 gives some examples of how the arrival rate and service time may be communicated.

Table 2-1. *Arrival Rate and Service Time Descriptions*

Description	Arrival Rate (Work/Time)	Service Time (Time/Work)
Fifty transactions arrive into the system each minute, each consuming 25 ms of CPU time.	50 trx/min	25 ms/trx
Twenty-five transactions arrive into the system each second. The five 3.4GHz CPUs can process a transaction in 28 ms.	25 trx/s	28 ms/trx
Five transactions enter the system every 5 ms. It takes a CPU 4 ms to service a transaction.	1 trx/ms = 5/5 trx/ms	4 ms/trx
Each server can service a transaction in 3 seconds. Every 10 seconds, 350 transactions enter the system.	35 trx/s = 350/10 trx/s	3 s/trx = 3/1 s/trx
Preliminary testing has shown the application consumes about 20 seconds of server CPU time to complete an order. We process around 500 orders every hour.	$0.139\,orders/s = \dfrac{500 orders}{1hr} * \dfrac{1hr}{60m} * \dfrac{1m}{60s}$	20 s/order

We refer to how active or how busy a server is as the *busy rate*, the *busyness*, or simply the *utilization*. For example, if a server is busy 65% of the time, its utilization is 65% (didn't mean to insult your intelligence). When a server is busy around 70% of the time, it cannot process transactions immediately upon their arrival. When this occurs, the transaction is placed into a queue.

The Queue

Let's face it, no one likes to wait in a queue (also called a *line*). Not only is this irritating, but we know deep down that had better planning occurred, we wouldn't have to wait. It's one of those preventable things in life that happens, and there isn't much we can do about it.

When a transaction enters a computing system, it enters one of many queues. We will, of course, abstract, simplify, and model this behavior. A transaction remains in the queue until its turn to be serviced by a transaction processor.

Let's talk about a queue data structure for a second. A queue is a very simple data structure. It's essentially a linked list with a head and a tail. Transactions are pushed onto the queue (enqueue) and popped off of the queue (dequeue). The queues we model will be simple first in/first out (FIFO) queues.

The queue length provides us with additional information. The maximum utilization a server can sustain is 100%. Once a server nears 100% utilization, we know response time is *bad*, but we don't know just how bad it is. The queue length gives us the "how bad is it?" information. I find this information particularly useful in diagnosing existing performance issues, but it can also be valuable when forecasting.

There are many queuing configuration variations. For example, transactions can defect to another queue (think of moving to a shorter line at McDonald's), transactions can go in priority queues (think of a diplomatic line at a passport control), and certain transactions always go to the head of the queue (think of someone cutting in line at a theme park). While these variants and others do appear in computing systems, our models do not need to be this detailed and granular. Thankfully, our relatively simple queuing models will sufficiently grasp the characteristics of an Oracle-based system.

When a transaction waits in a queue, it waits Q_t time. The units are time per transaction. For example, transactions may wait in the queue for an average of 5 seconds, or 5 s/trx. The letter Q represents the length of the queue, and its unit is simply the number of transactions. For example, the queue length could be 15 transactions, or 15 trx.

As I mentioned earlier, when a server is around 70% busy, it usually cannot immediately process a transaction. It may seem strange that while the server is 30% idle (that is, not busy), the average transaction cannot be immediately served and therefore must queue. We'll dig into why this occurs in Chapter 5. But for now, just realize that when a server starts getting busy, transactions start to queue, the queue length increases, and performance starts to degrade.

Transaction Flow

Now that we have discussed arrivals, transaction processors, and queues, we can talk about transaction flow. When a business transaction is submitted, it flows throughout the computing system consuming CPU, IO, memory, and network resources. Sometimes a transaction doesn't have to wait in a queue and can immediately be serviced; other times, it must wait in a queue first. But the point is that a transaction flows throughout the system, repeatedly queuing and being serviced until it completes and exits the system.

During the life of a transaction, if we add up all the service time and all the queue time, we can determine the transaction's time spent in the system. This "time in the system" is commonly known as the *response time*. Response time is the most important term in forecasting, and it's also one of the simplest. Response time is service time plus queue time:

$$R_t = S_t + Q_t$$

The complications arise in defining exactly what is *service time* and what is *queue time*. Remember that service time is when a transaction is actually being serviced, and queue time is when a transaction is doing nothing but waiting to be serviced. It is easy for people to brush these definitions off as simplistic and of no real value. Don't be fooled.

While an Oracle DBA will think of service time as CPU time and everything else as queue time, not everyone views response time like this. An IO subsystem engineer may view service time as data-transfer time, and see rotational delay and disk head movement as queue time. Memory specialists will have their own definitions of service time and queue time. People feel most comfortable relating response time to their frame of reference. It's just easier.

But problems arise when you want to communicate with people outside your frame of reference. So you must be extremely careful when discussing response time and educate your audience about what you consider to be service time and queue time.

Most models focus on a single computing system component. For example, a model may be built specifically for modeling a CPU subsystem, as opposed to an IO subsystem or the network subsystem. While this may be perfectly appropriate, understand that this single component approach is usually not as precise as a multiple component approach. Multiple component models are more complicated than single component models and typically used in forecasting-related products.

When a real transaction enters a real system, it does not enter the CPU queue, wait, get serviced by a CPU, and then exit the system. It's obviously much more complicated than that. The transaction may enter the CPU subsystem, enter the IO subsystem, move back into the CPU subsystem, and then exit. There is feedback; there is a chain of events in every transaction's life; and there are many detailed happenings that we do not deal with. This is fine as long as our model captures enough reality to be useful.

When performance is being forecasted, we look closely at the inputs (service time and number of servers) and the outputs (queue time, queue length, utilization, and response time). These numbers are the foundation of our analysis. A terrific way to communicate these numbers is to graph them. The most common graph, which I will repeatedly reference in this book, is known as the *response time curve*.

The Response Time Curve

Of all the ways to communicate risk, the response time curve is one of the best. The response time curve allows us to communicate very technical situations in an easily understandable format. Our risk mitigation strategies will undoubtedly result in response time change. Understanding and explaining this change will help everyone understand why and how a strategy makes sense. Don't underestimate the simplistic power of the response time curve.

The response time curve is simple. Take a look at the response time curve graph in Figure 2-1. The vertical axis is the response time. For simplicity, think of how long it takes a query to complete. Keep in mind that response time is the sum of the service time and the queue time. The horizontal axis is the arrival rate. We slide to the right as more transactions enter the system per unit of time.

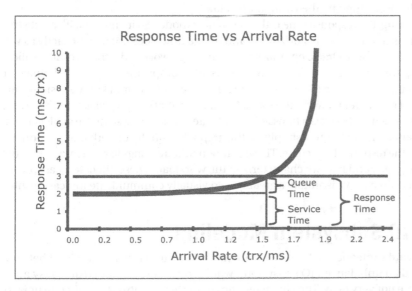

Figure 2-1. *Graph of the classic response time curve. This example shows at an arrival rate of 1.55 trx/ms the response time is 3 ms/trx, the service time is 2 ms/trx, and the queue time is 1 ms/trx.*

Notice that when the arrival rate is small, the response time is equal to the service time; that is, there is no queuing. But as more transactions enter the system per unit of time (that is, the arrival rate increases), queuing will eventually occur. Notice that just a little queuing occurs at the beginning. But as the arrival rate continues to increase, at some point (after 75% utilization), the queue time will skyrocket. When this occurs, the response time also skyrockets, performance slows, and users get extremely upset.

While at a university, I had a job answering the computer operations room telephone. The phone could handle multiple lines, and since I could talk with only one person at a time, sometimes I had to put someone on hold. When things were calm and someone called, I would listen to their request, handle the call, hang up, and then wait for the next call. That's when the job was relaxing. However, if the call arrival rate increased enough, someone would call while I was already talking to someone on the other line. As a result, someone had to wait their turn, or in forecasting terms, they queued. I noticed that once the rate of calls caused people to queue, it took only a slight increase in the call arrival rate before there were many people in the queue and they were waiting a long time. It was like everything was calm, and then WHAM!, everyone was queuing.

You might have experienced this yourself with your computer systems. Performance is fine, yet the system is really busy. Then for any number of reasons, the system activity increases just a little, and WHAM!, performance takes a dive. And you sit back and say, "What just happened? Everything was going fine and the workload didn't increase that much."

What happened to both of us is that we hit the famous rocket-science-like term, *elbow of the curve* (also known as the *knee of the curve*). At the elbow of the curve, a small increase in the arrival rates causes a large increase in the response time. This happens in all queuing systems in some fashion, and it is our job to understand when and under what conditions the elbow of the curve will occur.

It's difficult for me to convey the depth of insight you'll receive by studying the response time curve. Knowing how to shift the curve up, down, left, and right will significantly aid your IT understanding. This is so important that I'll spend more time specifically in this area in Chapter 5, which covers queuing theory in more detail.

When forecasting, the response time is the based on a model. So it's not real; it's an abstraction. Service time is never perfectly horizontal, and queue time does not occur exactly as we plan in real systems. All those Oracle optimizations and messy workload issues we talked about earlier muddy up things a bit. However, transactions and computing systems do behave in a queuing-like manner. They must—it's their nature. I've been asked how I know a system will respond this way. The answer is always the same. I simply say that's how transactions behave . . . and so do humans when we become a transaction and enter a queuing system like at McDonald's.

Your confidence should not rely simply on the graph, but on the underlying components, which resulted in the response time curve. These components are things like the forecast model, the numbers of servers, and how we characterized the workload. These affect forecast precision. The response time curve is simply a great way to visually communicate forecast results.

CPU and IO Subsystem Modeling

Have you ever heard someone say, "Our CPUs are not balanced." Probably not. But I bet you have experienced an unbalanced IO subsystem, where some devices were really busy and other devices were not very busy. The characteristics of these two subsystems dictate how to model them.

Look closely at Figure 2-2. Which one more closely represents a CPU subsystem, and which one represents an IO subsystem?

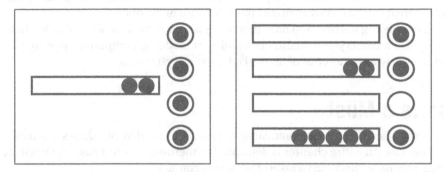

Figure 2-2. *CPU and IO subsystems have fundamentally different queuing structures and therefore are modeled differently.*

Does it make a difference which CPU services a transaction? Generally, it does not. Does it make a difference which IO device services a transaction? It most certainly does (data is read and written from/to a specific device). This question alone dictates the queuing model on the left in Figure 2-2 as a better representation of a CPU subsystem. An IO transaction must read or write data from a specific device (that is, a server), and as a result, it will be routed to that device's queue. The only possible IO subsystem model is the one on the right.

In a CPU subsystem, generally any CPU can service any transaction. As a result, there needs to be only one queue. The benefits are tremendous compared to IO subsystem queuing. With an IO subsystem, there must be a queue for each device. This can cause major IO bottlenecks because, while one queue may be completely empty, another queue can be very active. Because there is a single CPU queue and all CPUs feed off of that one queue, there will never be a transaction waiting for a CPU while there is an available CPU. But an IO subsystem can have transactions needing IO service that can't get serviced while there are idle IO devices. A simple IO subsystem simulation vividly shows that even a perfectly balanced IO subsystem will result in transactions queuing at an IO device, while at the same time, there are idle IO devices.

In a CPU subsystem, we model one queue being shared by multiple CPUs. We model an IO subsystem as having one queue for each device. It's important to remember that we are modeling, and not exactly duplicating, the real system. At this point, if you are struggling with accepting that we can adequately model something so complex so simply, just remember how much we can learn about cars, rockets, and railroads by studying their models.

We can glean some other interesting bits of knowledge from these models. Notice that in a CPU subsystem, a single large transaction will not block other transactions from receiving CPU service. Yet a single large IO transaction can block an entire device, forcing all the other transactions needing to be serviced by that same IO device to wait! IO subsystem vendors have developed all sorts of proprietary algorithms to reduce this impact.

Fast-food restaurants provide a plethora of queuing examples. Comparing one restaurant to another is a great way to learn about queuing systems. Because we walk into McDonald's and have to queue before we are served (that is, our order is taken), some type of queuing system must exist. While there are exceptions, most McDonald's order-taking queuing systems are configured the same. Is it more like a CPU subsystem (one queue, multiple servers) or like an IO subsystem (one queue for each server)? Have you ever got stuck in the wrong queue? Remember that parent who pulls out a big list of items just as she is asked what she wants? Ugh! This is exactly what a transaction needing IO experiences when it must wait for a long transaction to complete before it can be served or simply move forward in the queue.

Life is full of queuing systems. You have probably just never thought about it much before. I suspect this will change! As you read this book and start modeling computing systems, you will begin to see the world as a series of networked queuing systems.

Method Is a Must

We are at the point where we can start forecasting. But hold on, I need to introduce some method before chaos ensues. An entire chapter is dedicated to methodically forecasting Oracle performance (Chapter 6), so this is just a taste of what is to come.

A good method provides structure with freedom. A bad method breeds unbearable bureaucracy and kills creativity along with freedom. Because forecasting is a "science thing" (it is, after all, reproducible), we should be able to develop a repeatable method.

We can choose from many forecasting methods. Every capacity planning book includes some type of method. The method I present is tailored specifically for the realities of Oracle systems—realities such as the workload is messy, there are multiple forecasting models, and there is usually someone or some company (think vendor) who wants you to fail. A solid method will help you work and explain not just *what* you are doing, but *how* you are doing it.

The method I have used for years works exceptionally well with real-life Oracle systems (production or planned). This method involves six steps:

Step 1: Determine the study question. Every forecasting exercise, no matter how simplistic or complex, is based on a fundamental question or need. Find out what that question is, get everyone involved and agree to it, and don't sway from answering that question.

Step 2: Gather workload data. The study question will give you clues as to what data you need. Gather it, store it, and get ready to use it.

Step 3: Characterize the workload data. Raw data is not all that useful. You will need to transform this raw workload data into a format that is useful for people when forecasting and also appropriate for forecast model input. While characterizing a workload can be very simple, a precise forecast requires a well-characterized workload.

Step 4: Develop and use the appropriate model. You have many modeling options. But your study question, available workload data, and characterization options will lead to an obvious model choice.

Step 5: Validate the forecast. If possible, you want to determine (that is, validate) the precision and usefulness of your forecasts. A responsible forecast includes a good understanding of actual precision. It's not good enough to say, "This model always yields good precision." You have to measure the precision. Some models inherently do this for you; others do not. "Professional" capacity planners get irate if you have not validated your forecast, so be prepared.

Step 6: Forecast. As you can see, it takes quite a while before you actually start forecasting. Unless you are using a professional product, you will spend a significant amount of your time doing tasks that are not related to analysis. When you forecast, you are learning about IT service and risk, and you are developing strategies to mitigate the risk and to mitigate service-level breaches.

Personally, I'm not a big method guy. But I also recognize that forecasting can be so engaging that it's easy to get carried away and lose sight of what you're really trying to accomplish. Having a solid method in place will allow you to repeatedly and consistently provide your company with true forecasting value.

Data Collection

If you're going to forecast, you need to have some input data. Regardless of your model type (benchmark, simulation, or mathematical), you will need data inputs. Even when forecasting future production systems (think new implementations), you'll need some performance data. For folks not familiar with Oracle, this can be a little overwhelming. However, I think you'll find that while there is a sometimes-dizzying array of possibilities, it's very straightforward. And remember to keep it simple.

Usually, you have collected a bunch of raw data that is not all that useful in its initial form. You will then need to transform the raw data into a format that is useful for the people doing the actual forecasting and also for forecast model input. The process of transforming the raw data is known as *workload characterization*. I've devoted an entire chapter to workload characterization (Chapter 7) to handle the harsh realities of an Oracle environment.

If you will be gathering the data yourself (as opposed to a professional data collector), gather just what you need, gather as infrequently as possible, and try to use standard tools like sar and sqlplus. The more data you gather and the more frequently you probe a system, the more likely you will negatively impact the system.

Professional data collectors can be extremely complex. This is due to the need to handle a lot of data collection, movement, and management, all without negatively impacting the system. Most homegrown collectors are very specific and targeted, and therefore do not need to be as complicated. For example, they may collect only a few Oracle system-level statistics (as opposed to Oracle session-level data) and some operating system statistics.

When gathering your own data, be sure all sources start and stop collection at the same time. You don't want your operating system data to represent only part of your Oracle data collection. When a partial overlap or crossover occurs, the data becomes totally worthless. The danger is that you will still have performance data to enter into the forecast model, but the forecasts will be worse than wrong—they will be misleading. This is why you will want to script and automate your data gathering. Remove as much manual intervention as possible. This will result in clean and confident data.

Example 2-1. Gathering CPU and Oracle Data

Dan was asked how much more work the database server could handle before it "runs out of gas" and response time becomes intolerable. One of Dan's first tasks is to gather Oracle workload and CPU utilization data. In this exercise, we'll follow Dan as he gathers and transforms the data into information that we will enter into the basic forecasting formulas later in the chapter.

While Dan ran two separate routines when gathering data from Oracle and the operating system, their execution was timed so the collected data covered the same 300-second (5-minute) period.

One of the first decisions Dan must make is what exactly constitutes the arrival rate. Throughout this book, you'll learn about the many workload-related statistics and how to validate their affect on forecast precision. Dan decided to use the Oracle internal statistic *user calls* to represent the workload; that is, the arrival rate.

Dan must now gather Oracle workload data. As with most Oracle internal statistics, the values increase over time. To determine what occurred within a specific period of time, an initial statistic snapshot (S_0) and an ending statistic snapshot (S_1) must be taken. Then simply subtract the initial value from the ending value to get the snapshot period activity ($S_1 - S_0$). To determine the arrival rate, divide the period workload activity by the snapshot duration time (T). Here is the formula:

$$\lambda = \frac{S_1 - S_0}{T}$$

The following is the code snippet Dan used to collect the raw Oracle workload data. As noted, Dan decided the Oracle statistic user calls (uc) will represent the arrival rate.

```
SQL> select name, value
  2  from v$sysstat
  3  where name = 'user calls';

NAME        VALUE
----------- ----------
user calls    5006032


SQL> exec sys.dbms_lock.sleep(300);

PL/SQL procedure successfully completed.

SQL> select name, value
  2  from v$sysstat
  3  where name = 'user calls';

NAME        VALUE
----------- ----------
user calls    5007865
```

Placing the collected Oracle workload data into the formula, Dan derived an arrival rate of 6.11 uc/s.

$$\lambda = \frac{S_1 - S_0}{T} = \frac{5007865uc - 5006032uc}{300s} = \frac{1833uc}{300s} = 6.11uc/s$$

CPU subsystem information was gathered using the standard Unix sar -u command. Dan used the following sar command to take a 5-minute CPU subsystem activity snapshot. The average CPU utilization, or busyness, will be the sum of the CPU user time (shown as %usr) and the CPU system time (shown as %sys). Looking at the sar command's output, you can see user time is 27% and system time is 8%, so the average CPU utilization is 35%. Dan wrote this number down, as he will use it a little later.

```
sar -u 300 1
SunOS soul 5.8 Generic_108528-03
10:51:00  %usr  %sys  %wio %idle
10:56:00   27    8     0    65
```

Now that Dan knows the CPU utilization (35%) and the arrival rate (6.11 uc/s), he is ready to use the essential forecasting formulas.

If you have access to a production Oracle machine, I suggest you immediately gather workload data just as I've described. In the next section, we will get to the formulas, and you can apply the workload data you gathered.

As you can see, gathering useful workload data does not need to be overly complicated. With that said, there are a number of things we did and did not do in this example that may result in an irresponsible forecast. But the process you are going through is valuable, and you'll start to develop an inherent sense of your system. You are now equipped with some data and ready to learn about the essential forecasting formulas.

Essential Mathematics

The core forecasting formulas are relatively simple and straightforward. After you do a few basic forecasts, you'll start to develop a kind of feel for your system and the general cause-and-effect relationships. I realize this is not very mathematical, but part of forecasting is helping people to grasp the raw forecast numerics. If your audience develops an understanding and a feel for the forecasting relationships, then they are more likely to embrace your conclusions.

Table 2-2 provides a quick review of the key variables, along with their symbols and definitions.

Table 2-2. *Key Variables for Essential Forecasting Mathematics*

Variable	Definition	Example
λ	The arrival rate is how much work enters the system within a period of time.	10 trx/ms
S_t	Service time is how long it takes a server to service a single transaction and is represented as time per transaction.	2 ms/trx
U	Utilization is the busyness of a server and is represented as a simple percentage.	83%
Q	Queue length is simply the length of the queue. For Oracle systems, we typically do not want transactions waiting in the queue.	0 trx
Q_t	Queue time is how long a transaction waits in the queue before it begins to be served. This is represented as time per transaction.	0.02 ms/trx
R_t	Response time is service time plus queue time and is represented as time per transaction.	2.02 ms/trx
M	Number of servers is how many servers are servicing transactions	24 servers

The Formulas

It's time to introduce the essential forecasting formulas. Notice that while there are similarities between the CPU and IO formulas, the response time formulas are distinctly different. The differences are the result of their queuing systems. As you'll recall, a CPU subsystem is modeled as having a single queue serving one or more servers, whereas an IO subsystem is modeled as having a single queue servicing each device.

These are the essential CPU and IO subsystem forecasting formulas:

$$U = \frac{S_t \lambda}{M}$$

$$Q = \lambda Q_t$$

$$R_{t-cpu} = \frac{S_t}{1-U^M}$$

$$R_{t-io} = \frac{S_t}{1-U}$$

$$R_t = S_t + Q_t$$

If you're like me, formulas are simply a tool. Before I feel comfortable using a tool or a formula, I need to develop a trust and a feel for it. Simply saying that response time is service time plus queue time is great, but when I picture users getting upset because queue time has increased, which causes the response time increase, I can agree with it and embrace it. To help you develop a trust for these formulas, let's walk through a few thought experiments.

CPU thought experiment 1: What happens to CPU utilization when the arrival rate increases? If there is an increase in the workload, we expect the CPU utilization to increase. Using the CPU utilization formula, an increase in the arrival rate increases the numerator, which will cause the utilization to increase.

CPU thought experiment 2: What happens to CPU utilization when we use faster CPUs? If we replace our server's CPUs with newer, faster CPUs, then we expect the utilization to drop (assuming there is not an increase in workload). Since faster CPUs take less time to service a transaction, the service time will decrease. Using the CPU utilization formula, faster CPUs will decrease the service time, which will decrease the numerator, resulting in a decrease in CPU utilization.

CPU thought experiment 3: What happens to CPU response time when we use faster CPUs? If we switch to faster CPUs, we expect response time to improve; that is, to decrease. The faster CPUs will result in a service time decrease. Using the CPU response time formula, the service time decrease will decrease the numerator, resulting in a response time decrease.

CPU thought experiment 4: What happens to CPU response time if utilization increases? We expect performance to decrease; that is, response time to increase if CPU utilization increases. Using the response time CPU formula, if the utilization increases, the denominator will decrease, causing the response time to increase.

CPU thought experiment 5: What happens to CPU response time if we increase the number of CPUs? This is a tricky one! We know from experience that response time should decrease when additional CPUs are implemented. Using the CPU response time formula, if the number of CPUs increases, U^M will decrease (think 0.5^1 versus 0.5^2), so $1 - U^M$ will increase, and the denominator will increase, causing response time to decrease!

IO thought experiment 1: What happens to IO response time if faster devices are implemented? We expect IO response time to drop because the devices can do the work faster. Using the IO response time formula, service time will decrease with the faster devices, causing the numerator to decrease, resulting in a decrease in response time. Remember that a decrease in response time is an improvement in performance.

IO thought experiment 2: What happens to IO response time if we increase the number of devices? The big assumption here is IO activity will be perfectly spread across all disks. With today's sophisticated (and expensive) IO subsystems, this is not an unreasonable assumption. This requires the use of two formulas. First, using the utilization formula, if the number of servers (devices) increases, the denominator increases, so the utilization decreases. Second, using the IO response time formula, if the utilization decreases, the denominator will increase, causing the response time to decrease!

Now that you have a feel and some trust for the formulas, let's take the workload data we previously gathered and apply it to the formulas, which should result in a real-world scenario.

The Application

Suppose that management wants to know if the current system can handle the upcoming quarter-end close. The quarter-end close is expected to triple the current peak workload.

What management is really asking is if any response time change will significantly slow key business processes to such an extent that business service levels will be negatively affected and possibly breached. So we need to figure out what will happen to response time and utilization when workload increases by 200%. (A workload double is a 100% increase, and a workload triple is a 200% increase.)

Previously in this chapter (in Example 2-1), we gathered data and determined the peak arrival rate was 6.11 uc/s with CPU utilization at 35%. What I didn't tell you was the database server contains 12 CPUs. Now let's substitute our gathered statistics into the essential forecasting formulas.

$$U = \frac{S_t \lambda}{M}; S_t = \frac{UM}{\lambda} = \frac{0.35 * 12}{6.11\,uc/s} = 0.69\,s/uc$$

$$R_t = \frac{S_t}{1 - U^M} = \frac{0.69\,s/uc}{1 - 0.35^{12}} = 0.69\,s/uc$$

$$R_t = S_t + Q_t$$

$$Q_t = R_t - S_t = 0.69\,s/uc - 0.69\,s/uc = 0$$

$$Q = \lambda Q_t = 6.11\,uc/s * 0.00\,s/uc = 0.00$$

In themselves, service time and response time do not provide any immediate value. After all, what does a response time of 0.69 uc/s mean? We get the valuable results when we start increasing the arrival rate while keeping the service time and the number of CPUs constant, and watch what happens to forecasted utilization and response time.

Look closely at Table 2-3. The peak workload is 6.11 uc/s, which represents a 0% workload increase. This is commonly called the *baseline*. All forecasts are based on a specified baseline. As we increase the baseline workload arrival rate to 10%, the arrival rate also increases to 6.721 uc/s. If we increase the baseline workload arrival rate to 20%, the arrival rate increases to 7.332 uc/s. We continue increasing the workload arrival rate until the response time skyrockets off the charts. At each arrival rate increase, we calculate the expected utilization, response time, and queue length based on the service time (0.69 s/uc), the number of CPUs (12), and the adjusted arrival rate.

Table 2-3. *Systematically Varying One Aspect of Forecast Input Variables and Then Forecasting Results in a Forecast Scenario*

Inputs		Outputs		
% WL Increase	**Arrival Rate**	**Busy**	**Response Time**	**Queue Length**
0	6.110	0.351	0.690	0.000
10	6.721	0.386	0.690	0.000
20	7.332	0.422	0.690	0.000
30	7.943	0.457	0.690	0.000
40	8.554	0.492	0.690	0.001
50	9.165	0.527	0.690	0.003
60	9.776	0.562	0.691	0.007
70	10.387	0.597	0.691	0.015
80	10.998	0.632	0.693	0.031
90	11.609	0.668	0.695	0.063
100	12.220	0.703	0.700	0.124
110	12.831	0.738	0.708	0.236
120	13.442	0.773	0.723	0.442
130	14.053	0.808	0.748	0.814
140	14.664	0.843	0.792	1.500
150	15.275	0.878	0.874	2.815
160	15.886	0.913	1.041	5.582
170	16.497	0.949	1.470	12.874
180	17.108	0.984	3.857	54.186
190	17.719	1.019	−2.748	−60.920
200	18.330	1.054	−0.785	−27.034

Figure 2-3 shows the classic response time curve graph. The horizontal axis is the increasing arrival rate, and the vertical axis is the forecasted response time. Numerically, we can state that response time starts to dramatically increase somewhere around mid 70% utilization, which is around 13 uc/s. Graphically, it's easy to see that at around 13 uc/s, we enter the elbow of the curve.

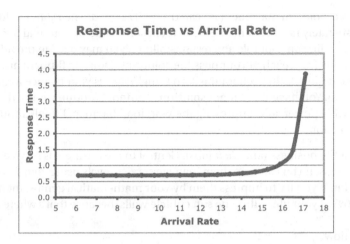

Figure 2-3. *A graphical representation of the classic response time curve based on Table 2-3 data*

Management needs to know what's going to happen with a 200% workload increase. Well, not a whole lot is going to be happening. At around a 110% workload increase (just over a double, or 2X, workload increase), performance is going to take a significant hit, and the business is going to suffer. It is extremely unlikely that the system can handle a triple, or 3X, workload increase. Let's look at how to communicate our numeric forecast results to management.

What Management Needs to Know

What you should tell management is entirely different than what you should tell the technical folks. You just don't go to your manager, show him a table full of numbers or even a pretty graph, and say, "Looks like we're in deep trouble, boss." If the likelihood of a problem occurring is high, management needs to know its options and needs to grasp the central issues. Based on our example, a simple presentation related to the following five points could be presented:

- **Workload is expected to triple (200% increase) at the upcoming quarter-end close.** Double-check this and get everyone to agree. If they don't agree, then obviously the results don't mean a whole lot.

- **There is significant risk that service levels will become unacceptable.** Make sure everyone understands that it's not even close. Bad things will probably happen, and it will be so severe the business will suffer. It's not debatable; it's going to happen.

- **Significant business interruption will start to occur at around 110% workload increase.** Management needs to know that just over a 2X workload increase, performance will tank, yet everyone expects the workload to increase by 3X. So, obviously, something must be done.

- **The CPU subsystem is at risk of not providing enough power.** (We did not investigate the IO subsystem, but let's assume the IO subsystem will not be at risk.) Let management know it's not the IO subsystem. The problem clearly rests and is focused on the CPU subsystem. So the solution needs to also be centered around the CPU subsystem.

- **The solution is . . .** At this point, management is scared—really scared. Their jobs could be at risk, and they desperately need your help. So give them some solid options and perhaps your opinion. Depending on your role and responsibilities, you may need to provide cost and expected benefits from each of your possible solutions. Don't be flippant and provide solutions at the depth of, "Just reboot the dern thing!" Now is your chance to be a shining IT professional. You have three main solutions centered around tuning the system, buying more CPU power, and improving the workload balance. I'll talk more about this in the next section.

Management cares about the business (and *their* jobs). Central to the business is service levels meeting the business needs. If you can help them manage service levels using your forecasting prowess, you'll be a star. If you try to impress them by your mathematical genius, then I hope you enjoy spending 70% of your life within the soft cubicle walls, because that's where you'll stay.

Management needs to know:

Will agreed-upon service levels (implied or otherwise) be breached? Explain this in terms of risk or likelihood. You can then frame your solutions directly at the identified risks. It closes the loop of, "Here's the risk. Now here's how to mitigate that risk."

Where does the risk reside? Since we are focusing on the database server, you will need to graphically explain in large blocks where the database server fits into the IT architecture. Don't get fancy. Display only a few blocks on the screen. Details and precision are not necessary, and will distract and confuse management. What is required is the general recognition of where the risk resides. Let management know if it's the CPU system, the IO subsystem, the memory subsystem, or the network subsystem that is going to run out of gas.[1]

When is the expected risk going to occur? Most forecasting work looks into the future, so there is a good chance it will be necessary to explain *when* forecast service levels will be at risk. Focus on what the forecasts are communicating, not what you personally believe will occur.

What can be done to mitigate the identified risk? As I mentioned, at this point, management is scared, and they desperately need your help. It's always a good idea to come up with multiple risk mitigation strategies. Simply saying, "Well, we need five more CPUs" may not be an option for budget or political reasons. So you should have another option. Be careful not to overstep your authority and position of responsibility. If you are not involved in the cost side of things, clearly provide information for the financial people. But be careful about recommending a solution unless you are aware of most of the issues.

If you transform your raw forecasts into "what management needs," you are truly managing performance, managing service levels, and adding a tremendous amount of value to your company. While desirable, it is extremely rare that management receives a well-thought-out presentation based on a solid technical analysis without the presentation focusing on the technical analysis. Do perform a rock-solid technical analysis, but take the time to transform the analysis into a presentation targeted for management. Focus on what management needs to know, not on the forecasting-related technicalities. This is where the value of the forecast lies.

---

1. The phrase "running out of gas," while not technical, is one of those global communication terms that everyone understands.

Risk Mitigation Strategies

So how do you develop these risk mitigation strategies that I keep talking about? Honestly, it's a combination of science, art, experience, and understanding your environment. Keep in mind that it's typically not our decision to pick the final solution. Either intentionally or unintentionally, we may not be aware of many factors. Besides the obvious budget constraints, there could be reasons related to timing, availability, politics, expenditures, legal, upgrades, patches, and expected new hardware. The list goes on and on. So unless you are tasked with specifying the best answer, don't. Providing your management with choices and explaining the costs and benefits of those choices from your perspective and then translating into an SLM perspective is extremely valuable to your company.

The next step is to develop multiple strategies to mitigate the identified risk. I have found that by framing strategies around three basic options/strategies, I'm able to better communicate. The three basic options are tune, buy, and balance. Continuing with the example introduced in Example 2-1, that would mean our basic options are to tune the application and Oracle, buy more CPU capacity, and better balance the existing workload. We'll take a look at all three.

Tuning the Application and Oracle

When tuning occurs, the workload applied to the operating system is effectively reduced. A simple calculation shows that if the original workload increases by 70%, but we tune the application by 20%, the net result is only a 50% workload increase. That is significant!

You need a good technical team to responsibly come up with a percent-tuning forecast. Simply reducing the most offending SQL statement's response time by 20% does not translate into an overall 20% workload reduction. This is especially true, for example, if a SQL statement is IO-intensive but the expected bottleneck will be the CPUs. It's best to be very conservative and have a well-thought-out plan of attack before suggesting this option.

While I just mentioned reducing a 70% workload increase by 20% nets a 50% workload gain, this is actually overly aggressive, resulting in too much workload. A more accurate estimation occurs when you apply the workload decrease (the tuning) *before* the workload increase. The more accurate workload increase is actually closer to 36%. So this makes more sense, first I'll show you the formulas, followed by an example.

Here are the variables:

W_f = Forecasted workload increase

W_i = Initial workload increase

W_r = Expected workload reduction

And here is the simple formula:

$$W_f = W_i - W_r$$

This is a more accurate workload increase formula:

$$W_f = (1 - W_r) * (1 + W_i) - 1 = W_i - W_r - W_r W_i$$

In a way, tuning the application is an investment. When tuning, you are investing money into making the application more efficient. This will reap rewards for the entire life of the application. When you buy additional capacity, the excess capacity will eventually be used. The downside to tuning is that it takes time and money, and it's difficult to estimate how much of a positive impact the tuning will actually have.

Example 2-2. Tuning to Reduce the Workload

Suppose the current workload is 50 trx/s, the workload is expected to increase by 70%, and the performance team members feel very confident they can tune the overall application by at least 20%. What is the net workload change in terms of percentage and actual workload and also the final workload?

We apply the simple formula:

$$W_f = W_i - W_r = 70\% - 20\% = 50\%$$

The simple formula predicts a 50% net workload gain, which is an additional 25 trx/s (25 trx/s = 50 trx/s X 50%). The final workload would be 75 trx/s.

Then we apply the more accurate workload increase formula:

$$W_f = (1 - W_r) * (1 + W_i) - 1 = (1 - 20\%) * (1 + 50\%) - 1 = 0.8 * 1.5 - 1 = 0.2 = 20\%$$

The more accurate formula predicts only an additional 20% workload gain, which is an additional 10 trx/s (10 trx/s = 50 trx/s × 20%). The final workload would be 60 trx/s.

Personally, I would forecast using both formulas. The simple formula is easier for people to grasp. Also, the forecast will more likely oversize the system rather then undersize it. It's no problem to perform multiple similar forecasts, so do them both. That is a great way to get an additional data point, which helps to better understand the situation.

Buying More CPU Capacity

While the objective of performance tuning is never to recommend purchasing additional hardware capacity, it is very common to recommend securing additional hardware when forecasting. Capacity management (and more specifically, forecasting) is intimately connected to IT financial management. This is especially true when forecasting is routinely used for budgeting, planning, and purchasing decisions. So if you are a performance-centric person, don't feel like you are failing when more capacity is required. Acquiring more capacity is normal, and in many cases, the right thing to do.

Buying more CPU capacity (or any transaction processor/server component, for that matter) comes in three flavors: more CPUs, faster CPUs, or more and faster CPUs. We will go into this in more detail in Chapter 5, but for now, please accept the following:

- More hardware increases arrival rate capacity.

- Faster hardware processes transactions faster and also increases arrival rate capacity.

- More and faster hardware gives you a big boost in both performance and arrival rate capacity.

Let's look at quick examples of the more hardware and the faster hardware options.

Example 2-3. Using Faster Hardware

Suppose the vendor is pitching new CPUs that are 20% faster and he swears they will dramatically increase performance. Management wants to know if this is really true. If so, management will work with the finance team to perform a cost-benefit analysis and possibly budget the new hardware acquisition.

Increasing CPU speed reduces CPU service time, so the service time will be reduced by 20%. The current number of CPUs is two, the current CPU utilization is 65%, and Oracle is processing (the arrival rate) 12.5 user calls each millisecond. We expect the workload to increase 30%, so management wants this to be included in our work. The math looks like this:

1.   Forecast any missing variables based on the current situation. We have been given everything except the CPU service time.

$$M = 2cpus$$
$$U = 65\%$$
$$\lambda = 12.5\,uc/ms$$
$$S_t = \frac{UM}{\lambda} = \frac{0.65*2}{12.5\,uc/ms} = \frac{1.3}{12.5\,uc/ms} = 0.104\,ms/uc$$

2.   Forecast the utilization and response time with the workload increase using the existing hardware configuration. The only variable change is the arrival rate.

$$M = 2cpus$$
$$S_t = 0.104\,ms/uc$$
$$\lambda = 12.50\,uc/ms*(1+30\%) = 16.250\,uc/ms$$
$$U = \frac{S_t\lambda}{M} = \frac{0.104\,ms/uc*16.250\,uc/ms}{2} = \frac{1.690}{2} = 0.845 = 85\%$$
$$R_t = \frac{S_t}{1-U^M} = \frac{0.104\,ms/uc}{1-0.845^2} = \frac{0.104\,ms/uc}{1-0.714} = \frac{0.104\,ms/uc}{0.286} = 0.364\,ms/uc$$

3.   Forecast the utilization and response time with both the workload increase and the faster CPUs. Notice the variable change in both the service time and arrival rate.

$$M = 2cpus$$
$$\lambda = 12.50\,uc/ms*(1+30\%) = 16.250\,uc/ms$$
$$S_t = 0.104\,ms/uc*(1-20\%) = 0.0832\,ms/uc$$
$$U = \frac{S_t\lambda}{M} = \frac{0.083\,ms/uc*16.250\,uc/ms}{2} = \frac{1.349}{2} = 0.675 = 68\%$$
$$R_t = \frac{S_t}{1-U^M} = \frac{0.083\,ms/uc}{1-0.675^2} = \frac{0.083\,ms/uc}{1-0.456} = \frac{0.083\,ms/uc}{0.544} = 0.153\,ms/uc$$

Switching the old CPUs out and replacing them with the new faster CPUs along with the expected workload increase, our forecast predicts the utilization will decrease from 85% to 68%. That's a very nice 15% utilization improvement (85% – 68%)! Response time dropped from 0.364 ms/uc to 0.153 ms/uc! That's a whopping 58% response time decrease! This is all good news, because without the new CPUs, when the workload increases by 30%, utilization will increase to 85%. At 85% utilization, the system will be well into the elbow of the curve, and service levels will most likely be negatively affected. So in this situation, it appears the vendor was right on the money.

Example 2-4. Adding More Hardware

We are asked to determine if upgrading our current two CPU database server to four CPUs will be necessary given the workload is expected to increase by 30%. If we decide it is necessary, management will work with the finance team to perform a cost benefit analysis and possibly budget the new hardware acquisition. The computing system details are the same as in Example 2-3.

As we discovered in Example 2-3, a 30% workload increase causes the CPU utilization to increase to 85% (see step 2). This is well within the elbow of the curve, and performance will definitely be impacted. So our solution would be to tune the system, balance the workload (explained in the next section), or add additional CPU power. In Example 2-3, we added CPU power by switching to faster CPUs. For this example, we will add two more CPUs.

Let's start by forecasting the utilization and response time with both the workload increase and the additional CPUs. The service time does not change because we are not using the new faster CPUs.

$$M = 4\,cpus$$
$$\lambda = 12.50\,uc/ms * (1 + 30\%) = 16.250\,uc/ms$$
$$S_t = 0.104\,ms/uc$$
$$U = \frac{S_t \lambda}{M} = \frac{0.104\,ms/uc * 16.250\,uc/ms}{4} = \frac{1.690}{4} = 0.423 = 42\%$$
$$R_t = \frac{S_t}{1 - U^M} = \frac{0.104\,ms/uc}{1 - 0.423^2} = \frac{0.104\,ms/uc}{1 - 0.179} = \frac{0.104\,ms/uc}{0.821} = 0.127\,ms/uc$$

In this exercise, we are investigating if adding two CPUs will allow service levels to be met. They most definitely will be met! The two additional CPUs drop the utilization from an unfortunate 85% to a very comfortable 42%. And response time plummets by 65% from 0.364 ms/uc down to 0.127 ms/uc. (For details, see Exercise 2-3, step 2.) So the additional CPUs are technically a viable solution.

From a *buy* perspective, we have quickly identified two alternatives: faster CPUs and more CPUs. What management must do now is perform a return on investment and cost benefit analyses for our *tune*, *buy*, and *balance* options (see next section).

Balancing Existing Workload

I've never had a client whose workload was perfectly balanced. There are always peaks and valleys. The valleys represent opportunity. While this may not be viewed as forecasting, it definitely falls under capacity management and SLM, so it's worth mentioning.

Traditionally, focusing on batch processing provides the most likely opportunity to balance the workload. This is due to the fact that we typically have some level of control over batch processing. With online processing, users will work when they need to work. Most large Oracle systems push a tremendous amount of batch work through their systems. Very carefully scheduling and prioritizing typically yields a massive workload decrease during peak processing time.

To get started, determine which batch processes are running during the peak time. This could be during quarter-end processing. Work with the application system administrators and the department heads and try to spread out or reduce the activity during those peak hours. Perhaps there is also an ad hoc reporting system. Can that be disabled just during peak quarter-end processing? Using our example, if you can reduce the batch workload by 30% during quarter-end processing, you have effectively neutralized the expected workload increase!

Example 2-5. Forecasting for Bob's Manager Frank

This example will take all that we have learned but add a disturbing (though realistic) twist to the situation. (I think it is important to add interesting twists to exercises and case studies because real life is rarely kind.)

Bob's manager Frank (who is actually Bob's wife's cousin's brother's friend) needs to reduce the cost of the company's Oracle database license. Since the database license is based on the number of CPUs, Frank asked Bob to determine if it would be possible to remove CPUs from the database server without breaching service levels.

Bob has repeatedly observed that the 26 CPU HP server is usually running at around 28% busy (utilization) during peak processing time (month-end close).

Using our essential forecasting formulas, here is how Bob solved the problem.

Bob was given:

$$M = 26cpus$$
$$U = 28\%$$

The strategy is to determine the change in CPU response time. Here is the formula:

$$R_t = \frac{S_t}{1 - U^M}$$

Bob has a problem. While he knows the number of CPUs (M) and the CPU utilization (U), he does not have the service time (S_t). The formula for deriving the service time is:

$$U = \frac{S_t \lambda}{M}; S_t = \frac{UM}{\lambda}$$

And now he has another problem! While he knows the utilization (U) and the number of servers (M), he does not know the arrival rate (λ). So he is going to set the arrival rate (λ) to 1 and solve for the service time (S_t). This is perfectly fine, because he is not trying to convey the actual numeric service time and response times. He is trying to communicate if service levels will be breached. This can be accomplished by understanding when response time skyrockets. If Bob needed to stand up and say, "The average service time is . . . ," then this method would not work. But because he is simply using the number to show a change (the response time), it's OK. You'll also notice Bob is not using any units like transactions or time like milliseconds. That's because it doesn't make any difference. Because, again, he wants to determine the change in response time, not the actual response number. Setting the arrival rate:

$$\lambda = 1$$

$$S_t = \frac{UM}{\lambda} = \frac{0.28 * 26}{1} = 7.280$$

Now that he knows the service time (S_t), the CPU utilization (U), and the number of CPUs (M), he can derive the response time (R_t).

$$R_t = \frac{S_t}{1-U^M} = \frac{7.280}{1-0.28^{26}} = \frac{7.280}{1.000} = 7.28$$

The derived response time of 7.28 will be the baseline. As Table 2-4 shows, he will now slowly reduce the number of CPUs, calculate the revised CPU utilization, and calculate the revised response time.

Table 2-4. *As the Number of CPUs Is Reduced, Utilization and Response Increase*

No. CPUs	% Busy	Response Time	Queue Time	RT % Change
26	28%	7.2800	0.0000	0
25	29%	7.2800	0.0000	0.0%
24	30%	7.2800	0.0000	0.0%
23	32%	7.2800	0.0000	0.0%
22	33%	7.2800	0.0000	0.0%
21	35%	7.2800	0.0000	0.0%
20	36%	7.2800	0.0000	0.0%
19	38%	7.2800	0.0000	0.0%
18	40%	7.2800	0.0000	0.0%
17	43%	7.2800	0.0000	0.0%
16	46%	7.2800	0.0000	0.0%
15	49%	7.2801	0.0001	0.0%
14	52%	7.2808	0.0008	0.0%
13	56%	7.2839	0.0039	0.1%
12	61%	7.2981	0.0181	0.2%
11	66%	7.3585	0.0785	1.1%
10	73%	7.5977	0.3177	4.4%
9	81%	8.5471	1.2671	17.4%
8	91%	13.7424	6.4624	88.8%
7	104%	-23.0429	-30.3229	-416.5%
6	121%	-3.3232	-10.6032	-145.6%

Figure 2-4 shows the response time graph, but the horizontal axis is the number of CPUs, not the arrival rate. As you can see, how many CPUs can be removed becomes obvious. Once there are only around 13 CPUs, response time change begins to significantly increase.

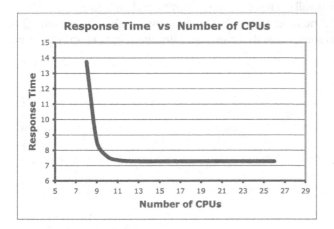

Figure 2-4. *A response time curve with a twist: the horizontal axis is the number of CPUs as opposed to the traditional arrival rate. Once there are around 13 CPUs, we enter the elbow of the curve.*

Looking at the numerical forecasts in Table 2-4, you can see that the response time doesn't start to significantly change until the number of CPUs is down to around 13. So does Bob tell his boss that he can remove 13 CPUs (26 CPUs initial – 13 CPUs remaining)? Absolutely not! It is extremely rare that someone would ever recommend a solution pegged next to the elbow of the curve. This leaves no room for workload growth, spikes in the workload, forecasting precision limitations, paranoia of breaching service levels, and the fudge factor.[2] Bob doesn't have enough information to responsibly answer Frank's question. However, using what he does know, he could say, "Assuming the workload does not increase and there are no significant workload spikes, 11 CPUs (26 CPUs initial – 11 CPUs = 15 CPUs remaining) could be removed from the database server without service level breaches."

Summary

We have covered a lot in this chapter—everything from core forecasting definitions and formulas to how to transform technical information to information meaningful to management. At this point, you should have a good understanding and feel for the relationships between service time, queue time, utilization, servers, and response time. The response time curve should also begin to settle and become a natural way for you to communicate complex forecasting topics.

---

2. According to Wikipedia, "Fudge factor is a margin over and above the required resources such as time, capital, human capital, or cost required for a certain project. Sometimes, fudge factors may be factors other than resources, e.g. a margin of error above the minimum error on a measurement. A fudge factor is also a number used in an equation to make it match current theories. This is usually derided as a false number, but one famous case that later turned out to be correct is the Planck constant. Additionally, the cosmological constant has gone back and forth between being a real value and a fudge factor."

You are ready to do some forecasting! If you have access to a production Oracle system, gather some data and do some forecasts. There is nothing more satisfying then actually doing the things you just have learned. But remember that there is much more to forecasting than just the numbers. While you'll quickly learn about the process of forecasting, randomly gathering a small snapshot of data and performing some forecasts will not result in a responsible or valuable forecast.

Now that you have a solid foundation and understand the essentials of forecasting Oracle performance, it's time to discuss some areas that can have a dramatic impact on your forecast precision.

CHAPTER 3

■ ■ ■

Increasing Forecast Precision

Chapter 2 presented the essentials, including data collection, the basic forecasting formulas, and how to deal with some uncomfortable realities. Once you get familiar with the essential forecasting formulas and you've performed a few forecasts, you'll start to wonder how you can increase forecast precision. Increasing forecast precision may be simpler than you think.

This chapter focuses on taking the essentials to the next level. First, we'll look at some common forecasting "gotchas." Then I will introduce you to other forecasting models, baseline selection, and a better response time formula. We'll also look at how to calculate better averages. I think you'll be surprised that, with just a little more effort, your forecasts can be significantly more precise.

Forecasting Gotchas!

What we did in Chapter 2 was valid and purposeful, but if you aren't careful, your forecasts will be irrelevant and, even worse, misleading. I conveniently sidestepped a number of forecasting gotchas. Here are some of the most common pitfalls:

Small number of workload samples: The exercises and case studies in Chapter 2 were based on a single workload data sample. The problem is Oracle systems are very dynamic, and any one activity snapshot will likely not represent its complexity. So, how frequently should data be gathered and how do we best summarize this data? Both of these questions will be addressed in this chapter and Chapter 7.

Frequent workload sampling: The beauty of rapidly sampling data is that you get a lot of data and are less likely to miss something important. However, Oracle systems fluctuate rapidly, and focusing on any one short-duration snapshot will probably not be a good system representation. And don't forget that the more frequently a system is probed, the more likely the probing will affect the very system under investigation. Later in this chapter, in the "How to Average Diverse Values" section, I'll present how to combine multiple samples into a single representative sample. Don't be too impressed by those who espouse the virtues of rapid data sampling. There is always a cost when sampling.

Unvalidated forecast: An unvalidated forecast is a dangerous thing. If you have a gun, you need to know if it's loaded, whether you're going to use the gun or store the gun. If you are going stand up in front of your peers and your management, you had better know if, for example, your forecast precision is plus or minus one CPU or five CPUs. Most forecast models have inherent precision capabilities, and usually you have the opportunity to statistically determine the precision.

Simplistic workload characterization: In the Chapter 2 case studies and examples, we characterized the system workload based solely on CPU utilization and the Oracle internal statistic *user calls*. That is very simplistic. As you gain in forecast experience, you'll learn that some of the most simplistic workload characterizations will yield amazing forecast precision. Added complexity does not always equate to added precision. Never assume a complex workload characterization yields high-precision forecasts until it has been validated.

Single component forecast model: All the models presented in this book will focus on one computing system subsystem. For example, our essential forecasting formulas in Chapter 2 focused on either the CPU subsystem or the IO subsystem, but not both. Because subsystems are constantly interacting with each other, a single component forecast model is inherently less precise than a multiple component model. Perhaps the precision is sufficient for your needs. If so, then you're OK. To reflect subsystem interaction, most forecasting products use multiple component forecast models.

How to avoid and appropriately deal with each of these gotchas and many others will be presented in the pages of this book. Being aware of the gotchas is the first step in avoiding them!

Model Selection

Model selection is more a science than an art. While we like to talk and think about all the model possibilities, when it comes right down to making the decision, the situation will generally govern the model you choose. Many forecast models are available, each with its own advantages. Five models are commonly used when forecasting Oracle performance.

Each of us tends to have a natural affinity for one model. But it is important to gain a practical working knowledge using all five models. Over time, you'll be exposed to many different forecasting situations. Being skilled in just one modeling technique will eventually limit you. Worse is when someone tries to use a forecast model that is not a natural fit for the given situation. It's like trying to put a square peg into a round hole—it may work, but it's painful and there probably is a better way. You should be comfortable using multiple forecast models.

Questions to Ask

As you learned in Chapter 2, every forecasting exercise has at its core a central question that must be answered. This is called the *study question*. After the study question has been agreed upon, whether formally or informally, your will start thinking about the most appropriate forecast model. When I go through the process of selecting a forecast model, I ask myself a number of questions to help methodically select the best model or models. It is very common for multiple models to be appropriate.

Following are the issues to consider:

Single or multiple components: Each forecast model focuses on either one or more subsystems. All the models presented in this book are single component models. Most forecasting products use multiple component models.

Model input data: All forecast models require input data, but some models require application-centric data and others require more Oracle internal-centric data. If your study question is related to a specific business process or business activity, it is best if the forecast model can receive this type of data as an input. If this is not possible, a translation must be made between the business process or activity and a more technical workload (for example, *user calls*). Data translation or transformation always reduces forecast precision. If possible, use a model that can accept the most pertinent data directly and without translation or transformation. For example, suppose you are asked to determine how many orders an order-entry system can handle each hour before response time skyrockets. This question is to be answered in relation to orders and response time. Using an Oracle internal statistic may be more technically convenient, but since the question demands an answer related to orders, it will be much simpler and probably more precise to use a model that can accept order data.

Production or planned system: Some models require production-like data. Others work fine with good guesses, broad boundaries, or transaction samples.

Model precision capability: Each forecast model has a predisposed forecast precision capability. Matching required forecast precision with potential forecast model precision is very important to ensure financial, time, and precision expectations are met. Spending three months on a low-precision forecast is just as disastrous as spending three hours on a high-precision forecast. If the study question is closely related to service levels or response time, a more precise model will be required. In contrast, when budgeting or exploring various architectural options, a low-precision model should be fine. A good strategy is to start with a low-precision forecast. Then, if necessary and appropriate, conduct a higher-precision forecast.

Project duration: Each model tends to find itself more involved with projects of a similar duration. For example, low-precision models will typically be involved with very short (perhaps running only minutes) projects, whereas high-precision models are more likely to be used with more precision-aggressive projects. However, if you automate the entire forecasting process or use a vendor product, even precise forecasts can be performed relatively quickly.

To help solidify these rather abstract model selection guidelines, let's look at a quick example. Example 3-1 shows how these considerations are applied to a specific case. In the next section, I will introduce each of the forecast models presented in this book. I will then lead you through this example again plus one additional exercise with the objective of selecting the most appropriate forecast model.

Example 3-1. Applying Model Selection Evaluation Criteria

Suppose our company is going to add 250 more Oracle Manufacturing users to the system next month and our manager wants to know if the CPUs can handle the load. Here is how this situation maps to the five model selection considerations:

- **Single or multiple components:** Since we are concerned with only CPU activity, we need only a single component forecast model. At this point, any of the forecast models presented in this book would qualify.

- **Model input data:** We are given the number of additional users and we know they are going to use the Oracle Manufacturing product. This is very application-centric. Since we need to know if the CPU subsystem can handle the increased load, at a minimum, we will need to forecast CPU utilization. We would like to use a model that will take application-related data as input and output CPU subsystem-related information.

- **Production or planned system:** The system is already in production, so we have a potential wealth of existing workload data. That gives us many forecast model options.

- **Model precision capability:** We are not asked about response time specifics and there is no reference to specific service levels or even response time. We only need to know "if" something is going to happen. If we are very conservative in our forecasts and allow for a lot of potential forecast error, we should be able to use a low-precision forecast model. Again, this leaves us with many forecast model options.

- **Project duration:** We do not have any specific information about the project duration. So we must ask. Don't assume you have a month or only an hour. Since we don't know the project duration, we can't eliminate any forecast models.

For this example, the only model selection constraint concerns application-centric input data. As you'll see, this constraint still leaves us with two forecast model options.

Fundamental Forecasting Models

One of the most exciting aspects of forecasting is that we get to work with many different forecast models. It keeps us alert and provides an endless supply of unique forecasting situations. If you are just starting to forecast, however, at times it can be overwhelming. But don't worry—equipped with the experience of using just a handful of forecasting models, you'll be prepared to tackle Oracle database server-related forecasting.

In Chapter 2, we discussed the essential forecasting mathematics. In upcoming chapters, we'll dive deep into ratio modeling, regression analysis, and queuing theory modeling. The following sections provide a quick overview of the forecasting models we have covered and what is to come.

Simple Math

As the name states, the simple math model is simple. It's almost embarrassing to write about, but the model is practical. Anyone involved in forecasting uses simple math, usually without ever thinking about it.

For example, if we know an Oracle client process consumes 10MB of nonshared resident memory and plans are to add another 50 users (resulting in 50 additional client processes), then the system will require 500MB of additional memory. Because there is no queuing involved with simple math, it's appropriate only for forecasts like memory, basic IO predictions, and basic networking. I would resist using simple math for CPU, semi-precise IO, and advanced network predictions.

Simple math can be used for single component forecasts. The model can take as input either application or technical metrics, and the input data can be retrieved from a production system or from estimations. Simple math is usually involved with short-duration projects. The precision is usually low, but sufficient when used appropriately.

Essential Forecasting Mathematics

The essential forecasting formulas were presented in Chapter 2. They will become second nature. While these formulas are very straightforward, they can produce relatively precise forecasts. It all depends on the quality of the data being fed into the formulas. Even the most sophisticated and precise forecast models adhere to the principles of the essential forecasting mathematics.

The essential formulas are single component. They usually take as input technical metrics, and the input data can be retrieved from a production system or from estimations. This model is usually used with short-duration projects.

Ratio Modeling

Ratio modeling is a fantastic way to make quick, low-precision forecasts. Two colleagues and I developed the ratio modeling technique back in the mid-1990s, in response to finding ourselves in situations where we simply had to deliver a forecast, yet we did not have the time to use an alternative model.

Ratio modeling works very well when you are quickly budgeting hardware, quickly assessing and exposing technical risk, validating alternative technical architecture designs, and especially when sizing packaged applications. The technique enables you to define the relationship between process categories (such as batch processes) and a specific system resource (such as the CPU).

Ratio modeling produces no statistical data and is not formally validated, so it is a truly back-of-the-envelope forecast technique. While this technique is unsettling to many laboratory-type capacity planners, it is extremely powerful when appropriately used.

Ratio modeling is a single component model. It receives as input both technical and application-centric metrics, and the input data is retrieved from both production systems and from estimations. Ratio modeling usually is involved with short-duration projects. Sometimes using the word *project* is even a stretch when talking about ratio modeling.

Regression Analysis

Regression analysis is one of my personal favorites. It's a fantastic way to forecast because it pushes you to automate data collection, provides standard industry-accepted statistical validation, can produce very precise forecasts, and is very simple to use.

While most forecasting mathematics applications are based around changing the physical hardware configuration, regression analysis is typically used to determine how much of some *business activity* can occur before the system runs out of gas. For example, suppose you have a production system and are asked to determine the maximum number of orders the system can be expected to process within a single hour. This is a perfect fit for regression analysis.

Regression analysis is a single component model. It can receive input from both technical and application metrics, and the input data is retrieved from a production system (or a benchmark). It usually is involved with projects that last at most a month. While the initial project may last a month, if the process is automated, an updated forecast can take only minutes.

Queuing Theory

Queuing theory is basically an upgrade to essential forecasting mathematics. Queuing theory is a wonderful forecasting technique because it is so versatile. It can be used for forecasting as well as helping people understand a current performance issue. Plus it can be used for both low-precision and high-precision forecasts. We have already touched on queuing theory in the previous chapter, and in the "Response Time Mathematics" section later in this chapter, we'll go even deeper. Then Chapter 5 will focus on appropriately applying queuing theory in a wide variety of uncomfortable yet real-life situations.

Multiple component queuing theory models can become quite complex. This is especially true when higher precision is desired. Product-quality forecasting models will undoubtedly be deeply entrenched in advanced queuing theory plus their own proprietary algorithms. In this book, the queuing theory models, while more complex than the essential forecasting mathematics, will be easily understood by those involved in IT.

The queuing theory models I'll present are single component models. They can receive input from both technical (that is, Oracle and the operating system) or application (such as orders, invoices, paychecks, and so on) sources, and the input data is retrieved from either a production or proposed system. Project duration can vary significantly based on the precision required and data collection issues.

Now that you have had an introduction to the models presented in this book, Examples 3-2 and 3-3 show how you might actually go through the model selection process.

Example 3-2. Selecting a Low-Precision Model

This is the same situation as in Example 3-1. Our company is going to add 250 more Oracle Manufacturing users to the system next month and our manager wants to know if the CPUs can handle the load. Here is how this situation maps to our possible forecasting models:

- **Simple math:** This will not meet our requirements since we are focusing on the CPU subsystem. We need a model that is more mathematically rigorous to better capture the system characteristics.

- **Essential forecasting mathematics:** This could possibly meet our requirements, but because one of the key inputs is the number of Oracle Manufacturing users, we would either use the number of users as the workload or relate some more technical metric to a manufacturing user. When we go down this path, precision immediately drops and we start making a lot of assumptions, so let's hope there is a better alternative.

- **Regression analysis:** This is a possibility because we are not focusing on hardware alternatives like adding or removing CPUs. We need only a single component model, so that's another plus. To use regression analysis, we must have production-like data, so the project duration must be considered. One of the difficulties with using regression analysis is you won't know the precision until after you go through the entire forecasting process. Regression analysis is a possibility if we have a few weeks to gather data. If our boss wants an immediate answer, then we need an alternative.

- **Queuing theory:** This will probably not work well because we will need to translate the number of users to an arrival rate. At least with regression analysis we will immediately know the forecast precision, whereas with queuing theory, we will have to do some additional validation work. Queuing theory shines when gathering detailed data and it's summarized into a few values. Queuing theory also provides response time breakdowns, which are beyond what we need. The precision we are being asked to provide can be met without going to the trouble of performing a potentially complex and time-consuming workload gathering and characterization process. Let's hope we can find a better alternative.

- **Ratio modeling:** This will work well if we have the appropriate ratios. As you might expect, part of ratio modeling is calculating the ratios. Once the ratios are calculated, they can be quickly used without gathering additional data. The precision, single component, production system, and the project duration requirements all support using ratio modeling. If our boss wants an immediate answer and we have the ratios, ratio modeling will work. Otherwise, just as with regression analysis, we will need to collect data.

For this example, we need more information about how long we have to answer the question. We also need to verify that this can be a low-precision forecast, and we need know if there is existing ratio or other collected performance data. Either ratio modeling or regression analysis will most likely be good model candidates.

Example 3-3. Selecting a Service-Level-Centric Model

Suppose we are responsible for ensuring that service levels are met for our company's most critical production Oracle database server. In addition to the expected 50% workload increase, we want to forecast using fast CPUs (50% faster) and also the effect of using an improved IO cache (IO service times expected to be 15% faster). We need to know if our existing system can handle the load without breaching service levels. If service levels are going to be breached, we must provide multiple solutions to mitigate the risk. If service levels will be met easily, we are to recommend reducing the hardware to help reduce hardware costs and any associated software licensing costs. This is a routine exercise for us, and we have plenty of historical performance data available. Which model is the most appropriate?

When someone talks about service-level breaches, you should immediately think high risk and expect to use a higher-precision model. Knowing when service levels will be breached typically requires knowing changes in response time. While we have a general idea when response time will begin to skyrocket (at around 80% utilization), that is probably not good enough. So be careful. Let's go with the assumption, which would need to be verified, that we will need to forecast utilization and changes in the response time.

Since utilization and response time change must be forecast, most of our forecasting model options are immediately disqualified. Simple math, ratio modeling, and even regression analysis won't work. While regression analysis can provide high-precision forecasts, it will not provide the response time details we need. In addition, only our basic forecasting formulas and queuing theory can simultaneously handle inputs like service time and changes in the hardware configuration (for example, changing the number of CPUs).

It appears we have both the time and the data needed to use queuing theory. This will allow us to answer the study question with strong precision. While we could probably use the essential forecasting formulas, the effort required to bring the precision up a notch will be well worth the effort, especially considering the importance of the forecast. We will talk about some of these precision-enhancing changes later in this chapter, in the "Response Time Mathematics" section.

At this point, you should have a clear understanding that there are many forecast model options from which to choose. I'm also hoping that you're getting more familiar with selecting the best model or models for a particular forecast. Don't expect a high level of comfort when selecting a forecast model until you've done it a few times. There are many intricacies, and each forecasting situation is slightly different. It will take a while and some experience before you get comfortable.

Baseline Selection

"Now with 15% less fat!" Statements like these beg the question yet provide no reasonable way for us to ask, "15% of what?" It makes a huge difference—15% of 1 kilo is significantly different than 15% of 50 grams. Forecasting is very similar.

All forecasts require input data, and most forecasts are based on a specific situation, time, workload, and hardware configuration. For example, if you want to forecast the number of CPUs required to meet service levels when the workload doubles, you absolutely must know the workload. After all, you can't double something you know nothing about. It's like walking into a store and asking, "Can I please have a double?" The store employee would give you a strange look and try to figure out if your question is to be taken seriously. If so, she will ask you something like, "What would you like a double of?" OK, it's true that if you walked into a hamburger joint and asked for a "double," the employee might be able to interpret and assume you mean a double burger. But there must be context and previous understanding for any reasonable attempt to respond to the question. When forecasting, we must know the context related to any change we would like to forecast.

To identify our change context, we use a special word called the *baseline*. It's a simple word but is preeminently important when forecasting Oracle performance. Suppose you wanted to know how much more workload a system could process before response time skyrocketed. Before we can forecast "more workload," we must know the baseline workload. For example, the baseline workload could be the daily peak workload of 1,534 trx/s. This peak workload would be part of the baseline.

Once the concept of the baseline is understood, the obvious question becomes how to determine the best baselines. Usually, there is no single best baseline. Oracle workloads are so dynamic that picking a single moment in time and basing all your forecasts on that single moment is shortsighted and risky. Usually, multiple baselines are perfectly acceptable. A strong forecast analysis will perform multiple scenarios, each with a different baseline.

For example, suppose between 9 a.m. and 10 a.m., and between 2 p.m. and 3 p.m. are the CPU subsystem's busiest times, with an average utilization of 45%. Between 9 a.m. and 10 a.m., there were 2,500 general-ledger transactions and 150 order-entry transactions processed. But between 2 p.m. and 3 p.m., there were 500 general-ledger transactions and 450 order-entry transactions processed. These workloads are very different. Which should be the baseline? The answer is both. Run your same forecast scenarios but with different baselines. Forecasting using multiple baselines will give you a much broader and deeper understanding of how your system will behave under real-life workload conditions.

It's not always easy to determine the appropriate baselines. Usually, baselines are related to various peak-processing times. It's unusual for IT to make capacity plans based on typical daily usage. IT usually wants to ensure service levels are met during the busiest times—that is, the peak times. A complicating factor occurs, as with the previous example, when various peak workloads are diverse. For example, the peak could be measured by CPU utilization, IO utilization, or system transaction activity. Any one of these could be used to determine the peak activity.

Suppose that the peak transaction processing times occur on Fridays at 3 p.m., but peak IO utilization may occur at noon at the end of each month. What is the true peak? I find that creatively displaying workload data both numerically and graphically helps to locate and select good baselines.

A good tool or product will allow you to view your workload in ways that naturally highlight potential baselines. For example, OraPub's HoriZone product allows the workload to be sorted by any workload component, such as transactional activity, CPU utilization, or IO utilization. Figure 3-1 shows an example of selecting a baseline using OraPub's HoriZone SLM product.

Baseline Selection											
HORIZONE Workload Snapshots									[return to forecast] [reset ordering]		
			System Workload			CPU Subsystem			IO Subsystem		
Current Baseline	Workload Gathering Time	Database	TRX (trx/ms) Descending	IO (kb/trx)	CPU (ms/trx)	CPU Busy (%) Descending	CPU Number	CPU Service Time (ms/trx)	IO Busy (%)	IO Active Devices	IO Service Time (ms/trx)
○	30-Jun-06 10:30:00	weln01p	0.0824	9.9767	1.6368	44	24	1.6368	8	46	9.9767
○	30-Jun-06 10:30:00	anap	0.0220	1.1992	0.3162	44	24	0.3162	8	46	1.1992
○	30-Jun-06 09:30:01	weln01p	0.0893	18.6946	3.0166	42	24	3.0166	9	46	18.6946
○	30-Jun-06 09:30:01	camsft1p	0.0604	28.9822	8.8834	42	24	8.8834	9	46	28.9822
○	30-Jun-06 09:30:01	anap	0.0021	0.7470	0.7742	42	24	0.7742	9	46	0.7470
○	28-Jun-06 16:30:00	weln01p	0.0653	11.2437	1.9912	38	24	1.9912	9	46	11.2437
○	28-Jun-06 16:30:00	camsft1p	0.0529	52.0306	9.6524	38	24	9.6524	9	46	52.0306
○	28-Jun-06 16:30:00	anap	0.0086	37.0427	1.3648	38	24	1.3648	9	46	37.0427
○	30-Jun-06 08:30:00	weln01p	0.0677	24.6812	2.9108	37	24	2.9108	9	46	24.6812
○	30-Jun-06 08:30:00	camsft1p	0.0219	156.8143	12.4349	37	24	12.4349	9	46	156.8143
○	30-Jun-06 08:30:00	anap	0.0055	23.6458	2.4907	37	24	2.4907	9	46	23.6458
○	28-Jun-06 15:30:00	weln01p	0.0852	12.7820	2.2171	37	24	2.2171	9	46	12.7820
○	28-Jun-06 15:30:00	camsft1p	0.0393	101.0311	11.2117	37	24	11.2117	9	46	101.0311
○	28-Jun-06 15:30:00	anap	0.0294	0.3303	0.2305	37	24	0.2305	9	46	0.3303
○	29-Jun-06 09:30:00	weln01p	0.1215	16.1934	2.6010	33	24	2.6010	10	46	16.1934
○	29-Jun-06 09:30:00	camsft1p	0.0641	33.0163	4.9647	33	24	4.9647	10	46	33.0163
○	29-Jun-06 09:30:00	anap	0.0037	1.9825	0.5154	33	24	0.5154	10	46	1.9825
○ ⊘	28-Jun-06 09:30:00	weln01p	0.1142	14.6500	2.5300	32	24	2.5300	14	46	14.6500
○ ⊘	28-Jun-06 09:30:00	camsft1p	0.0778	52.1993	3.9193	32	24	3.9193	14	46	52.1993
○ ⊘	28-Jun-06 09:30:00	anap	0.0031	4.2432	1.1422	32	24	1.1422	14	46	4.2432

Figure 3-1. *Using OraPub's HoriZone, the workload has been sorted by CPU utilization (descending) and then by transaction activity (descending).*

Selecting good baselines is so important that it's a good idea to get input from others. I ask the business managers when their business is most active. I ask IT managers the same question. Then I look at the actual workload activity from multiple perspectives (CPU utilization, transactional activity, and so on). Then I'll select the most likely baselines, present them to key people, and once approved, run the same forecast scenarios for each baseline. This method reduces the risk of a botched project, because I'm considering baselines from a number of different and valid perspectives.

Response Time Mathematics

While our essential forecasting formulas can produce stellar results, it doesn't take a whole lot of extra effort to improve their precision. As you have seen, the essential formulas are great for back-of-the-envelope forecasts and for double-checking more precise models. But it is well worth your time and effort to understand their shortcomings, how to eliminate these shortcomings, and also how to implement the improved math in your forecasting tools.

Erlang C Forecasting Formulas

While our essential forecasting formulas forecast utilization perfectly, they tend to underestimate response time. More precisely, they underestimate queue time. This means that we will be led to believe our Oracle systems can process more work then they actually can. That's bad. By using the *Erlang C* function, our response time forecasts can be improved. Figure 3-2 shows an example of using both methods. Notice that the essential forecasting-based response time does not enter the elbow of the curve until after the Erlang C-based response time curve.

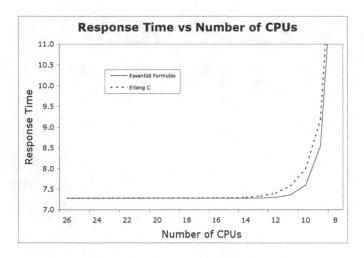

Figure 3-2. *An example of the differences in response time calculation formulas*

The Erlang C function is actually quite famous in forecasting circles, so you may want to know just a little more about the man behind the math. Agner Krarup Erlang (1878–1929) was the first person to study the problem of telephone networks, and his work won him international recognition. Not until the 1960s was his work theory applied to computing systems. His formula is the underlying mathematics still used today in complex telephone networks and computing system forecasting. He was born at Lønborg, in Jutland, Denmark, and had one brother and two sisters. He was extremely smart and had a natural inclination toward scientific research. However, he was considered to be a fantastic teacher, even though his friends called him "The Private Person." He loved travel, mathematics, and the natural sciences. He was known to be a charitable man. He never married but devoted all his time and energy to his work and studies. He sounds like someone I would want to get to know.

When the Erlang C function is used, we do not apply the essential forecasting response time formulas. Instead, we have a single new queue time formula that can be applied to both CPU and IO subsystems. But it's a little tricky. Actually, the Erlang C function is appropriate for only single queue systems. That's fine for CPU subsystems because we model them with a single queue. But you'll recall that an IO subsystem is modeled with each device having its own queue. So we have a slight problem.

The work-around is to chop up the IO subsystem into multiple single-queue, single-server systems. Now we can apply the Erlang C formula. Since each single-queue, single-server IO subsystem is mathematically the same, investigating just one of the systems is enough to understand the entire IO subsystem. We are assuming the IO subsystem has perfectly balanced IO across all the IO devices. Considering today's advanced IO subsystems, this not an unreasonable assumption.

Here's how we make this work for both CPU and IO subsystems. We need to know the number of queues in the entire CPU or IO system (Q_n). We model a CPU subsystem with only one queue ($Q_n = 1$). We model an IO subsystem with each device being serviced by its own queue. Therefore, the number of IO queues will be equal to the number of IO devices (Q_n = number of IO devices).

In this context, a *device* could be a physical hard drive, a partition on a hard drive, a RAID array containing many hard drives, a volume, and so on. The list is endless. The key is whatever you define a device to be, that definition is constant throughout the entire forecasting process.

Using the sar -d or iostat command to dictate what a device is provides a device definition that everyone can see and makes the collection of IO-related statistics more straightforward. Having a single and easily understood device definition allows us to ask questions such as, "What will happen to performance if we add ten more devices?" If the definition of a device is unclear or inconsistent, than general device-related forecasting questions don't make any sense or the underlying forecast model must be much more complex. For example, the forecast model would need to understand the difference between a single physical device, a five-device array, and solid-state devices. This is possible, but starting down this road can result in an extremely complicated model that actually becomes less precise. Again, remember to keep things as simple as possible.

While the variable M is the number of servers in the system, the variable m is defined to be the number of servers *for each queue* in the system. A CPU subsystem has only one queue in the system, but that one queue is associated with all the CPUs. So when modeling CPU subsystems, m is the number of CPUs. For IO subsystems, each device has its own queue, so the number of servers for each queue is always one.

We also need to know the arrival rate at each queue (λ_q). I simply added a q subscript to indicate that the arrival rate is for each queue, not the entire system (λ_{sys}).

For CPU subsystems, there is only one queue, so obviously the entire system arrival rate (λ_{sys}) equals the arrival rate at the one queue (λ_q). But for IO subsystems, the arrival rate at each queue (λ_q) is the system arrival rate (λ_{sys}) divided by the number of IO devices—that is, the number of queues in the system (Q_n). Here's the formula for calculating the arrival rate at each queue (λ_q) for *both* CPU and IO subsystems:

$$\lambda_q = \frac{\lambda_{sys}}{Q_n}$$

Suppose there are 90 transactions entering the IO subsystem each second (λ_{sys}) and there are 10 IO devices (Q_n). So while the system arrival rate (λ_{sys}) is 90 trx/s, the arrival rate at each queue (λ_q) would be 9 (90 / 10). The service time (S_t) would remain the same and the number of servers per queue (m) is 1.

We have a new queue time function (Q_t), based on the Erlang C (E_c) function:

$$E_c = ErlangC\left(m, S_t, \lambda_q\right)$$

$$Q_t = \frac{E_c S_t}{m\left(1 - U\right)}$$

Notice that when the utilization (U) reaches 100%, the denominator becomes 0 and queue time (Q_t) become infinity (which means your formulas and spreadsheets will blow up).

We will continue to use the same utilization (U) and queue length (Q) formulas. The only difference is the use of the arrival rate for each queue (λ_q). And remember, m is the number of servers per queue, not the number of servers in the system.

$$U = \frac{S_t \lambda_q}{m}$$

$$Q = \lambda_q Q_t$$

Here is the Erlang C formula in all its glory:

$$E_c(m, S_t, \lambda_q) = \frac{\dfrac{\left(m S_t \lambda_q\right)^m}{m!}}{\left(1 - m S_t\right) \displaystyle\sum_{k=0}^{m-1} \dfrac{\left(m S_t \lambda_q\right)^k}{k!} + \dfrac{\left(m S_t \lambda_q\right)^m}{m!}}$$

In its mathematical form, this formula doesn't do us a whole lot of good. We still need Erlang C math that we can codify and use ourselves. You have a few options. First, a free queuing theory spreadsheet that uses Erlang's formulas is available from OraPub, at www.orapub.com/tools. You can also search for "Erlang C" on the Internet. Finally, the following Perl script (ErlangC.pl, also available at www.orapub.com/tools) implements the Erlang C function into the new forecasting formulas. You can run the code exactly as it is presented. Just change the initial variables, and you're all set! If all you want is the virgin Erlang C function, just rip it out of the following code.

```perl
#!/usr/bin/perl
# ErlangC.pl     More precise forecasting mathematics using Erlang C
# Created by Craig Shallahamer on August 3, 2006

my $queues              =  1  ; # Queues in entire system
                                # For CPU subsystem will be 1
                                # For IO  subsystem will be number of devices
my $servers             = 24 ; # Servers per each queue
                                # For CPU subsystem will be number of CPUs
                                # For IO  subsystems will be 1
my $service_time        = 4.0; # units example: ms/trx
my $system_arrival_rate = 5.0; # units example: trx/ms

my $queue_arrival_rate  = $system_arrival_rate / $queues ;
my $queue_traffic       = $service_time * $queue_arrival_rate ;

my $rho                 = $queue_traffic / $servers ;
my $ErlangB             = $queue_traffic / ( 1 + $queue_traffic ) ;

# Jagerman's algorithm
my $m=0;
my $eb=0;
for ($m=2;$m<=$servers;$m++) {
    $eb = $ErlangB;
    $ErlangB = $eb * $queue_traffic / ( $m + $eb * $queue_traffic ) ;
}
```

```
my $ErlangC = $ErlangB / ( 1 - $rho + $rho * $ErlangB ) ;

my $utilization = ( $service_time * $queue_arrival_rate ) / $servers ;

my $queue_time = ( $ErlangC * $service_time ) /
                ( $servers * ( 1 - $utilization ) ) ;

my $response_time = $service_time + $queue_time ;

my $queue_length  = $queue_arrival_rate * $queue_time ;

print "\n";
print "Forecasting Oracle Performance by C. Shallahamer \n\n";
print "More Precise Queueing Mathematics with Erlang C \n\n";
print "System arrival rate     = $system_arrival_rate \n";
print "Queues in system        = $queues \n";
print "Queue arrival rate      = $queue_arrival_rate \n";
print "Servers per queue       = $servers \n";
print "Queue traffic           = $queue_traffic \n";
print "Erlang C                = $ErlangC \n";
print "Utilization             = $utilization \n";
print "Service time            = $service_time \n";
print "Queue time              = $queue_time \n";
print "Response time           = $response_time \n";
print "Queue length            = $queue_length \n";
print "\n";
```

You may be surprised to find that sometimes this code snippet blows up or reports strange figures like a negative queue time. It's actually supposed to do that! A queuing system becomes unstable when the workload arriving into the system is greater than the system can ever process; that is, the average utilization becomes greater than 100% and the queue length goes to infinity. The system is then given the highly scientific name of "an unstable system." So if you see errors, division by zeros, and so on when forecasting, don't jump to the conclusion that the model has an error. It could just be the system is unstable and the model has not trapped the error. Interestingly, some simulation products will simply produce a runtime error when the system becomes unstable.

An important caveat is that it is easy to mess up the arrival rates when using the Erlang C formulas. If you remember to calculate both the system arrival rate (λ_{sys}) and then the arrival rate at each queue (λ_q), you'll be fine. Even better is to use a program to help!

Take a close look at Table 3-1. It shows how to use the Erlang C enhanced forecasting formulas. The table examples are not related to the exercises, but do relate to each other. In this table, the CPU subsystem contains 64 CPUs and the IO subsystem contains 950 IO devices.

Table 3-1. *Erlang C Forecasting Formulas for a CPU Subsystem with 64 CPUs and an IO Subsystem with 950 IO Devices*

Name	Symbol/Formula	Examples
Service time	S_t	1.350 ms/trx (CPU) 8.500 ms/trx (IO)
Servers per queue	m	64 CPUs/queue 1 IO device/queue
System arrival rate	λ_{sys}	40 trx/ms
Queues in subsystem	Q_n	1 CPU queue 950 IO queues
Queue arrival rate	$\lambda_q = \dfrac{\lambda_{sys}}{Q_n}$	$\lambda_{q-cpu} = \dfrac{\lambda_{sys}}{Q_{n-cpu}} = \dfrac{40\,trx/ms}{1} = 40.000\,trx/ms$ $\lambda_{q-io} = \dfrac{\lambda_{sys}}{Q_{n-io}} = \dfrac{40\,trx/ms}{950} = 0.042\,trx/ms$
Erlang C	$E_c = ErlangC\left(m, S_t, \lambda_q\right)$ ErlangC.pl, OraPub spreadsheet	$E_{c-cpu} = ErlangC(64, 1.350, 40) = 0.129$ $E_{c-io} = ErlangC(1, 8.5, 0.042) = 0.358$
Utilization	$U = \dfrac{\lambda_q S_t}{m}$	$U_{cpu} = \dfrac{\lambda_{q-cpu} S_{t-cpu}}{m_{cpu}} = \dfrac{40.0\,trx/ms * 1.35\,ms/trx}{64} = \dfrac{54}{64} = 0.844 = 84\%$ $U_{io} = \dfrac{\lambda_{q-io} S_{t-io}}{m_{io}} = \dfrac{0.042\,trx/ms * 8.500\,ms/trx}{1} = 0.357 = 36\%$
Queue time	$Q_t = \dfrac{E_c S_t}{m(1-U)}$	$Q_{t-cpu} = \dfrac{E_{c-cpu} S_{t-cpu}}{m_{cpu}\left(1 - U_{cpu}\right)} = \dfrac{0.129 * 1.350\,ms/trx}{64(1 - 0.844)} = 0.017\,ms/trx$ $Q_{t-io} = \dfrac{E_{c-io} S_{t-io}}{m_{io}\left(1 - U_{io}\right)} = \dfrac{0.358 * 8.500\,ms/trx}{1(1 - 0.357)} = 4.720\,ms/trx$
Queue length	$Q = \lambda_q Q_t$	$Q_{cpu} = \lambda_{q-cpu} Q_{t-cpu} = 40.0\,trx/ms * 0.017\,ms/trx = 0.680$ $Q_{io} = \lambda_{q-io} Q_{t-io} = 0.042\,trx/ms * 4.720\,ms/trx = 0.198$

With the Erlang C mathematics introduced, it's time for some examples. The following three examples use Erlang C math and contrast the essential forecasting math with the more precise (Erlang C-based) response time formulas. Example 3-4 and Example 3-6 focus on the CPU subsystem, whereas Example 3-5 focuses on the IO subsystem.

Example 3-4. Using Erlang C Math for a CPU Subsystem Forecast

Suppose a transaction arrives in the system once every 0.20 second and there are 24 CPUs, which can process a transaction in 4 seconds. Using both the essential forecasting formulas and the Erlang C formulas, what will be the CPU subsystem's utilization, response time, and queue length?

The arrival rate was given in seconds per transaction, so we need to invert it like this:

$$\lambda_{sys} = \frac{1\,trx}{0.20s} = 5.0\,trx/s$$

There is one queue (Q_n), and there are 24 servers for each queue (m):

$$m = 24;\ Q_n = 1$$
$$\lambda_q = \frac{\lambda_{sys}}{Q_n} = \frac{5.0\,trx/s}{1} = 5.0\,trx/s$$
$$S_t = 4.0\,s/trx$$

We can easily calculate the utilization (U), but for the queue length (Q) and the queue time (Q_t), we need Erlang C:

$$U = \frac{S_t \lambda_q}{m} = \frac{4.0\,s/trx * 5.0\,trx/s}{24} = \frac{20}{24} = 0.83 = 83\%$$

When using the ErlangC.pl script, set the system arrival rate as 5 (λ_{sys}), the service time to 4 (S_t), the number of queues in the system to 1 (Q_n), and the number of servers per queue to 24 (m). Here are the results:

```
$ perl ErlangC.pl

Forecasting Oracle Performance by C. Shallahamer

More Precise Queueing Mathematics with Erlang C

System arrival rate    = 5
Queues in system       = 1
Queue arrival rate     = 5
Servers per queue      = 24
Queue traffic          = 20
Erlang C               = 0.298072299793829
Utilization            = 0.833333333333333
Service time           = 4
Queue time             = 0.298072299793829
Response time          = 4.29807229979383
Queue length           = 1.49036149896914
```

Now that we know the Erlang C results, we can calculate the queue time (Q_t), response time (R_t), and the queue length (Q):

$$Q_t = \frac{E_c S_t}{m(1-U)} = \frac{0.298*4.000\,s/trx}{24*(1-0.83333)} = \frac{1.192\,s/trx}{24*0.16667} = \frac{1.192\,s/trx}{4.00008} = 0.298\,s/trx$$

$$R_t = S_t + Q_t = 4.000\,s/trx + 0.298\,s/trx = 4.298\,s/trx$$

$$Q = \lambda_q Q_t = 4\,trx/s * 0.298\,s/trx = 1.192$$

The Erlang C-based queue time is 0.298 s/trx, resulting in a response time of 4.298 s/trx. Our essential forecasting formula response time results in 4.05 s/trx and is as follows:

$$R_{t-cpu} = \frac{S_t}{1-U^M} = \frac{4}{1-0.83333^{24}} = \frac{4}{1-0.01258} = \frac{4}{0.98742} = 4.051\,s/trx$$

The difference of 0.25 s/trx may not seem like much, but that's about a 6% difference. This is significant! Later in this chapter, in the "Contrasting Forecasting Formulas" section, I discuss the differences between the two formulas.

Example 3-5. Using Erlang C Math for an IO Subsystem Forecast

Suppose our IO subsystem consists of 450 RAID arrays, and each array can service a transaction in 19.4 ms. It has been determined that around 4,500 transactions arrive at the IO subsystem each second. Using both the essential forecasting formulas and the Erlang C formulas, what will be the IO subsystem's utilization, response time, and queue length?

Don't get confused by the mention of a "RAID array." An array, filer, or a physical disk can be modeled as a queuing theory server. The trick is each "device" must have the same characteristics. For example, it would be much more complicated to model an IO subsystem containing flash memory, an EMC array, and standard SCSI devices.

As with any forecasting problem, ensure unit consistency. We were given time in both seconds and milliseconds. Let's standardize on milliseconds:

$$\lambda_{sys} = \frac{4500\,trx}{1s} * \frac{1s}{1000ms} = 4.5\,trx/ms$$

There are 450 devices and 450 queues (Q_n), and there is one server for each queue (m):

$$m = 1;\ Q_n = 450$$

$$\lambda_q = \frac{\lambda_{sys}}{Q_n} = \frac{4.5\,trx/ms}{450} = 0.010\,trx/ms$$

$$S_t = 19.4\,ms/trx$$

We can easily calculate the utilization (U), but for the queue time (Q_t) and queue length (Q) we need Erlang C:

$$U = \frac{S_t\lambda_q}{m} = \frac{19.4\,ms/trx * 0.010\,trx/ms}{1} = \frac{0.194}{1} = 0.194 = 19.4\%$$

When using the ErlangC.pl script, the system arrival rate is 4.5 (λ_{sys}), the number of queues in the system (Q_n) is 450, and the number of servers per queue is 1 (m). Here are the results:

```
$ perl ErlangC.pl

Forecasting Oracle Performance by C. Shallahamer

More Precise Queueing Mathematics with Erlang C

System arrival rate    = 4.5
Queues in system       = 450
Queue arrival rate     = 0.01
Servers per queue      = 1
Queue traffic          = 0.194
Erlang C               = 0.194
Utilization            = 0.194
Service time           = 19.4
Queue time             = 4.66947890818858
Response time          = 24.0694789081886
Queue length           = 0.0466947890818858
```

Now that we know the Erlang C results, we can calculate the queue time (Q_t), response time (R_t), and the queue length (Q):

$$Q_t = \frac{E_cS_t}{m(1-U)} = \frac{0.194 * 19.400\,ms/trx}{1*(1-0.194)} = \frac{3.764\,ms/trx}{1*0.806} = \frac{3.764\,ms/trx}{0.806} = 4.669\,ms/trx$$

$$R_t = S_t + Q_t = 19.4\,ms/trx + 4.669\,ms/trx = 24.069\,ms/trx$$

$$Q = \lambda_q Q_t = 0.010\,trx/ms * 4.669\,ms/trx = 0.047$$

Notice that although the average IO device utilization is only 19%, there is a slight queue with transactions waiting an average of 4.669 ms before they are serviced. Even at low utilizations, because each server has its own queue, it is more likely that transactions will bunch up. This does not happen with a single queue CPU subsystem, and hence queuing does not set in until the utilization is much higher in a CPU subsystem.

The Erlang C-based queue time is 4.669 ms/trx, resulting in a response time of 24.069 ms/trx. As the following shows, the essential forecasting formula response time also results in 24.069 ms/trx.

$$R_{t-io} = \frac{S_t}{1-U} = \frac{19.4}{1-0.194} = \frac{19.4}{1-0.194} = \frac{19.4}{0.806} = 24.069\,ms/trx$$

Interesting! So sometimes the essential forecasting formulas match the Erlang C-based formulas. I'll discuss this in more detail after the next example.

Example 3-6. Using Erlang C Math for Another CPU Subsystem Forecast

Suppose our CPU subsystem consists of 32 CPUs that can process a transaction in 0.012 ms. The workload (that is, the system arrival rate) has been determined to be 2,200 trx/ms. Using both the essential forecasting formulas and the Erlang C-based formulas, what will be the CPU subsystem's utilization, response time, and queue length?

$$\lambda_{sys} = 2200 \, trx/ms$$

There is one queue (Q_n), and there are 32 servers for each queue (m):

$$m = 32; \ Q_n = 1$$

$$\lambda_q = \frac{\lambda_{sys}}{Q_n} = \frac{2200 \, trx/ms}{1} = 2200 \, trx/ms$$

$$S_t = 0.012 \, ms/trx$$

We can easily calculate the utilization (U), but we need Erlang C to calculate the queue time (Q_t), response time (R_t), and queue length (Q):

$$U = \frac{S_t \lambda_q}{m} = \frac{0.012 \, ms/trx * 2200 \, trx/ms}{32} = \frac{26.4}{32} = 0.825 = 83\%$$

When using the ErlangC.pl script, set the system arrival rate to 2200 (λ_{sys}), the service time to 0.012 (S_t), the number of queues in the system (Q_n) to 1, and the number of servers per queue to 32 (m). Here are the results:

```
$ perl ErlangC.pl

Forecasting Oracle Performance by C. Shallahamer

More Precise Queueing Mathematics with Erlang C

System arrival rate      = 2200
Queues in system         = 1
Queue arrival rate       = 2200
Servers per queue        = 32
Queue traffic            = 26.4
Erlang C                 = 0.215343208481877
Utilization              = 0.825
Service time             = 0.012
Queue time               = 0.000461449732461164
Response time            = 0.0124614497324612
Queue length             = 1.01518941141456
```

Now that we know the Erlang C results, we can calculate the queue time (Q_t), response time (R_t), and queue length (Q).

$$Q_t = \frac{E_c S_t}{m(1-U)} = \frac{0.2153 * 0.012 \, ms/trx}{32 * (1 - 0.825)} = \frac{0.003 \, ms/trx}{32 * 0.175} = \frac{0.003 \, ms/trx}{5.600} = 0.000 \, ms/trx$$

$$R_t = S_t + Q_t = 0.012 \, ms/trx + 0.000 \, ms/trx = 0.012 \, ms/trx$$

$$Q = \lambda_q Q_t = 2200 \, trx/ms * 0.000 \, ms/trx = 0.00$$

Because the Erlang C-based queue time is 0, the response time is equal to the service time of 0.012 ms/trx. Our essential forecasting formula response time result is also 0.012 ms/trx.

$$R_{t-cpu} = \frac{S_t}{1 - U^M} = \frac{0.012}{1 - 0.825^{32}} = \frac{0.012}{1 - 0.002} = \frac{0.012}{0.998} = 0.012 \, ms/trx$$

Contrasting Forecasting Formulas

Using new formulas is practical only if they make a difference. One thing I quickly learned when forecasting was that if I could *not* explain my method, and to a lesser extent, the mathematics, people tended to *not* trust the results. It's the classic situation where if people do not understand something, they immediately question its validity. This is why the thought experiments in Chapter 2 are so important. It helps you and the people you work with to get a feel for the queuing theory-related relationships.

When the mathematical calculations become more complicated, I tend to not use them unless there is a clear advantage. I ask myself, "What is the benefit in using something more complicated?" It's a valid question, because people tend to hide behind complexity, hoping no one will ask questions. Complexity increases the chance of error, so there must be a good reason for increasing complexity.

While the essential forecasting formulas tend to underestimate queue time, and the Erlang C-enabled formulas are supposed to provide an exact queue time calculation, what does this really mean to us? As our previous examples demonstrated, sometimes using the essential forecasting mathematics calculates the queue time just as well as using the Erlang C formulas. The difference—that is, the error in the essential forecasting formulas—is not constant, but depends on both the utilization (U) and the number of servers per queue (m).

Take a close look at Figure 3-3. The vertical axis is the difference in queue times; more specifically, the queue time calculation of the essential forecasting mathematics minus the Erlang C mathematics. Notice the dramatic drop in the slope. This shows the essential forecasting math underforecasts (produces an optimistic forecast of) the queuing effect. Interestingly, with only a few servers (three to twelve) the difference is relatively significant even at lower utilizations. But with just one, two, or more than twelve servers, the queue time difference diminishes.

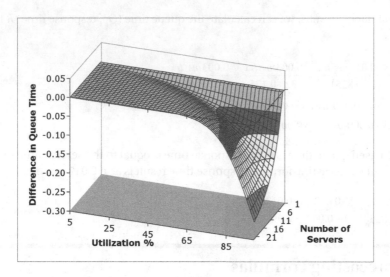

Figure 3-3. *Differences in queue time formulas*

Table 3-2 is organized by how most Oracle servers are configured. Most CPU subsystems are configured with 2, 12, 24, 32, or 64 CPUs. Performance analysts start paying attention when the CPU utilization surpasses 70%, and pay very close attention when it's into the mid-80% range; above that, performance is probably breaching service levels.

Table 3-2. *Sample Differences in Response Time Calculations, with Service Time of 1 ms/trx and the Arrival Rate Manipulated to Achieve the Desired Utilization*

Number of Servers Per Queue	0% to 70% Busy	71% to 85% Busy	86% to 100% Busy
1 to 2	0.00 to 0.00	0.00 to 0.00	0.00 to 0.00
3 to 5	0.00 to 0.05	0.00 to 0.07	0.03 to 0.10
6 to 12	0.00 to 0.04	0.05 to 0.11	0.09 to 0.20
13 to 24	0.00 to 0.01	0.03 to 0.06	0.08 to 0.26
25 to 32	0.00 to 0.00	0.00 to 0.07	0.07 to 0.28
33 to 64	0.00 to 0.00	0.00 to 0.05	0.03 to 0.30

So what does all this mean? Well, if you are forecasting a two CPU Linux server, as Table 3-2 shows, regardless of the response time math used, the response times difference is zero. When forecasting, we typically pay close attention to when utilization creeps over 70%. All but the smallest database servers will exhibit a significant difference in the response time calculations. So with larger database servers, you should always use the Erlang C formulas if possible.

Remember the example in Chapter 2 about Bob's boss Frank? In Chapter 2, we used only the essential forecasting formulas. Figure 3-2, shown earlier in the chapter, is the graph showing the differences in response time. Now let's take a look at the actual numeric results, as shown in Table 3-3.

Table 3-3. *Sample Differences in Queue Time and Response Time Calculations*

CPUs (*m*)	% Busy (*U*)	Essential R_t	Essential Q_t	Erlang C R_t	Erlang C Q_t	Q_t % Diff
26	28%	7.2800	0.0000	7.2800	0.0000	0.00%
25	29%	7.2800	0.0000	7.2800	0.0000	0.00%
24	30%	7.2800	0.0000	7.2800	0.0000	0.00%
23	32%	7.2800	0.0000	7.2800	0.0000	0.00%
22	33%	7.2800	0.0000	7.2800	0.0000	0.00%
21	35%	7.2800	0.0000	7.2800	0.0000	0.00%
20	36%	7.2800	0.0000	7.2800	0.0000	0.00%
19	38%	7.2800	0.0000	7.2801	0.0001	0.00%
18	40%	7.2800	0.0000	7.2804	0.0004	-0.01%
17	43%	7.2800	0.0000	7.2812	0.0012	–0.02%
16	46%	7.2800	0.0000	7.2831	0.0031	–0.04%
15	49%	7.2801	0.0001	7.2883	0.0083	–0.11%
14	52%	7.2808	0.0008	7.3009	0.0209	–0.28%
13	56%	7.2839	0.0039	7.3314	0.0514	–0.65%
12	61%	7.2981	0.0181	7.4033	0.1233	–1.42%
11	66%	7.3585	0.0785	7.5736	0.2936	–2.84%
10	73%	7.5977	0.3177	7.9949	0.7149	–4.97%
9	81%	8.5471	1.2671	9.1932	1.9132	–7.03%
8	91%	13.7424	6.4624	14.6508	7.3708	–6.20%
7	104%	–23.0429	–30.3229	–23.0429	–30.3229	0.00%
6	121%	–3.3232	–10.6032	–3.3232	–10.6032	0.00%

As we would expect, the difference in response time increases as the number of CPUs decreases, causing the utilization to increase. Even before we get deep into the elbow of the curve, the queue time difference is more than 5%. This is why it's always a good idea to use the Erlang C-enabled formulas.

Average Calculation

Improving our forecasting formulas is just one way to improve forecast precision. We can do a host of other things. One of the most important and yet commonly overlooked ways to improve precision is to properly calculate averages.

Precise formulas are great, but if you put bogus data into them, well, you'll get bogus forecasts. What is so insidious about forecasting is that you may never know your forecast is worthless, and so you'll mislead others and yourself.[1] In the next chapter, I'll present the core statistics you'll need to survive when forecasting, but before that, I need to talk about the *average*.

We enter only a few numbers into our forecasting formulas. These few numbers are supposed to represent an extremely complex and fluid Oracle system. We need every trick we can think of to make these numbers the best they can be. Our concern over averages relate to arrival patterns, service time patterns, and also a lot of sample data. First, we'll discuss arrival patterns, and then we'll discuss a better way to average a lot of samples.

The Right Distribution Pattern

When we talk about utilization, service time, and arrival rates, we're really talking about the average utilization, average service time, and average arrival rate. I didn't mention this earlier because I didn't want to further complicate matters.

When most people think of an average, a normal distribution comes to mind. That is, it's just as likely a number will be greater than the average as it will be less than the average. For example, if I said the average student age in my classes is 27 plus or minus 7, you would immediately assume most students are between 20 and 34. While the normal distribution works great in many situations, when we work with arrival rates and service times, we need to use a different distribution.

Take a look at Figure 3-4. Suppose the figure represents a one-minute snapshot of people arriving into an office building. While the average arrival rate is 6 people per minute, their arrival patterns, or distributions, are very different. Different arrival or service time distributions make a significant difference in forecast response time and queue length.

Figure 3-4. *Two different arrival patterns that have the same average arrival rate*

If you worked at a fast-food restaurant, which would you prefer: customers walking into the restaurant perfectly spaced with an even arrival pattern or customers arriving in two big groups? Of course you would want the even arrival pattern, because you know from experience that the average queue will be shorter and more consistent. (We'll get into this a lot more in Chapter 5.)

---

1. One way to prevent making potentially embarrassing (and career-shortening) mistakes is to perform the same forecast using different forecast models. For example, to help ensure I didn't botch my math when writing this book, I used simulation, Erlang C, and the essential forecasting formulas for every exercise and case study. This is another advantage to using a product instead of doing the grunt work yourself.

The accepted arrival and service time pattern for modern database servers is called the *exponential distribution*. It's very different than the normal distribution. The exponential distribution is shown in Figure 3-5. The vertical axis is the likelihood the arrival rate (or service time) will be the value shown on the horizontal axis (actually the value divided by the mean). This means it is more likely that a value less than the mean will be chosen than a value that is greater than the mean. A normal distribution is just as likely to produce a value greater than the average as it is to produce a value that is less than the average. An exponential distribution is less likely to produce a value twice the average than it is to produce a value half the average. A little more practically, the arrival (or service time) pattern will have a lot of values less than the mean and few values greater than the mean.

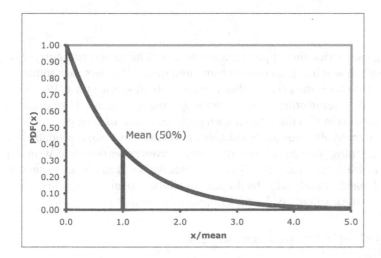

Figure 3-5. *Probability density function (PDF) of the exponential distribution*

The Erlang C formulas assume an exponential distribution, which is one reason why they are more precise than the essential forecasting formulas. But just as important as using the correct distribution is deriving a single best value that represents many samples.

How to Average Diverse Values

Averages are supposed to represent a group of samples. But sometimes the samples are so diverse that the average doesn't represent the samples very well. When forecasting, this can cause imprecision. If you have never thought about this, it will seem strange, but take a look at Table 3-4. What's the average service time?

Table 3-4. *Determining the Average Service Time*

Transaction	Arrival Rate (trx/m)	Service Time (min/trx)
GL Journal entry	10	10
Web hit	500	2
Order entry	2	25

Most people would say the average service time is 12.3:

$$12.3 = \frac{10 + 2 + 25}{3} = \frac{37}{3}$$

However, is 12.3 a good service time representation for a *web hit* or an *order entry*? No. Even stranger is there are 500 web hits each minute compared to only 2 orders each minute. So wouldn't it make sense to have the average closer to the web hit service time? When we influence an average based on some other value, we are *weighting* the average. I like to call the average calculation that results in 12.3 the *straight average* or the *standard average*.

Besides properly characterizing your workload, using a weighted average is probably the most precision-enhancing thing you can do! To derive a better average service time, weight it based on its associated arrival rate. First, multiply each transaction's arrival rate by its service time. Then add them all together and divide by the sum of all the arrivals. Here is how the weighted average service time is calculated for the example in Table 3-4:

$$S_{t:wa} = \frac{(10*10) + (500*2) + (2*25)}{10 + 500 + 2} = \frac{100 + 1000 + 50}{552} = \frac{1150}{552} = 2.08$$

Doesn't an average of 2.08 just feel better than 12.3? It captures the essence or the characteristic of the service time. Just imagine the difference in utilization, queue time, queue length, and response time using these different values would produce! Here is the actual weighted average formula in math geek format:

$$S_{t:wa} = \frac{\sum_{i=0}^{i=n}(\lambda_i S_{t:i})}{\sum_{i=0}^{i=n}\lambda_i}$$

Example 3-7 contrasts forecasting results when using a standard average and a weighted average. As you'll see, the differences can be shocking!

Example 3-7. Using Standard Average vs. Weighted Average Data

Suppose we wanted to forecast IO utilization and response time. Peak processing occurs over a one-hour duration on Tuesday afternoons. The data was gathered using the Unix `iostat` command. To perform our forecasts and to validate the forecasted utilization, the queuing theory model requires the number of devices, the arrival rate, and the average service time. Table 3-5 shows the collected data, and Table 3-6 shows summary information.

Table 3-5. *Detailed IO Device Statistics*

IO Device	R+W Reqs/ms	Service Time (ms)
c4t13d1	27.19	8.21
c4t13d2	17.27	17.94
c4t13d3	13.96	4.42
c4t13d4	11.36	13.92
c4t13d5	64.50	11.88
c4t13d6	14.57	6.97
c4t13d7	21.33	4.38
c4t14d0	14.88	2.83
c4t14d1	14.89	10.85
c4t14d2	36.74	7.44
c4t14d3	72.40	18.45
c4t14d4	19.69	3.81
c4t14d5	29.76	18.46
c4t14d6	23.67	6.37

Table 3-6. *Summary IO Device Statistics*

Description	Data
Number of devices	14
Total reqs/sec	382
Straight average S_t(ms)	9.71
Weighted average S_t (ms)	11.26

Notice the average service time differences. The straight average is 9.71 ms, and the weighted average is 11.26 ms. This may not seem like much, but look closely at Table 3-7. The far-left column is the arrival rate. The next four columns are based on the straight average service time calculation, followed by forecasts based on the weighted average service time.

Table 3-7. *Determining the Good Average Value Can Significantly Affect Forecast Precision*

| System Arrival Rate (req/s) | Straight Average Service Time | | | | Weighted Average Service Time | | | | |
	Service Time (s/req)	Busy %	Essential RT (s/req)	Erlang C RT (s/req)	Service Time (s/req)	Busy %	Essential RT (s/req)	Erlang C RT (s/req)	Diff Erlang C RT
0.00	0.0097	0%	0.0097	0.0097	0.0113	0%	0.0113	0.0113	–14%
48.77	0.0097	3%	0.0100	0.0100	0.0113	4%	0.0117	0.0117	–14%
97.55	0.0097	7%	0.0104	0.0104	0.0113	8%	0.0122	0.0122	–15%
146.32	0.0097	10%	0.0108	0.0108	0.0113	12%	0.0127	0.0127	–15%
195.10	0.0097	14%	0.0112	0.0112	0.0113	16%	0.0133	0.0133	–16%
243.87	0.0097	17%	0.0117	0.0117	0.0113	20%	0.0140	0.0140	–16%
292.65	0.0097	20%	0.0122	0.0122	0.0113	24%	0.0147	0.0147	–17%
341.42	0.0097	24%	0.0127	0.0127	0.0113	27%	0.0155	0.0155	–18%
390.19	0.0097	27%	0.0133	0.0133	0.0113	31%	0.0164	0.0164	–19%
438.97	0.0097	30%	0.0140	0.0140	0.0113	35%	0.0174	0.0174	–20%
487.74	0.0097	34%	0.0147	0.0147	0.0113	39%	0.0185	0.0185	–21%
536.52	0.0097	37%	0.0155	0.0155	0.0113	43%	0.0198	0.0198	–22%
585.29	0.0097	41%	0.0163	0.0163	0.0113	47%	0.0212	0.0212	–23%
634.06	0.0097	44%	0.0173	0.0173	0.0113	51%	0.0229	0.0229	–24%
682.84	0.0097	47%	0.0184	0.0184	0.0113	55%	0.0249	0.0249	–26%
731.61	0.0097	51%	0.0197	0.0197	0.0113	59%	0.0273	0.0273	–28%
780.39	0.0097	54%	0.0212	0.0212	0.0113	63%	0.0302	0.0302	–30%
829.16	0.0097	58%	0.0229	0.0229	0.0113	67%	0.0337	0.0337	–32%
877.94	0.0097	61%	0.0248	0.0248	0.0113	71%	0.0382	0.0382	–35%
926.71	0.0097	64%	0.0272	0.0272	0.0113	74%	0.0441	0.0441	–38%
975.48	0.0097	68%	0.0300	0.0300	0.0113	78%	0.0521	0.0521	–42%
1024.26	0.0097	71%	0.0335	0.0335	0.0113	82%	0.0636	0.0636	–47%
1073.03	0.0097	74%	0.0380	0.0380	0.0113	86%	0.0817	0.0817	–54%
1121.81	0.0097	78%	0.0437	0.0437	0.0113	90%	0.1142	0.1142	–62%
1170.58	0.0097	81%	0.0516	0.0516	0.0113	94%	0.1895	0.1895	–73%
1219.35	0.0097	85%	0.0629	0.0629	0.0113	98%	0.5580	0.5580	–89%
1268.13	0.0097	88%	0.0806	0.0806	0.0113	102%	–0.5911	N/A	N/A
1316.90	0.0097	91%	0.1121	0.1121	0.0113	106%	–0.1932	N/A	N/A
1365.68	0.0097	95%	0.1839	0.1839	0.0113	110%	–0.1155	N/A	N/A
1414.45	0.0097	98%	0.5117	0.5117	0.0113	114%	–0.0823	N/A	N/A
1463.23	0.0097	101%	–0.6538	–0.6538	0.0113	118%	–0.0640	N/A	N/A

Look at the differences between the essential and Erlang C response time results. There are no differences! That's because with IO subsystems, the number of servers per queue is only one, and when there are one or two servers per queue, the error is virtually zero.

However, look at the far-right column in Table 3-7. This column shows the difference between Erlang C response time calculations based on the standard service time average and using the weighted service time average. The response time difference is very significant. From the start, the service time difference causes an immediate 14% response time difference, which continues to increase to nearly 90%! Figure 3-6 shows the stunning difference graphically.

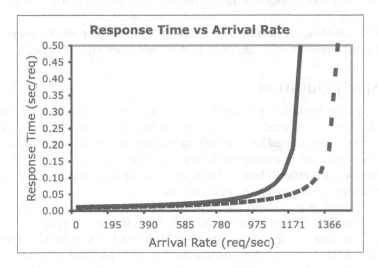

Figure 3-6. *Using a weighted average service time can make a significant response time difference. The dotted line is based on a straight average.*

As this example shows, using a weighted average instead of a straight average can have a significant effect on your forecasts. In this example, had we made recommendations based on the straight average, we would have expected our IO subsystem to handle a workload that it probably would not have been able to endure. As a result, we would have been surprised when the IO subsystem response time skyrocketed and service levels started to breach—all because we got lazy and did not use a weighted average. Considering how simple it is to calculate a weighted average and the potential benefits of doing so, always use a weighted average unless you have a very good reason to do otherwise.

Case Study: Highlight Company

We have covered a lot over the past few chapters. In this chapter alone, I've introduced forecasting gotchas, additional forecasting models, more advanced forecasting mathematics, baselines, and weighted averages. These are important and will significantly impact your forecasts. But all this information can be overwhelming, and applying it in a real-life situation can, at first, be daunting. A case study will help solidify these new concepts so they become useful and not just interesting factoids.

Our case study is a forecast for the Highlight Company, which is an electric light recycler (the company gathers, recycles, and resells electric lights). Over the past few years, Highlight's sales have steadily risen. Company executives are looking for ways to increase sales and market share.

We're busy at work and minding our own business. On Friday afternoon, just when we're getting ready to leave for a relaxing holiday, our manager casually stops by and says, "Highlight just acquired a tungsten mine. All the new company's business processes will immediately cease, and on Monday, they will begin using our existing systems. That's not going to be a problem, is it?"

While this situation is unsettling, it's not all that uncommon. If you are prepared in advance, you'll find that answering questions like these can easily be done within a couple of hours.

Determine the Study Question

The first thing to do is clearly understand the study question. What the boss just asked can be translated to "Can our database server handle the increased workload?" But there is a serious problem here, because the word *increased* has not been quantified. However, even without workload increase details, we can still perform some forecasts and present our results to management. Obviously, someone will eventually have to decide what the expected workload increase will be, but that should not stop us from doing our initial analysis.

There are many ways the scope of our work can be defined. While a Request For Proposal (RFP) and a project proposal will typically define the project's scope, it is always a good idea to confirm the scope with the project manager. The scope must be defined, or you will not know the bounds of your work. For this case study, let's assume that we are to consider only the CPU and IO subsystems. Networking and memory are out of scope.

Gather and Characterize Workload

Next, we must gather workload data and characterize it, so it's useful while forecasting and also for forecast model input. Fortunately, we've been collecting workload data over the past few months (good job!). How we will characterize our workload is partly based on the selected forecast model. Looking ahead, since we'll be using our Erlang C-based forecasting formulas and considering the study question, a very simple workload characterization is required.

Computing system activity will be grouped into three interrelated categories: CPU activity, IO subsystem activity, and application workload. A single general application workload category will be used. For this example, the Oracle internal statistic user calls will represent the application workload. Through the math, we will link these three categories together. Establishing a relationship among the workload components is essential for a more complete and true computing system model.

Select the Forecast Model

While we've been thinking about using Erlang C-based queuing theory for our forecasting model, we need to carefully consider our other options:

- Simple math is not good enough because it does not consider queuing, and queuing is obviously important when forecasting CPU and IO subsystem response time.

- Ratio modeling is not appropriate because our study question is centered on the entire workload, not specific workload portions like OLTP or batch work. In addition, ratio modeling has a very low precision (and is not statistically validated), so if we can avoid using it, we will.

- Regression analysis works best when the study question relates to one or more key business processes. We could use the general workload (that is, the arrival rate) and relate that to CPU and IO utilization, but why do that when we can use queuing theory, which obviously considers queuing? So regression analysis is not a good choice.

- Essential forecasting mathematics could be used. The study question relates to increasing the general workload and is concerned about changes in response time. However, with just a little bit more effort, we could use our Erlang C-enabled forecasting formulas.

Since we already have the Erlang C functions built into a spreadsheet, we don't need to use the ErlangC.pl script and run it a bunch of times, consolidate the data, and graph it. Our best option is to use our Erlang C queuing theory formulas.

Forecast and Validate

Before we start plugging numbers into our spreadsheet, for both the CPU subsystem and the IO subsystem, we need to determine the service time, the number of servers, and the arrival rate. Since we have been collecting data for three months, we have many possibilities. Now we need to determine the baseline.

The Baseline

The baseline must be carefully selected, as all our forecasts will be based on the baseline. When we present a 50% workload increase, it will be a 50% baseline workload increase. So we had better choose wisely.

There are many ways to view workload data. We want to focus on ways to quickly locate peak activity. One of the easiest ways to determine peak activity is to simply query the data directly from Oracle. Another option is to place the data into a spreadsheet. One way OraPub's SLM product, HoriZone, help users select the baseline is by displaying data in a spreadsheet-like format with the ability to quickly apply different sorting options. An example of this is shown in Figure 3-1 earlier in this chapter.

Another option is to graph the workload data. There is an infinite number of ways to graph workload data. Graphing is helpful when peak workloads express themselves in a variety of ways. For example, the peak activity may be when the arrival rate is the highest, when the CPU utilization is the highest, or perhaps when the IO utilization is the highest. Or the peak may be some combination of all three, which is usually the case. This is why it is usually best to select and forecast based on multiple baselines.

After carefully observing workload data from a graphical and spreadsheet perspective, a few baselines where selected. In this case study, we will forecast using one of these baselines. The baseline chosen for this case study has a peak application workload of 323.243 ktrx/ms (thousands of trx/ms), 32 CPUs with an average utilization of 33%, and 60 active IO devices with an average utilization of 45%.

This information can be gathered easily from any Oracle database and operating system. Notice the CPU and IO service times were not gathered. Sometimes the data we need is simply not available; other times, we want to derive the data. Since we cannot gather CPU service time, we must derive it. We could have gathered the IO service time. However, the forecast precision will be better if we use a common Oracle-centric arrival rate for both the CPU and IO subsystems. Using a common arrival rate will establish a link, or relationship, between the CPU, IO, and application subsystems. This leaves only one unknown variable: the service time. So out of necessity, we will derive the CPU service time, but for higher precision, we will derive the IO service time.

Remember that a CPU subsystem is modeled with one queue for all servers (Q_n), and the number of servers for each queue (m) is the number of CPUs. Here are our baseline CPU forecasts:

$$\lambda_q = \frac{\lambda_{sys}}{Q_n} = \frac{323.243\,ktrx/ms}{1} = 323.243\,ktrx/ms$$

$$U = \frac{S_t\lambda_q}{m}$$

$$S_t = \frac{Um}{\lambda_q} = \frac{0.330*32}{323.243\,ktrx/ms} = \frac{10.560}{323.243\,ktrx/ms} = 0.033\,ms/ktrx$$

$$E_c\left(m,S_t,\lambda_q\right) = E_c\left(32,0.033,323.243\right) = 0.000$$

$$Q_t = \frac{E_c S_t}{m\left(1-U\right)} = \frac{0.000*0.033\,ms/trx}{1\left(1-0.330\right)} = \frac{0.000\,ms/trx}{0.670} = 0.00\,ms/trx$$

$$R_t = S_t + Q_t = 0.033\,ms/trx + 0.000\,ms/trx = 0.033\,ms/trx$$

For the IO subsystem, we know the number of devices and the arrival rate, but not the service time. We model an IO subsystem with one queue for each server (m). Since there are 60 IO devices, there will be 60 queues (Q_n). Here are our baseline IO forecasts:

$$U = 0.45$$

$$Q_n = 60$$

$$\lambda_q = \frac{\lambda_{sys}}{Q_n} = \frac{323.243\,ktrx/ms}{60} = 5.387\,ktrx/ms$$

$$m = 1$$

$$S_t = \frac{Um}{\lambda_q} = \frac{0.450*1}{5.387\,ktrx/ms} = 0.084\,ms/ktrx$$

$$E_c\left(m,S_t,\lambda_q\right) = E_c\left(1,0.084,5.387\right) = 0.450$$

$$Q_t = \frac{E_c S_t}{m\left(1-U\right)} = \frac{0.450*0.084\,ms/trx}{1\left(1-0.450\right)} = \frac{0.0378\,ms/trx}{0.65} = 0.058\,ms/trx$$

$$R_t = S_t + Q_t = 0.0835\,ms/trx + 0.058\,ms/trx = 0.1415\,ms/trx$$

CPU and IO Forecasts

In themselves, baseline queue times and response times are of little value. After all, by itself, milliseconds per transaction do not mean anything to the end user or us. The useful information is where the response times changes and what influences the change. Table 3-8 shows the CPU forecasts, and Table 3-9 shows the IO forecasts. Focus on what arrival rate increase causes a significant response time change.

Table 3-8. *The Case Study CPU Forecasts*

Arrival Rate Increase	Arrival Rate	Utilization	Service Time	Response Time	Response Time Change	Pct RT Change
0%	323	33.0%	0.033	0.033	0.000	0.000
10%	356	36.3%	0.033	0.033	0.000	0.000
20%	388	39.6%	0.033	0.033	0.000	0.000
30%	420	42.9%	0.033	0.033	0.000	0.000
40%	453	46.2%	0.033	0.033	0.000	0.000
50%	485	49.5%	0.033	0.033	0.000	0.000
60%	517	52.8%	0.033	0.033	0.000	0.000
70%	550	56.1%	0.033	0.033	0.000	0.000
80%	582	59.4%	0.033	0.033	0.000	0.000
90%	614	62.7%	0.033	0.033	0.000	0.000
100%	646	66.0%	0.033	0.033	0.000	0.001
110%	679	69.3%	0.033	0.033	0.000	0.002
120%	711	72.6%	0.033	0.033	0.000	0.003
130%	743	75.9%	0.033	0.033	0.000	0.006
140%	776	79.2%	0.033	0.033	0.001	0.010
150%	808	82.5%	0.033	0.034	0.001	0.016
160%	840	85.8%	0.033	0.035	0.002	0.028
170%	873	89.1%	0.033	0.037	0.004	0.050
180%	905	92.4%	0.033	0.040	0.008	0.099
190%	937	95.7%	0.033	0.050	0.017	0.245
200%	970	99.0%	0.033	0.128	0.095	1.555
210%	1002	102.3%	0.033	−0.019	−0.052	−1.148

Table 3-9. *Case Study IO Forecasts*

Arrival Rate Increase	Arrival Rate	Utilization	Service Time	Response Time	Response Time Change
0%	323	45.0%	0.0835	0.152	0.000
10%	356	49.5%	0.0835	0.165	0.014
20%	388	54.0%	0.0835	0.182	0.030
30%	420	58.5%	0.0835	0.201	0.049
40%	453	63.0%	0.0835	0.226	0.074
50%	485	67.5%	0.0835	0.257	0.105
60%	517	72.0%	0.0835	0.298	0.146
70%	550	76.5%	0.0835	0.355	0.204
80%	582	81.0%	0.0835	0.440	0.288
90%	614	85.5%	0.0835	0.576	0.424
100%	646	90.0%	0.0835	0.835	0.683
110%	679	94.5%	0.0835	1.519	1.367
120%	711	99.0%	0.0835	8.353	8.201
130%	743	103.5%	0.0835	−2.387	−2.538

Let's look at these tables (Table 3-8 and Table 3-9) and their associated figures (Figure 3-7 and Figure 3-8) a little more closely. The initial arrival rate change is 0% because the first row is the baseline. (I purposely chose the arrival rate increments to make the tables useful and also so the tables would fit on a page.)

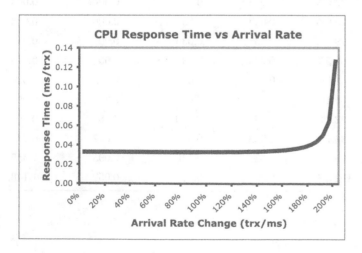

Figure 3-7. *The CPU subsystem response time curve*

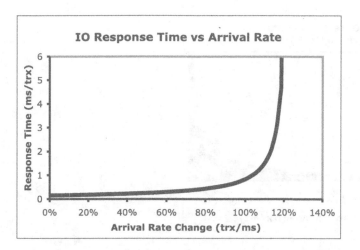

Figure 3-8. *The IO subsystem response time curve*

Notice the IO response time contains significant queue time even at the baseline ($Q_t = R_t - S_t$) and continues to increase as the workload increases. There is significant queue time, even with an average utilization of only 45%! This is easy to see graphically in Figure 3-8 because there is a slope to the response time curve before the elbow of the curve occurs. This is the result of the one-queue-per-server configuration and is very realistic. In contrast, with the CPU subsystem shown in Figure 3-7, queuing does not set in (that is, the response time does not significantly change) until the utilization is around 80% (150% workload increase). The CPU queue time is virtually zero and then skyrockets because there are 32 CPUs. If the system had fewer CPUs, the slope, while still steep, would have been more gradual.

To determine when the response time begins to significantly affect performance, it is helpful to look at response time from an overall system perspective, not just a CPU or an IO perspective. It is also important to understand which subsystem becomes the initial bottleneck. Take a close look at Figure 3-9. Our focus is not on the actual response time, but on the response time *change*. While the system response time is slowing increasing (mostly due to IO queue time), once the IO queue time really kicks in at around a 90% workload increase, very quickly IO queue time becomes the clear response time component and just clobbers performance.

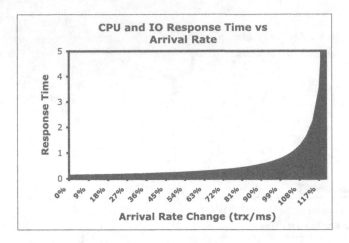

Figure 3-9. *The system response time vs. workload change*

Validation

Before we can present the forecast results to management, we must validate the forecasts. The validation statistically determines forecast precision and helps us determine the usefulness of the results.

Management and IT need to understand if the precision is plus or minus 2% versus plus or minus 20%. Since every forecast exercise has either an implied or explicitly stated precision goal, the precision must be determined. The validation process provides the opportunity to establish the precision.

If the forecast precision is unacceptable, the validation is said to have failed. A failed validation can be caused by, for example, a poor workload characterization, a poorly selected model, or a very complex workload.

As stated earlier, workload data is being gathered, so there is no shortage of data to validate the forecasts. The validation process is actually very simple. At a basic level, the predicted values are compared to the actual values. Then we can statistically determine the average, standard deviation, skew, data distribution, and so on.

A proper validation includes a solid statistical analysis, and since that is presented in the next chapter, this case study does not contain a proper validation. The validation process is presented in more detail in Chapter 6. For the remainder of this case study, assume the forecast precision was within acceptable limits.

What We Tell Management

While the mathematics, the tables, and the graphs are informative, we must translate the raw data into management information. We can summarize the situation and our risk mitigation strategies as follows.

Here's the situation:

- We need to get a better idea of the acquired company's workload compared to our workload. While the forecast mathematics we used can yield pretty good precision, the unknown workload and how it was characterized will not produce a high-precision forecast. As a result, our forecasts must be very conservative.

- *Assuming* the acquired company's workload is like ours, adding their workload to our workload (100% workload increase), our system may be able to support the increased workload without a breach in service levels. But it's very close, and there is a very high likelihood service levels will be breached. The users should expect a significant performance slowdown.

- The IO subsystem will be the bottleneck. The CPU subsystem is looking very good and is not at risk until nearly a 180% workload increase.

Here's what we can do to mitigate the risk:

- Understand their workload better by creating reasonable boundaries. Let's try to bound the acquired company's workload compared to ours. For example, is it possible the company could have a workload twice our workload, three times, and so on? Keep asking questions like these until all sensible boundaries have been tried, and then stop. The stopping point is the worst case (and going the other way, the best case) scenario. Perform a number of scenarios and use those to present to management.

- Reduce peak workload. If there is a good chance service levels will be breached, then identify all noncritical IO-intensive processes and investigate running them at nonpeak times or less often.

- Investigate adding additional IO capacity. We can run additional scenarios increasing the number of IO devices and their IO device speed.

- Continue gathering workload data and perform forecasts soon after the new users are online.

Summary

If you made it through the mathematics in this chapter, then you'll be fine. I tried to keep the math as straightforward as possible, not skip steps, and show you the algebra as we worked through the exercises. By now, you know the math is just one piece of this chapter and just one way to increase forecast precision.

Interesting, just as there are ways to increase forecast precision, there are also ways to *decrease* precision. Being aware of the gotchas covered at the beginning of this chapter will help you avoid needlessly reducing precision. If you are a little uncomfortable selecting the appropriate forecast model, don't worry. I have devoted complete chapters to using queuing theory, regression analysis, and ratio modeling models.

I can't overemphasize the importance of using a weighted average, using Erlang C-enabled formulas, and selecting the appropriate baselines when forecasting. Expending a little extra effort in these areas will significantly improve forecast precision.

This chapter is a kind of turning point. You now have the fundamentals behind you and are ready to dig deeper into other areas. These areas will allow you to comfortably and confidently work with others who have spent years forecasting Oracle performance.

Finally, while this chapter has been technical in nature, remember it is not the technical details that are valuable to your company. Your company needs information about risk, service-level breaches, and how to mitigate potential problems. Forecasting is not an end in itself. It is simply a tool that management can use to properly manage IT service levels.

## CHAPTER 4

Basic Forecasting Statistics

Don't skip this chapter, and don't go looking for mass quantities of caffeinated beverages! This chapter is both condensed and specifically created for forecasting professionals. I promise you the value of your work will dramatically increase by using a few simple statistics. As you'll see, statistics is both relevant and extremely important to your understanding of forecasting and also for your career.

Statistics is a topic I avoided for many years during my academic and professional life. But it finally caught up with me, and I had to figure it out. The first book I tried to glean statistical meaning and methods from just about drove me nuts! Most "practical" statistics books are written like textbooks. They leave me with no doubt that the authors live in academic ivory towers and receive tons of pleasure out of trying to impress their readers with their ability to prove theorems and skip key steps that would make their work understandable. Thankfully, I met some people and found a couple of good books that allowed me to get a handle on the subject. A good friend and English colleague[1] turned to me said, "Have you seen Derek Rowntree's book, *Statistics Without Tears?*" With a title like that, I had to get the book, and from that point on, my statistical fears and the tears have vanished.

To my surprise, what I discovered is that statistics is a language designed to help me communicate uncertainty in new and powerful ways. Armed with basic statistical knowledge, the robustness of my work fabulously improved. What I learned, in part, is contained within this chapter.

What Is Statistics?

Statistics is one of those awkward words everyone uses but cleverly avoids defining, so I'll give it a shot. Statistics is a discipline and a method that describes a collection of data and provides calculations to characterize a set of measurements. Stated another way, statistics helps us to better understand data by allowing us to characterize the data in different ways. For example, we gain a better understanding of data by knowing its average, standard deviation, and skew. As Mr. Rowntree writes, a researcher in a firm's *statistics* department may use *statistics* (statistical methods) to gather and interpret *statistics* (data) about the revenue from sales of a new detergent, and may summarize his findings by quoting the *statistics* of "average sales per thousand of population" in various towns and "range of sales revenue from town to town." It's no wonder people are scared to death to define statistics!

---

1. Thank you very much Dr. Ian Carney for that short but vital conversation in our Portland, Oregon office many years ago!

I love basic statistics because it protects my work and reputation, provides my clients with additional relevant information, and increases the robustness of my work. My goal when using statistics is to better understand precision and to better communicate. If you try to impress or intimidate people, you'll just turn them off. And that's no way to develop trust, gain endorsements for your work, and rally people to support your recommendations.

When pressed for a specific number (for example, response time), I know someone wants an exact number and will hold me to it. But we all know that's impossible. When forecasting, using statistics allows me to describe forecast precision numerically. So while no one can provide an exact number (such as the response time will always be less than 3 seconds), by using statistics, I can express and communicate the forecast's expected precision. So, to avoid getting backed into a corner that no human being can escape, I sharpen my pencil and make a few simple statistical calculations.

I look at statistics as a way to increase communication and reduce confusion. Examples 4-1 and 4-2 show that by integrating simple statistics into our daily lives and into our work, we can better communicate. They show the value of adding even simple statistical statements to your work. This chapter will help you to explain, in management-level terms, your findings. I think you'll find your work will be more responsible, useful, and regarded with a much higher level of respect.

Example 4-1. Three Miles a Day?

Gabrielle told a group of people that she runs an average of 3 miles each day. Most people would assume she runs nearly every day and when she does run, she runs *about* 3 miles a day. But there are many correct interpretations! Gabrielle could run 6 miles every other day. Or perhaps she wakes up each Saturday and runs 21 miles! The point is, even without an attempt on her part to deceive or mislead, her statement can be interpreted many different ways. However, using some simple statistics, this ambiguity can be completely eliminated.

In this chapter, you'll learn how Gabrielle can better communicate by simply modifying her statement to something like, "I'd say that 90% of the time, I run 3 miles each day, plus or minus a quarter of a mile."

Example 4-2. Query Response Time

Annalisa was asked to determine how long a particular query takes. She said it takes 3 seconds. Yet when Gabrielle tested it, it took 4 seconds, Gabrielle says, "You told me this query takes 3 seconds, but when I ran it, it took 4 seconds! You are wrong." And Gabrielle is absolutely correct. Annalisa should have said that the query takes an *average* of 3 seconds. With very little additional effort, she could have added that 90% of the time, the query takes an average of 3 seconds plus or minus 2 seconds.

I love statements like this, because even if the query took 10 seconds, Annalisa would still be correct! By saying that *90%* of the time the query will take from 1 to 5 seconds, she is also saying 10% of the time, the query will take less than or greater than this range. By calculating the average and the plus or minus range, she has enhanced her professional work and reputation, and provided better information.

Sample vs. Population

While the *definition* of a sample and a population seem very straightforward, people tend to interchange them. A *sample* is what is actually measured. For example, if you executed and measured the response time of a query 50 times, your sample set would contain 50 individual samples. The *population* would be all the possible measurements of all the possible sample sets. Obviously, this is not practical and actually not possible in this situation.

A sample relates to actual measurements, and there are numerical descriptions that characterize the sample set. Based on these characterizations, we can learn many things about the measured samples. Commenting about a population is quite different.

For many practical reasons, a population is typically not measured. For example, when a countrywide survey is conducted, not every citizen is sampled. It just doesn't make financial and mathematical sense. But if we need to know certain things about the population, we will need to make *inferences* about the population based on our samples. The key word here is *inference*. When we refer to a sample, we are referring to the actual sample measurements. When referring to a population, we must refer to inferences we have made about the population based on the sample set.

The math relating to a sample set and the math related to a population are very different. The math related to a sample set will be presented next. We'll look at the math related to population in the "Making Inferences" section later in this chapter.

Describing Samples

A sample can be described, or characterized, in many ways, but these descriptions fall into two broad categories: numeric or visual. Both are important and can help us in our work.

Numerically Describing Samples

When a sample is characterized, we focus on its *central tendencies* and its *measures of dispersion*.

Central tendencies describe how the sample tends to center around a particular value. While the data may vary greatly and may look unbalanced visually, we can always characterize data by its mean, median, and mode(s). The mean is simply the straight average; the median is the middle number when the sample is sorted; and the mode(s) is the peak(s) we see when the sample data is stacked in histogram format. For our work, we are primarily interested in the average and, as mentioned in Chapter 3, the weighted average. To calculate the average in Microsoft Excel, use the average function.

Central tendencies provide only part of the story and, in themselves, will force self-imposed assumptions about a sample. To eliminate the ambiguity, we must quantify the dispersion of the data. If the sample data is tightly centered around the mean, then the dispersion is minimal. When data varies wildly, the dispersion will be relatively large. Typically, dispersion is calculated and represented by quartiles (dividing the data in four groups), deviation, variance, and the standard deviation. As you'll see, for our work, the standard deviation is the most important. To calculate the standard deviation in Excel, use the stdev function.

While it may seem obvious, it's easy to forget that normally distributed-based mathematics expects the sample set to be normally distributed. If the sample set is not normally distributed, the mathematics will still calculate a standard deviation, but will be misleading. Two simple ways to determine whether a distribution is normal are to calculate the statistic skew and to view the histogram.

A lesser-known statistic, *skew* is a measure of symmetry, or more precisely, the lack of symmetry. If a distribution is not skewed, it will look the same on the left and right of the mean. The skewness for a normal distribution is zero. A negative skew indicates the data is skewed to the left; that is, the top of the histogram is to the left of the mean. And, of course, a positive skew indicates the data is skewed to the right. Looking ahead, Figure 4-3 and Figure 4-5 have a skew of zero, which means they are perfectly normally distributed. However, Figure 4-6 has a skew of 0.38 (skewed to the right) and Figure 4-8 has a skew of –0.234 (skewed to the left).

In Excel, the skew function is available. A perfectly normal distribution will have a skew value of zero, but you'll be hard-pressed to see such values in real production Oracle systems.

Once you know the sample mean, the standard deviation, and the skew, you are equipped to make some rather astounding statistical statements! But this talk about statistics is meaningless unless we can use it in our work. Example 4-3 is just one way you can gather response time data and then apply simple statistics to help communicate what you discovered.

Example 4-3. Numerically Describing Response Time Samples

The Oswego Company wants to measure one of its key business processes. This process can be measured by executing a single SQL statement. The SQL statement was placed into the key_biz_process.sql script and run every 15 minutes (900 seconds). The following shell script was used to collect 4,000 samples.

```
#!/bin/sh
max_samples=4000
current_sample=1
while [ $current_sample -le $max_samples ]
do
echo "========"
echo "======== Sample $current_sample of $max_samples on `date` ====="
echo "========"
sqlplus trader/trader <<EOF
set timing on
@key_biz_process.sql
EOF
sleep 900
current_sample=`echo $current_sample + 1 | bc`
done
echo "==================="
echo "Sampling completed."
echo "==================="
```

The script was run and the output redirected into the sample.out file. To quickly grab the SQL statement's elapsed time, do something like this:

```
cat sample.out | grep Elapsed | awk -F: '{print $4}'
```

The raw data can then be pasted into a single spreadsheet column. From here, depending on your spreadsheet prowess, you're all set!

The Oswego Company ran the data collection script. As expected, 4,000 samples were gathered once every 15 minutes (every 900 seconds). The spreadsheet dutifully calculated the average elapsed time to be 4.67 seconds, the standard deviation to be 1.87 seconds, and the skew to be 0.35.

Because of the infinite possibilities of interactions within an Oracle system, it is very common for the standard deviation to seem unusually large.

On many production Oracle systems, using the data collection method shown in Example 4-3 could easily result in a distribution that is not normal. For example, if there were a workload peak at lunchtime and another at midnight, there would most likely be two statistical modes; that is, you would see two distinct sets of response times. Perhaps the lunchtime peak response time is 3.0 s/trx while the midnight peak response time is 5.3 s/trx. While the mean won't show this, the standard deviation should be strangely large. If we apply our skew formula and also create a histogram of our sample set (see Figure 4-4, later in the chapter), the two distinct response time peaks are easy to see.

If your situation is likely to have multiple modes, it will be more appropriate and informative to group the samples by their modes and then perform the statistical analysis for each group.

Going on a slight tangent, when sampling Oracle internal statistics, most of the *performance views*, as they are called, are reset when the Oracle instance restarts. As long as the Oracle system is running, the statistics keep increasing. Suppose Jordan needs to know the number of commits that occurred within a single hour. Each hour, she sampled the current commits value, resulting in a starting and ending value for each sample. By subtracting the starting value from the ending value, the number of commits for each hour is derived.

As I've hinted, when forecasting Oracle performance, numerical statistics are not enough. We need to visually inspect our data.

Visually Describing Data Samples

Numerically characterizing a sample is great when working with the math, but to help yourself and others better understand the data, it is a good idea to graph the data in a histogram format.[2] But just as important, a histogram allows us to quickly check if the data is normally distributed. Knowing our data is normally distributed is important because our mathematics requires our sample to be normally distributed.

In Chapter 3, I introduced the normal distribution and the exponential distribution. The normal distribution, shown in Figure 4-1, is known as the *bell curve* because it looks like a, ah, bell. A normal distribution sample set contains as many sample values less than the average as it does greater than the average. In contrast, the exponential distribution has more values less than the mean than greater than the mean. We use the exponential distribution when working with service times, arrival rates, and queuing theory. For sampling performance-related events like the number of commits per hour, number of orders entered per hour, or transaction response times, a normal distribution can be expected.

---

2. More formally, a histogram is a representation of a frequency distribution by means of rectangles whose widths represent class intervals and whose areas are proportional to the corresponding frequencies.

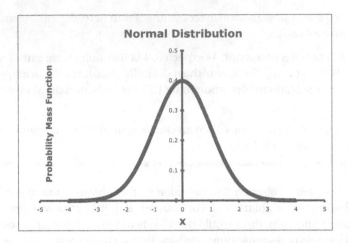

Figure 4-1. *The normal distribution with an average of 0 and a standard deviation of 1*

Using the results from Example 4-3, let's plot the normal distribution. Based on our numerical analysis, the response time average is 4.67 seconds and the standard deviation is 1.87 seconds. Figure 4-2 shows the normal distribution using these two inputs. To make the graphing simpler, feel free to use the statistical templates available at www.orapub.com/tools.

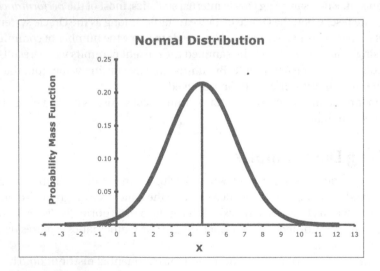

Figure 4-2. *The normal distribution with an average of 4.67 and a standard deviation of 1.87*

CAREFUL OF THE BUFFER CACHE!

If you plan on running queries in rapid succession, consider the effect of Oracle's data block buffer cache. Any DBA will tell you the first query in a series of executions is typically slower because the data is not cached in Oracle's data block buffer cache. In fact, it will take a few times running the same query before the response times settle down.

If you include the initial queries, your sample data will not be normally distributed. It is important to decide if the initial queries are to be included in your sample. This needs to be considered only if the queries are run in rapid succession. Perhaps the query is run once each hour to get a more user-realistic metric. In this case, every query execution is important. However you decide to set up your data collection process, don't forget to consider the caching effect.

As Figure 4-3 shows, histograms group sample data into what are called *bins*. Looking at the histogram, we can clearly see the data is grouped into 12 bins and is normally distributed. The first bin contains the number of sample occurrences where the response time was less than 773, which was three.

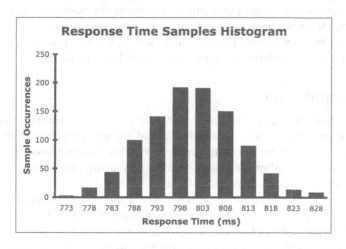

Figure 4-3. *Normally distributed performance data shown as a histogram. The skew is 0.*

Figure 4-4 is a good example of what a histogram will look like when there are two distinct peaks (statistically called *modes*). This is very common in Oracle environments, as there are typically various workload peaks throughout the day, week, month, and quarter, as well as any number of other peaks (for example, Christmastime). Characterizing complex Oracle workloads will be discussed in Chapter 7. The data shown in Figure 4-4 is based on 210 data points, with an average of 3.499, a standard deviation of 0.974, and a skew of 0.518. Without viewing the histogram, you might assume the data is normally distributed!

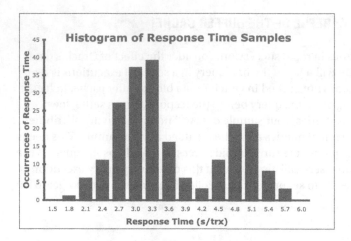

Figure 4-4. *Normally distributed multiple-mode performance data shown as a histogram*

In Chapter 9, other visual analysis techniques will be presented. The most important of these techniques is residual analysis. Residual analysis, along with the other techniques, helps us to understand if our forecasts are more precise in certain areas. For example, based on the workload and the model, forecasts below 60% utilization may be very precise, whereas forecasts above 60% utilization may not be very precise. Understanding where precision is higher and lower is very helpful when validating if the forecast system is appropriate.

Fully Describing Sample Data

Now that we've covered numerically and graphically describing our samples, it is time to combine the two. If the sample data is shown to be normally distributed and we know the sample mean and the sample standard deviation, we are equipped to make powerful observations. These observations can be described to others both numerically and visually, providing you with multiple ways to communicate your findings.

I don't want to trigger any traumatic experiences, but remember the back of your old university statistics books? Remember those graphs and the associated charts? Each graph represented a statistical distribution that can be seen by constructing a simple histogram. The associated chart shows the area under the curve at various positions on the graph. Table 4-1 shows selected areas under the normal distribution curve between the mean and the standard deviations. For example, about 34% of the area lies between the mean and one standard deviation. So if the mean is 12 and the standard deviation is 2, then 68% of our sample values are statistically between 10 and 14. How can I make such an outlandish statement? It's because the mean is 12, the standard deviation is 2, and of utmost importance, the sample data is normally distributed. If the data were not normally distributed, we would have to reference a different and more appropriate distribution.

Table 4-1. *Proportions Under the Normal Curve*

Standard Deviation (Interval Coefficient)	Area Between Mean and Standard Deviation
0.00	0.0000
0.25	0.0987
0.50	0.1915
0.75	0.2734
1.00	0.3413
1.25	0.3944
1.50	0.4332
1.75	0.4599
1.96	0.4750
2.00	0.4772
2.25	0.4878
2.50	0.4938
2.75	0.4970
3.00	0.4987
3.25	0.4994
3.50	0.4998
4.00	0.49997

Now let's put all this together. Based on Example 4-3, the average response time is 4.67, the standard deviation is 1.87, and the distribution is normal. Look closely at Figure 4-5. The x-axis is the sample response time. There are five vertical lines on the graph. The centerline is the response time average of 4.67. The other lines mark the standard deviations. For example, the line just to the right of the average is the average plus one standard deviation, and the line just to the left of the average is the average minus one standard deviation. I purposely moused over the line just to the right of the average. Notice the value shows 6.54, which is precisely the average plus one standard deviation (4.67 + 1.87).

Here's where statistics starts getting interesting and useful. We know that for a normal distribution, 68% of all the samples will be between plus and minus one standard deviation. Using our Example 4-3 data, 68% of our samples are between 4.67 plus and minus 1.87; in other words, 4.67 ± 1.87, or between 2.80 and 6.54. How do we know this? Because the data is normally distributed and we know the mean and the standard deviation.

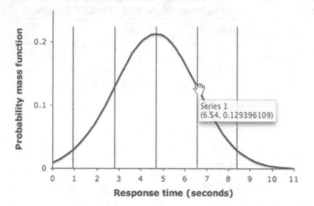

Figure 4-5. *Normally distributed data with standard deviation lines. The mean is 4.67, the standard deviation is 1.87, and the skew is 0.*

There are two key closely related words that you must understand. They are the *confidence level* and the *confidence interval*. I just mentioned 68%. That is a confidence level. The confidence level tells us how sure we can be a sample will reside in a section of a distribution. Simply put, the larger the confidence level, the more likely you are of selecting a particular sample. For example, using Example 4-3 and Figure 4-5, if you randomly choose one of your 4,000 samples, there is a 68% chance the sample response time will be between 2.80 and 6.54. That is because the 68% confidence level contains samples between the mean minus one standard deviation and the mean plus one standard deviation.

Here is another quick example. What is the likelihood you would pick a sample with a response time between 4.67 and 6.54? The mean is 4.67, and 6.54 is the mean plus one standard deviation. We are dealing with one standard deviation of area, which includes 34% of all our samples. So the answer is that there is a 34% chance of picking a response time sample that is between 4.67 and 6.54.

The confidence *interval* is simply the distance between the low value and the high value based on a chosen confidence level. Using Example 4-3 and Figure 4-5, with a confidence level of 68%, the confidence interval starts at one standard deviation below the mean (4.67 − 1.87 = 2.80) and ends one standard deviation above the mean (4.67 + 1.87 = 6.54), resulting in an interval of 3.74 (6.54 − 2.80). Notice that when the confidence level increases, so does the confidence interval. And when the confidence level decreases, so does the confidence interval.

Let's do this a little more formally. When there are 30 or more samples,[3] the confidence interval formula is:

$$CI = \bar{x} \pm Z * SD$$

---

3. Statistical formulas commonly have restrictions. One of the most common is the sample size. When calculating confidence intervals, two common distributions are used: the normal distribution and the t-distribution. Statisticians state when using the normal distribution for calculating confidence intervals, 30 or more samples are required. In contrast, the t-distribution requires less than 30 samples. The confidence interval formulas presented in this book are based on the normal distribution and therefore require 30 or more samples.

where *x-bar* is the average, *Z* is the interval coefficient (for example, 1.00 when the confidence level is 68%), and *SD* is the standard deviation.

Using Example 4-3, at the 68% confidence level, the confidence interval is calculated as follows:

$$CI = \bar{x} \pm Z * SD = 4.67 \pm 1.0 * 1.87 = 4.67 \pm 1.87$$

So the confidence interval is 4.67 plus or minus 1.87, which is the difference between 6.54 (the mean plus 1.87) and 2.8 (the mean minus 1.87). So once again, the confidence interval is 3.74.

To make our lives a little simpler, when discussing our work, it is common to use the 95% confidence level because it's simply the mean plus and minus two standard deviations. (Actually, it is the mean plus and minus 1.96 standard deviations.) Referring to Example 4-3, if we randomly chose one of our samples, there is a 95% chance we would pick a value of 4.67 ± 3.74. However, when getting a little more formal, I like to use the 90% confidence level, which is based on 1.645 standard deviations. When forecasting, 90% is usually sufficient. Table 4-2 shows some common confidence levels and their standard deviation relationships.

Table 4-2. *Common Confidence Levels and Their Standard Deviation Relationships*

Confidence Level and Usage	Standard Deviation Relationship
68% (casual work)	1 standard deviation
90% (serious work)	1.645 standard deviations
95% (casual work)	2 standard deviations
95% (serious work)	1.960 standard deviations
99% (casual work)	3 standard deviations

Creating a service level is not to be taken lightly. Service levels are typically measured, monitored, and integrated using an SLM system (for example, OraPub's HoriZone product). Defining when a service level is breached is more than codifying, "If the query takes longer than 3 seconds, we consider that a breach in service levels." Example 4-4 shows an example of how a service level can be more appropriately determined.

Example 4-4. Creating a Service Level

Bernice has been asked to create service levels and is considering managing the time it takes to commit an order. She timed a number of users entering orders. The following is the commit time data:

```
3.688, 2.768, 3.002, 2.848, 2.861, 3.276, 2.841, 3.688, 3.160, 3.284,
3.127, 3.562, 2.538, 3.861, 3.236, 2.745, 2.674, 3.208, 2.504, 3.202,
2.697, 2.549, 2.981, 3.059, 2.997, 3.189, 3.428, 2.620, 3.292, 2.728,
2.938, 3.233, 3.186
```

What would be a good threshold to detect if the order-entry level of service had significantly changed?

A solution would be to check if the commit times exceeded the 95% confidence level threshold. The data Bernice collected will serve as the baseline. Based on the 33 samples, the average commit time was 3.06 s, the standard deviation was 0.35 s, and the skew was 0.38 (more data is to the right of the mean than to the left of the mean). The skew is pretty good, so she hopes the data is normally distributed. If not, she will need to use a different distribution to determine the 95% confidence figures. Figure 4-6 is a histogram of the sample set.

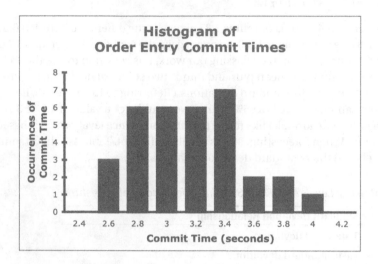

Figure 4-6. *Example 4-4 sample data in a histogram. The average commit time is 3.06 s, the standard deviation is 0.35 s, and the skew is 0.38.*

Clearly, the sample does not conform perfectly to a normal distribution. However, it's close enough. The bulk of occurrences are in the middle, and there is a tail on both sides. Plus, the data is skewed slightly, as both the skew calculation and histogram indicate. Plugging the mean and the standard deviation into the spreadsheet (available at www.orapub.com/tools and discussed in detail in Chapter 5) results in the normal distribution shown in Figure 4-7.

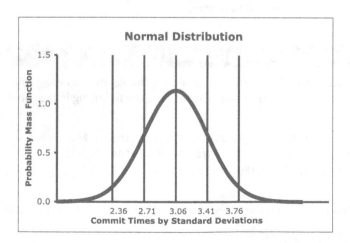

Figure 4-7. *The normal distribution with an average of 3.06 and a standard deviation of 0.35*

The upper half of the 95% confidence level is the mean plus two standard deviations. Since the mean is 3.06 and two standard deviations is 0.70, the upper end of the 95% confidence level is 3.76. While the sample order commit times can expect to reach 3.76 around 2.5%[4] of the time (one half of 5%), it is unlikely. To directly answer the question, a possible service level threshold could be 3.76 seconds. However, if this triggers too many false alarms, then use the 99% confidence level, which is around three standard deviations.

How to describe a workload can be more difficult than it initially seems. There are many ways to describe a workload. For example, it can be described as the average arrival rate, the peak arrival rate, how users feel about the workload, how systems are affected by the workload, and so on. Example 4-5 shows a common way to numerically describe a workload in transactions per second using basic statistics.

Example 4-5. Describing the Workload

Willy collected workload data over a period of one month resulting in 210 samples. While the data points are not shown, the average sample was 2.912 trx/s, the standard deviation was 0.406, and the skew was –0.234. Examine Figure 4-8 and Figure 4-9.

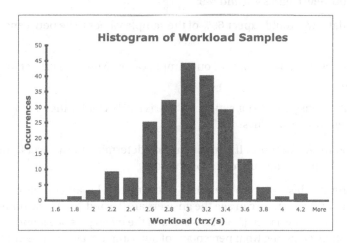

Figure 4-8. *Example 4-5 sample data in a histogram. The average sample is 2.912 trx/s, the standard deviation is 0.406, and the skew is –0.234.*

---

4. The 95% confidence level leaves 5% of the samples outside the two standard deviation range. Example 4-4 is not concerned if *both* the commit times exceed the mean plus two standard deviations (2.5%) *and* if the commit times are below the mean minus two standard deviations (2.5%). We are only interested if the commit time exceeds the mean plus two standard deviations, which statistically occured in only 2.5% of the samples.

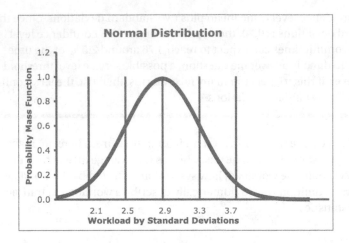

Figure 4-9. *The normal distribution with an average of 2.88 and a standard deviation of 0.46*

While the sample does not conform perfectly to a normal distribution, it's actually pretty close. The bulk of occurrences are in the middle, and there is a tail on both sides. Plus, the data is skewed only slightly, as both the skew calculation and the histogram indicate. Here are some questions to think about as you view Figures 4-8 and 4-9:

1. Based on our sample data, we would expect 68% of the sample values to be between what two values?

2. Based on our sample data, what percentage of our sample values would we expect to lie between 2.9 and 3.7?

3. If you were to randomly choose one of our samples, there is a 95% chance the sample value would be between what two values?

Take a few minutes to consider these questions. If you can quickly determine the answers, you have a solid understanding of the basics and are ready to move on.

Another way of asking question 1 is this: What are the values of the mean plus and minus one standard deviation? Looking at Figure 4-9, we can see the answers are 2.5 and 3.3. These numbers are the mean minus one standard deviation (2.5 = 2.9 – 0.4) and the mean plus one standard deviation (3.3 = 2.9 + 0.4). Question 2 is asking what percentage of our sample set lies between 2.9 and 3.7, which is two standard deviations. Table 4-1 (presented earlier in this chapter) shows that two standard deviations will contain around 0.478, or 47.8% of our sample. Question 3 is asking for the boundaries, which will contain 95%; that is, two standard deviations of our samples. The answer is between 2.1 and 3.7.

Making Inferences

So far in this chapter, I have referred to a specific sample set. Example 4-4 referred strictly to the commit time samples and made no attempt to predict future commit times or refer to non-sample commit times. That's because all the statistical mathematics presented so far relate to something that was actually measured. Whenever a reference is made to a nonsample, we are typically referring to the population. Because attempts are not made to physically measure the population, to describe or characterize the population, *inferences* must be made.

The difference between a measured sample and an inferred population can sometimes be very subtle, but it is extremely important to distinguish between the two in practice. If a reference is made to a sample or actual measurement, then we're referring to a sample. If a reference is in relation to a sample, but not specifically about the sample, then we're probably referring to the population. Table 4-3 contrasts the way we refer to samples and populations.

Table 4-3. *Referring to Samples vs. Populations*

Sample Talk	Population Talk
How long did the commits take on average?	How long can we expect commits to take?
How often are the redo logs switching?	How often will the redo logs switch?
What is the average customer query time?	What should the average customer query time be?
What is our peak workload?	What will the peak workload be next Tuesday?
We have determined batch jobs take an average of 30 minutes to complete.	We expect batch jobs to take around 30 minutes to complete.

Besides the obvious reference difference between samples and populations, there are significant mathematical formula differences. While both samples and populations have the same average, the dispersion calculation is very different. When working with samples, the main measure of dispersion is the standard deviation. When working with a population, the measure of dispersion is the *standard error*.

Officially, standard error is the average of all the standard deviations from all the possible samples. Since we don't measure the population, this must be inferred. The standard error is related to the standard deviation of a sample, the size of a sample, and the proportion of the population covered by a sample. Here's how we calculate the standard error (*SE*) when there are at least 30 samples:

$$SE = \frac{SD}{\sqrt{n}}$$

where n is the number of samples.

Referring to Example 4-5, the standard deviation is 0.406 and there are 210 samples. The standard error would then be:

$$SE = \frac{SD}{\sqrt{n}} = \frac{0.406}{\sqrt{210}} = \frac{0.406}{14.491} = 0.028$$

The beauty of this is that when referring to the population, it's the same as when referring to the sample, except we use the standard error instead of the standard deviation. For example, referring to Example 4-5, while 68% of our sample is between 2.91 ± 0.406, 68% of the population is between 2.91 ± 0.028.[5] That's a big difference!

You may be wondering why the standard error is less than the standard deviation, especially given the fact that the sample is based on actual measurements while the population standard error is inferred. It is a question that bothered me for many years until one of my students, who is a statistical wiz and who could communicate such an obvious and boring statistical question to an Oracle-minded person like myself, took the time to explain. He essentially said that I could think of the standard deviation calculation as being very conservative since only a part of the population is measured. When referring to the population, this conservatism has been removed, resulting in a standard error less than the standard deviation. Makes sense! Example 4-6 shows how simple it can be to calculate the standard error and then use it in describing the population.

Example 4-6. Describing a Possible Workload

In Example 4-5, Willy collected workload data over a period of one month resulting in 210 samples. The average was 2.912 trx/s, the standard deviation was 0.406, and the skew was –0.234. What can we expect the workload range to be 90% of the time?

Because the question is not asking about the sample, but what we can *expect*, we must use population mathematics. Otherwise, our mathematics will describe the sample, which is not what is being asked! We must first calculate the standard error.

$$SE = \frac{SD}{\sqrt{n}} = \frac{0.406}{\sqrt{210}} = \frac{0.406}{14.491} = 0.028$$

The 90% confidence level is not quite two standard errors from the mean. Table 4-2 (presented earlier in the chapter) shows that a 90% confidence interval relates to 1.645 times the standard error. First, we are dealing with a population and not a sample, so we are using the standard error, not the standard deviation. Second, to include 90% of the population, the 1.645 must be applied to both above the mean and below the mean (that is, plus and minus). Otherwise, we will have included just 45% of the population.

The confidence interval portion above the mean is 1.645×0.028, which is 0.046. Therefore, we can expect the workload range to be within 2.912 trx/s ± 0.046, which is from 2.87 trx/s to 2.96 trx/s, 90% of the time.

---

5. Actually, because the standard error (*SE*) relates to all the possible sample means, the confidence intervals also relate to all the sample means. For example, while I wrote we can statistically expect 68% of the population to be between 2.88 ± 0.028 (that is, the mean plus and minus one standard error), it is more correct to say 68% of all the sample means will be between 2.88 ± 0.028. However, I have been told by multiple statisticians that, in practice, we can use the standard error to characterize a population just like we use the standard deviation to characterize a sample. This is also confirmed in that the general population confidence interval is calculated as:

$$CI = \bar{x} \pm Z * \left(\frac{SD}{\sqrt{n}} \right)$$

where *x-bar* is the sample mean, *Z* is the interval coefficient, *SD* is the sample standard deviation, and *n* is the number of samples.

Equally important, the workload is expected to be less than 2.87 trx/s 5% of the time and greater than 2.96 trx/s 5% of the time. When someone asks you why the workload hit 5.5 trx/s when "you said" it would be between 2.87 and 2.96, remind them this range is statistically correct 90% of the time. The other 10% of the time the workload will statistically be either greater or less than those values . . . just as they observed! I use the word *statistically* quite a bit, because people tend to understand that statistics, like forecasting, is not exact. If someone wants something "more exact," then consider using the 99% confidence level.

Precision That Lies

Difficult as it may be to believe, there are actually people in this world who will use statistics with the intent to deceive others. Shocked as you are, you are now equipped to better catch these no-gooders in action. Let's start by looking at Figures 4-10, 4-11, and 4-12. Each of these figures forecasts the number of CPUs required to meet service levels using two different forecast models and, extremely important, at various confidence levels. Each forecast projects ten CPUs are needed, but their confidence levels and confidence intervals tell us much more about the usefulness of the forecasts.

Let's first consider Figure 4-10. Which forecast model is more precise: model A or model B? You learned that by changing the confidence level, the confidence interval will also change. However, both forecasts are shown at the same confidence level. This allows us to directly compare their confidence intervals and therefore their precision. When the confidence levels are the same, the smaller the confidence interval, the more precise the forecast. Since model B has a smaller confidence interval, its forecast is more precise. Ah, if only life were so perfect.

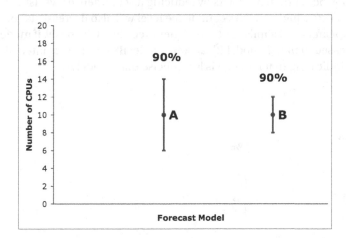

Figure 4-10. *Difficult to deceive when confidence levels are the same*

Next, let's consider Figure 4-11. This is the classic evil-vendor trick. The evil vendor using forecast model A would say, "It's easy to see that our model is much more precise than that vendor who uses model B!" Notice the confidence levels are clearly different! Suppose model A's forecast were shown at a confidence level of 95%. Notice that model A's confidence interval is plus and minus 2 CPUs at a confidence level of 68%. This means the standard error is 2.

Therefore, the confidence interval is close to ±4 at a 95% confidence level; that is, from 6 CPUs to 14 CPUs! Therefore, once we match the confidence levels, model A and model B have the same forecast precision! What makes situations like this even more deceptive is when the confidence levels are not shown or printed so small that no human could read the figure. To avoid falling for this trap, first match the confidence levels and then reexamine the confidence intervals.

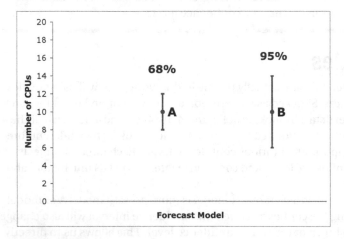

Figure 4-11. *Easy to deceive when confidence levels are different*

Look closely at Figure 4-12. This is a nasty (but stupid) trick where the model B group is trying to make its precision look better than model A's by reducing its confidence level (shown as 68%). As you have learned, decreasing model B's confidence level will also decrease its confidence interval, giving the appearance of similar or even higher precision. Obviously, if model A's confidence level were increased to match model B's at 90%, model B's confidence interval would be significantly larger, indicating that model B is less precise than model A.

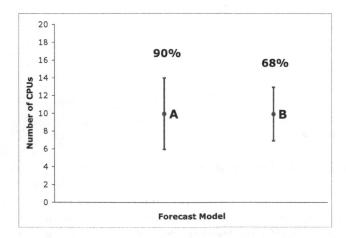

Figure 4-12. *Easy to deceive when confidence levels are reduced*

An even nastier trick (or a demonstration of a complete lack of statistical understanding), is to not show the confidence levels, as in Figure 4-13. Model A proponents will make all sorts of precision claims because there is no way to disprove them. Yet believing their claims would be foolish. The only way to compare precision is to make the effort and ask for the confidence levels. Unfortunately, even if you do ask, you will probably never get a reply!

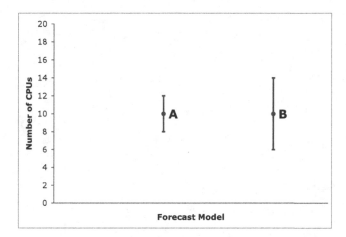

Figure 4-13. *Easy to deceive when confidence levels are not shown*

As you can see, there are many ways to deceive by cleverly shrouding the truth using statistical calculations and definitions. I hope this short section gave you the necessary confidence to stand up and ask presenters and authors the difficult questions (that they don't want you to ask).

Summary

The intention of this chapter was to demonstrate that statistics does not need to be complicated to be usable. I tried to keep the focus on the application of very specific areas of statistics and use many practical exercises. If you are comfortable and confident when using basic statistics in your forecasting work, then I have accomplished my goal.

Before the following chapters on forecasting models, methods, and workload characterization can be fully absorbed, the statistical concepts covered in this chapter must be understood. As you'll see, standard deviation, standard error, confidence levels, and confidence intervals are very important when forecasting. Without a solid basic statistical backing, you might recoil from making potentially very necessary and strong statements. Or even worse, you may be tempted to make unintentionally misleading or just plain wrong statements.

Finally, use statistics as a kind of weapon. Statistics will strengthen your work and your reputation. Most people are terrified of statistics. When your work contains understandable and appropriate statistics, and you're not trying to impress people with your statistical might, your audience will hugely respect your work. And when your work is respected, your recommendations are attributed added strength and meaning.

CHAPTER 5

■ ■ ■

Practical Queuing Theory

Queuing theory can be incredibly, well, theoretical! And it can put us to sleep. But when associated with real-life experiences, it comes to life and becomes very practical. Digging into the practical applications of queuing theory can be very satisfying and, in a way, life-changing.

Queuing systems are everywhere and all around us. Every moment of our lives, we are involved in a massive worldwide system of interwoven queues. Just as with computer systems, there is not simply a single CPU subsystem or a single IO subsystem. We encounter queuing system after queuing system, all networked and interconnected. We live our lives moving from one queuing system to the next. It's a strange and empty way to look at life, but after reading this chapter, I think you'll look at life a little differently than before.

There is a lot more to queuing theory than the Erlang C function and weighted averages. While important, they will not provide practical answers to questions like, "Which is better: faster CPUs or more CPUs?" These questions demand a deeper understanding. What you'll find is the answers to questions like this start with something similar to, "Well, it depends. . . ." While this may seem strange, after a few thought-bending exercises, you'll see what I mean.

In this chapter, using the foundation established primarily in Chapter 2, we'll consider variations with both computer and noncomputer system situations. We'll talk about notation, famous people, and a queuing theory spreadsheet. We'll end with a series of deceptively simple exercises. My goal with these exercises is to force you to think in ways you may have never thought before. Queuing theory that is applicable to our lives is one of the most important topics you'll ever study, and I hope this chapter will provide you with skills to take you beyond theory and formula.

Queuing System Notation

It's true—you can't escape queuing systems, so don't even try. From fueling your car, to ordering lunch, to talking with someone on the phone, you're organically part of the universal system of queues.

To help us understand and communicate queuing theory, a number of conventions and notations have been created. Figure 5-1 shows the two most important notations: the queue and the server.

Server

Queue

Figure 5-1. *Standard notation for a queue and a server*

I realize this is not too exciting or earth-shattering, but I will provide real-life applications to spice things up a bit. The beauty of this simple notation is that, because it is so simple, it can be used to communicate any number of queuing configurations. From fast-food to IO subsystems, the notation presented in Figure 5-1 can be used to both deepen our understanding of queuing configurations and also to communicate their meaning to others. Examples 5-1 through 5-4 focus on how to model various queuing systems. Some of these are computer-related, and some are just plan fun.

Example 5-1. Modeling a Four CPU Subsystem

Jeff was asked to do some CPU subsystem forecasting for the company's HR system. The CPU subsystem contains four CPUs. Using the notation presented in Figure 5-1, how would Jeff diagram his CPU subsystem?

If you'll recall from earlier chapters, a CPU subsystem is modeled with a single queue providing transactions to any available server. Because there are four CPUs in Jeff's system, there are also four servers, as shown in Figure 5-2.

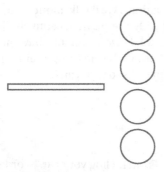

Figure 5-2. *Standard notation for a four CPU subsystem*

Example 5-2. Modeling a Four Device IO Subsystem

Marsha was asked to forecast when her company's very expensive IO subsystem would "run out of gas." She started by drawing a picture to model the IO subsystem. The IO subsystem contains four five-disk arrays. For a variety of reasons, she chose to model each disk array as a separate server. Using the notation presented in Figure 5-1, what would her IO subsystem model look like?

If you'll recall from earlier chapters, an IO subsystem is modeled with each server receiving transactions from its own queue. Therefore, there are four IO "devices," each being serviced by its own single queue. Since there are four IO devices, there are also four queues, as shown in Figure 5-3.

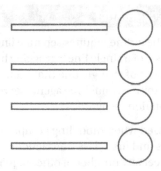

Figure 5-3. *Standard notation for a four device IO subsystem*

Example 5-3. Modeling McDonald's

Don't worry, I won't ask you to admit it, but you've probably been to a McDonald's. While there are exceptions, nearly all McDonald's restaurants use a standard queuing configuration for how people wait in line. How would you model this using the notation in Figure 5-1?

Let's see just how honest you are. When you walk into a McDonald's and have the arduous task of picking the best line, what is the first thing you do? Most people will tell you that they *only* look for the shortest line. But they are lying! I look for the shortest two or three lines, and then I apply additional super-advanced queuing criteria to the final line selection. Next, I look at the server (that is, the order-taker) and ask myself if I'm dealing with a 286 or a Pentium Pro! Finally, I look for anyone in the line with a list or a family lurking somewhere in the restaurant. Some people work the queuing system by, for example, having the husband and wife each pick a line. Then when there is a clear winner, one of them switches lines (known as *queue defection*). Fortunately, when we model Oracle-based systems, we don't need to model these advanced queuing situations.

Back to the example. McDonald's model is just like an IO subsystem in that each server has its own queue, as shown in Figure 5-4.

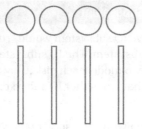

Figure 5-4. *Standard notation for modeling McDonald's order-taking*

Example 5-4. Modeling an Airline Check-in Area

Peter was given the task of modeling an airline check-in area. The airline requires separate lines for economy class and first class. The economy-class line consists of a single line zigzagging back and forth for what seems to be miles! The first-class line consists of a single line that seems to always be relatively short. Six agents service economy-class customers, and three agents service first-class customers. How would Peter model this using the notation in Figure 5-1?

This example introduces constraints that we have not addressed when modeling computing systems. In this example, there are economy-class transactions and first-class transactions. We can model transactions with different priorities, as well as to meet any number of other requirements. However, to simplify our models, I chose to represent the computing system transactions as having the same priority. Even with our relative model simplicity, our forecasts can be amazingly precise. Once a model becomes more complex, the input requirements, and therefore the data gathering requirements, become substantially more complex. If the data put into the model is not precise, regardless of a model's potential precision capability, the output will not be precise. Don't get trapped into believing that a complex model will always produce high-precision results.

The airline check-in area model looks like Figure 5-5.

Figure 5-5. *Standard notation for modeling a typical airline check-in area*

Little's Law

Besides Mr. Erlang, there are two other giants in queuing theory. The first I'll present is Little, and the second is Kendall.

John D.C. Little is not a professor of mathematics or even computer science! He is currently an Institute Professor and the Chair of Management Science at the MIT Sloan School of Management. His career has spanned five decades, and he has published technical papers in the areas of operations research methodology, traffic signal control, decision support systems, and marketing.

Mr. Little is best known for his operations research proof, known as Little's Law. His law was first proved in 1961! His theorem says the average number of customers in stable systems is equal to their average arrival rate, multiplied by their average time in the system. While there are a variety of symbols used to describe his law, one of the most commonly published representations is:

$$N = \lambda T$$

where:

- N is the average number in the system (that is, number being serviced and number in queue).

- λ is the average number of arrivals at some interval (that is, the arrival rate).

- T is the average time spent in the system (that is, the response time).

The system must be stable. This means, over a specified interval, the queue length is not growing to infinity. Another way to look at this is the average arrival rate equals the average throughput. Yet another way to look at this is the number of arrivals equals the number of departures.

Using our existing formulas, we cannot easily show Little's Law. While we know the number in the queue (the queue length), we don't know the number of customers being serviced. Little's term *average time in the system* is what we have been calling the *response time*.

When I first learned about Little's Law, I thought it was overly simplistic, not capable of complex computer system modeling, and based on limited thinking. What I didn't realize was that underneath the simple formula lies a deep practical and mathematical foundation. Little's Law is entirely independent of probability distributions (for example, the normal or exponential distribution). In fact, the distribution does not need to be defined or even assumed. This holds true for both the service time and the arrival rate!

I also failed to realize that the terminology makes it much easier to initially grasp than formal queuing theory. If you spend some time thinking about Little's Law and the associated formulas, you'll find they make common sense, and you will quickly develop a level of comfort with using them. So while they may seem overly simplistic, they are very useful and help solidify all we have learned so far.

Little's Law and the associated formulas make some symbol changes and add a couple of new ones. To be consistent with the industry and make it easier for you to understand other books, I have chosen to use the standard symbols that nearly all publications use. If you look closely at Table 5-1, you'll notice that you are already familiar with the symbols and their meanings. The only seemingly strange symbol is the letter L, which is always used to designate the number in the system. For example, L_w is the number of transactions waiting in the system.

Speaking with a more formal queuing theory tone, we would normally say this is the number of transactions waiting in the queue (Q).

Table 5-1. *Little's Laws Symbols and Their Meanings*

Symbol	Description	Example
T	Time in system (response time)	2.9 s/trx
L	Number in system	2.9 trx
L_w	Number waiting	0.9 trx
L_s	Number being served	2.0 trx
λ	Arrival rate	1.0 trx/s
M	Number of servers	3
U	Utilization	0.67
T_s	Service time	2.0 s/trx
S_r	Service rate	0.5 trx/s
T_w	Time waiting (queue time)	0.9 s/trx

Based on Little's Law, a handful of very useful formulas can be developed. Table 5-2 shows the key equations written out and in formula form. The first formula is the official Little's Law.

Table 5-2. *Formulas Based on Little's Laws*

Calculation	Formula
Number in system = arrival rate × time in system	$L = \lambda T$
Number in system = number waiting + number being served	$L = L_w + L_s$
Time in system = waiting time + service time	$T = T_w + T_s$
Number waiting = arrival rate × waiting time	$L_w = \lambda T_w$
Number being served = arrival rate × service time	$L_s = \lambda T_s$
Utilization = number being served / number of servers	$U = \dfrac{L_s}{M}$
Utilization = arrival rate / (service rate × number of servers)	$U = \dfrac{\lambda}{S_r M}$

The formulas probably don't seem all that useful. However, in some cases, they can solve problems that the queuing theory formulas presented so far cannot solve, at least not so eloquently. Examples 5-5, 5-6, and 5-7 show how Little's Law can be elegantly used.

Example 5-5. Validating Dylan's Workload Measurements

Dylan is a Unix administrator for a large database server. The server contains 64 CPUs, and the IO subsystem contains around 1,000 physical IO devices. All transactions are routed to a transaction processing (TP) monitor before entering the database systems. This enables transactional count and timing information to be easily collected.

One of the ways Dylan measures system workload activity is by calculating the number of transactions that are simultaneously present in the system. The workload is calculated in real time and displayed on his service level console. To ensure his systems are working correctly, he periodically manually checks the calculations.

He randomly gathered a workload activity sample. Between 8 a.m. and 9 a.m., the TP monitor summary log showed transactions were arriving at an average of 23.54 per second, the average response time was 0.56 second, and on average, there were 13.18 transactions in the system. Dylan needs to validate if there were really 13.18 transactions in the system. Here is how Dylan performed the validation:

$$\lambda = 23.54\, trx/s$$
$$T = 0.56\, s/trx$$
$$L = ?$$

Dylan then used the core Little's Law formula:

$$L = \lambda T$$
$$L = \lambda T = 23.54\, trx/s * 0.56s / trx = 13.18$$

As Dylan expected (since he developed the system himself, after all), both the TP monitor logs and the manual calculations matched, completing the validation.

Example 5-6. Determining Average Customer Time at Rashmi's Cafe

Rashmi works for a small independent cafe. She was asked to determine the average time each customer spends in the cafe during peak activity. This is not a simple service time and queue time situation, since customers also relax in the cafe. Rashmi decided to give Little's Law a little try.

Each sale receipt is time-stamped and includes what was ordered. Since not every customer orders a beverage, yet nearly every person in the cafe consumes a beverage, she has to look at each receipt and record the number of beverages ordered. This way, she can determine the number of customers that enter the cafe over any interval of time. The peak activity time occurs between 7:30 a.m. and 8:30 a.m., so Rashmi decided the interval should be 60 minutes. She also asked the barista to count the number of customers in the store between 7:30 a.m. and 8:30 a.m., every 15 minutes, and write it down on a piece of paper.

On a Friday morning during peak time, by counting the number of receipts, she determined 196 customers ordered 225 beverages. The barista checked his records and determined there was an average of 17 customers in the cafe. Rashmi now knows the arrival rate (λ) and the average number of customers in the cafe (L). She must determine the average time a customer spends in the cafe (T). Here is how Rashmi solved the problem:

$$\lambda = 225\,cust/hour$$
$$L = 17\,cust$$

She can use the core Little's Law formula:

$$L = \lambda T$$

She needs to find the time in the system (T), so doing a little algebra:

$$T = \frac{L}{\lambda}$$

plugging in the values and solving:

$$T = \frac{L}{\lambda} = \frac{17\,cust}{225\,cust/hour} = 0.0756\,hours * \frac{60\,min}{1\,hour} = 4.536\,min$$

Rashmi determined that, on average during peak cafe activity, the average customer spent about four and a half minutes in the cafe. Note that this holds true, regardless of the arrival and service time distributions.

Example 5-7. Determining HTTP Response Time

Peter is responsible for the response time of the company's 25 web servers. IT management has implemented a rather comprehensive SLM program, and as a result, all HTTP requests that hit one of the web servers must respond within 1.75 seconds. Peter knows there are many other layers of infrastructure below the web server (for example, the database server), but this is just one metric IT is gathering to measure service levels throughout the infrastructure.

By creating some shell scripts and scanning the web logs, Peter is able to determine the number of HTTP requests that occurred within any period of time. He created another shell script, which when run via cron, gathered the number of running HTTP processes. Peter chose the time interval to be 60 minutes for this particular exercise. The last data sample showed that 20,500 HTTP requests occurred over the 60-minute interval, and the cron script showed the average concurrently active HTTP processes to be three. Here is how Peter determined the average response time.

Peter decided to convert all timing information into seconds:

$$\lambda = \frac{20500\,req}{60\,min} * \frac{1\,min}{60s} = 5.694\,req/s$$
$$L = 3$$
$$T = ?$$

He can use the core Little's Law formula:

$$L = \lambda T$$

He needs to find the time in the system (T), so doing a little algebra:

$$T = \frac{L}{\lambda}$$

plugging in the values and solving:

$$T = \frac{L}{\lambda} = \frac{3}{5.694\,req/s} = 0.527\,s/req$$

Using Little's Law will equip you with an entirely new way to forecast performance. The formulas are simple to use, and the relative simplicity of the mathematics allows management to grasp, and therefore trust, the results. It's almost intuitive. When providing service-level metrics, don't forget about Little's Law.

Kendall's Notation

One of the contributions D. G. Kendall made to queuing theory was a quick and flexible notation to describe a wide variety of queuing system configurations. If you have heard others say things like, "We're using an MMM queuing theory model," then you have already heard the shortened Kendall notation.

Professor Kendall was a serious academic! Get this: He was born in 1918, graduated from Oxford in 1943, married in 1952, became a Doctor of Science at Oxford in 1977, became a Doctor of Science at Cambridge in 1988, was a professor of Mathematical Statistics at Cambridge from 1962 to 1985, published numerous papers, and received many awards. He pioneered stochastic geometry and became a world expert in probability and data analysis. Amazing!

Kendall's notation assumes a single queue system. As you know, this is fine when modeling CPU subsystems, but not IO subsystems (not to mention fast-food restaurants). So we'll need to expand his notation just slightly. Kendall's notation consists of three letters. Each placeholder represents a very specific characteristic of the queuing system. The shortened Kendall notation is simply $A/B/m$, where A represents the arrival pattern (that is, distribution), B represents the service time distribution, and m represents the number of servers in the system (not the number of servers per queue). By assigning the proper letters, any number of complex queuing systems can be quickly notated and communicated.

We can choose from many possible distributions. As mentioned earlier, for our work, we typically use the exponential distribution.

There is a higher-level pattern classification called *Markovian*. A Markovian pattern has some very special characteristics, which are very similar to real-life Oracle database systems. A Markovian pattern, among other things, means each transaction is independent of the other transactions. For example, just because an order is entered and a customer is queried at nearly the same time, that does not imply they are somehow related or dependent on one another; that is, one transaction does not depend on another transaction occurring. In contrast, when a person enters a fast-food restaurant, it is common for the next arrival to be related (as in father and son) to the previous arrival. For example, if I enter McDonald's and then Annalisa (one of my daughters) follows me, our arrivals are not independent. Computing system transactions typically arrive independently of other transactions.

The other Markovian characteristic we are concerned with is that the arrival times and the service times are exponentially distributed. As you can see, a Markovian pattern is a good match for most computing systems and, in particular, Oracle-based systems. Using Kendall's notation, the letter *M* designates a Markovian pattern.

For Oracle-based database systems, both the arrival and service time patterns are Markovian. So that's the how we get the first two *M*s when using Kendall's notation. The final character is shown as either a lowercase *m* or as the actual number of servers. So an M/M/m queuing system is appropriate for Oracle database systems. An M/M/12 queuing system is an appropriate way to represent a 12 CPU database system.

As I mentioned, Kendall's notation assumes a single queue. To enable IO subsystem modeling, multiple queues are needed. The most common extension to Kendall's notation is to simply place the number of queues in the system before the notation, and the final *m* becomes the number of servers *for each queue*. For example, 1xM/M/5 can model an Oracle database system with five CPUs, because each of the one queue(s) is associated with five servers. In contrast, a 5xM/M/1 system would represent an IO subsystem containing five devices, because each of the five queues is associated with a single server (that is, device).

Examples 5-8 through 5-12 demonstrate the flexibility of Kendall's notation. As you've already seen, queuing theory is not limited to computing systems. In fact, some of the most interesting (and sometimes complex) queuing-related configurations are related to traffic, networking, and fast-food restaurants. However, these systems may not be operating with M/M/m characteristics (but they can make terrific and interesting introductory examples).

Example 5-8. Modeling a Single CPU System

How would Pablo model a single CPU system using standard notation (Figure 5-1) and also using Kendall's notation?

Since there is one queue in the entire system and that one queue is sending transactions to the single server, the Kendall's notation is 1xM/M/1. Figure 5-6 is the diagram.

Figure 5-6. *A 1xM/M/1 queuing system*

Example 5-9. Modeling a Five CPU System

How would Drew model a five CPU subsystem using the standard notation (Figure 5-1) and also using Kendall's notation?

Since there is one queue in the entire system and that one queue is sending transactions to the five servers (that is, the CPUs), the Kendall's notation is 1xM/M/5. Figure 5-7 is the diagram.

Figure 5-7. *A 1xM/M/5 queuing system*

Example 5-10. Modeling a Four IO Device System

How would Todd model a four IO device system using standard notation (Figure 5-1) and also using Kendall's notation?

Since there are four queues in the entire system, and each of the four queues routes transactions to one device, the Kendall's notation is 4xM/M/1. Figure 5-8 is the diagram.

Figure 5-8. *A 4xM/M/1 queuing system*

Example 5-11. Modeling a Dual Web Server System

Maya administers the company's web servers. The company expects transaction activity to triple in the next six months. Transactions are randomly directed into one of the two web servers. Both web servers contain three CPUs. How would Maya model the web server system using standard notation (Figure 5-1) and also using Kendall's notation?

Since there are two web servers and she is modeling the CPU systems, there are two queues. Each queue is associated with three servers (that is, CPUs). Therefore, the Kendall's notation is 2xM/M/3. Figure 5-9 is the diagram.

Figure 5-9. *A 2xM/M/3 queuing system*

Example 5-12. Modeling an Airline Check-in Area

Reda is testing various queuing configurations to find an acceptable balance between customer queue time and the number of customer service agents. The trick is to minimize customer queue time, resulting in happy customers, while at the same time, minimize the number of customer service agents, resulting in happy management!

One of Reda's ideas is to have two lines: one for first-class passengers and the other for economy-class passengers. Two customer service agents will be dedicated to the first-class passengers, while four agents will service the economy-class passengers. How would Reda model the web server system using the standard notation (Figure 5-1) and also using Kendall's notation?

Because there are two classes of customers and they each are routed to a specific line (that is, queue), modeling this configuration requires two distinct queuing models: one for the first-class passengers and the second for the economy-class passengers. Both the first-class and economy-class configurations route their customers into a single line (that is, queue). Since the first-class configuration employs two agents, the Kendall's notation is 1xM/M/2. And because the economy-class configuration employs four agents, the Kendall's notation is 1xM/M/4. Figure 5-10 is the diagram.

Figure 5-10. *A 1xM/M/2 and a 1xM/M/4 queuing system*

As you can see, by combining Kendall's notation with our standard queuing diagramming method, many queuing configurations can be modeled, and all CPU and IO configurations we are likely to encounter can be modeled.

But the model is just the beginning. Once the model is properly diagramed or configured in our software tools, the underlying model mathematics must be selected (for example, essential forecasting mathematics or Erlang C), and the key parameters (for example, the arrival rate) must be entered. So far in this book, I have presented two mathematical-based model options: essential forecasting mathematics and an improvement using the Erlang C function. In the next section, we'll take this information, enter it into a spreadsheet, and solve many interesting problems.

The Queuing Theory Workbook

A few queuing theory spreadsheets are available for download. The spreadsheet used throughout this book is available for free at www.orapub.com/tools. If you are thinking of using a spreadsheet (instead of an expensive mathematical product) for queuing theory work, there is a good chance you will be challenged about its quality, so it is important that you know a little about the tool.

The spreadsheet is implemented in Microsoft Excel. In Excel terms, the spreadsheet is actually a *workbook* containing multiple *worksheets*. All the queuing theory functions are written in Visual Basic and implemented using macros. The queuing theory functions are based on standard queuing theory (Erlang C), and both the arrival rate and the service times are Markovian. So the core functions are not a recent invention or creation. They can easily be validated using the Erlangc.pl script presented in Chapter 3 (also available from www.orapub.com/tools).

Sometimes when using a queuing theory tool, the forecasted response time or queue length is a negative number, overflows, or results in a runtime error. Don't assume there is a problem with the tool. Just as when using the essential forecasting mathematics, when the forecasted utilization is greater than 100%, the system becomes unstable. Practically speaking, if this occurs in a real system, the run queues become so large that the server becomes unusable or shuts down. Many tools do not trap this event and simply show the pure mathematical result, which can be a negative queue length or response time. So when you use queuing theory mathematics and the results look strange, don't assume something is wrong with the tool. It is more likely that the workload the system is asked to process is simply too much.

Like any queuing program, the queuing theory workbook requires a few inputs. You will need inputs for the number of queues in the system, the number of servers per queue, the average arrival rate, and the average service time. Once all these values are entered, the spreadsheet will crank out the queue time, run queue length, and many other statistics. There are also some additional entries, which increase the result usefulness, including the units (such as trx), time (such as ms), lambda scale (such as 1.2), and the response time tolerance. The lambda scale is used to help scale the graph and can be adjusted until you're satisfied with how the graph looks.

Figure 5-11 is a partial screenshot of OraPub's queuing theory workbook. Notice two distinct cases have been entered. Case 1 has 12 CPUs, and Case 2 has 16 CPUs. Other than this, both cases have identical entries. Having two cases side by side enables both numerical comparisons (Figure 5-11) and also graphical comparisons, as shown in Figure 5-12.

Queuing Model Data Entry

	Description	Case 1 Values	Case 2 Values	Unit
3	Queues in system	1	1	#
4	Servers per queue	12	16	#
5	Service time	0.0300	0.0300	ms/trx
6	System Arrival rate	323.00	323.00	trx/ms
7	Response time tolerance	0.00		ms
9	Server Arrival rate	323.00	323.00	trx/ms
10	Traffic intensity	9.69	9.69	#
11	Utilization	80.8%	60.6%	#
12	Queue time	0.0050	0.0002	ms/trx
13	Queue length	1.6197	0.0692	#
14	Response time expected	0.0350	0.0302	ms/trx

Figure 5-11. *Partial screenshot of OraPub's queuing theory workbook (numerical input and analysis)*

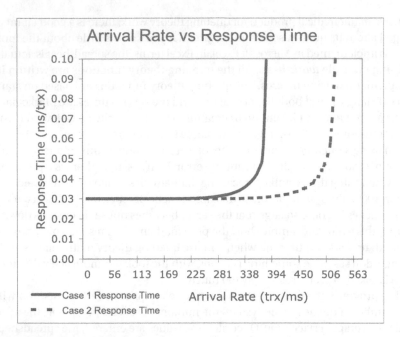

Figure 5-12. *Partial screenshot of OraPub's queuing theory workbook (comparison graph)*

Let's take a closer look at Case 1's numerical input and analysis shown in Figure 5-11. Case 1 is a CPU subsystem model, so there is only one queue in the system (cell B3). There are 12 CPUs, so there are 12 servers for each queue. I know it sounds strange saying, "12 servers for each queue," but speaking like this helps reduce data-entry errors. In Kendall's notation, this is a 1xM/M/12 queuing theory model. While Figure 5-11 does not show the data-entry points, the unit of work is trx (B26) and the unit of time is ms (B27). The entered unit of work and time are used throughout the workbook. For example, look at cell D5 in Figure 5-11. Notice the units are ms/trx (milliseconds per transaction). The entered service time and arrival rate are 0.030 ms/trx and 323.0 trx/ms, respectively. The response time tolerance was entered as zero. This is a good way to *remove* the response time tolerance from the graphs. With Erlang C queuing theory mathematics in mind, the server utilization (in cell B11, 80.8%), queue time (in cell B12, 0.0050 ms/trx), queue length (in cell B13, 1.6197), expected response time (in cell B14, 0.0350 ms/trx), plus many other statistics are calculated. As you would expect, the response time equals the service time (0.030 ms/trx) plus the queue time (0.0050 ms/trx).

Figure 5-12 is a screenshot from the case study comparison graph, which is the result of the numbers shown in Figure 5-11. The comparison graph shows both cases together. This highlights differences in the two queuing configurations and is a very effective communication tool. This graph makes the case differences so explicitly clear that you don't need to understand queuing theory to grasp the meaning.

Looking closely at Figure 5-12, notice the flat response time at 0.03 ms. Queuing does not set in until the arrival rate is around 281 trx/ms, so the response time is flat; that is, response time is equal to the service time. Because both cases use CPUs with identical service times, their lines overlap until queuing begins. However, once queuing sets in, because Case 1 has 12 CPUs and Case 2 has 16 CPUs, Case 1's response time begins to degrade (that is, increase) well before Case 2's response time. After the following examples, we'll spend more time analyzing the differences and the shifts in response time curves.

Let's start with a couple simple exercises using the queuing theory workbook, in Examples 5-13 and 5-14.

Example 5-13. Performing a Simple CPU Forecast

Using OraPub's queuing theory workbook, determine the utilization, queue length, queue time, and response time. Also determine the arrival rate when response time starts to significantly degrade. The CPU subsystem contains five CPUs, with a service time of 0.250 second (s). The arrival rate is 17.75 trx/s.

If you are following along using the spreadsheet, use both Figure 5-13 and this text as a data-entry guide. If you are not using the spreadsheet, pay close attention to Figure 5-13.

Queuing Model Data Entry

	Description	Case 1 Values	Case 2 Values	Unit
3	Queues in system	1	1	#
4	Servers per queue	5	16	#
5	Service time	0.2500	0.2500	s/trx
6	System Arrival rate	17.75	17.75	trx/s
7	Response time tolerance	0.00		s
9	Server Arrival rate	17.75	17.75	trx/s
10	Traffic intensity	4.44	4.44	#
11	Utilization	88.8%	27.7%	#
12	Queue time	0.3266	0.0000	s/trx
13	Queue length	5.7967	0.0000	#
14	Response time expected	0.5766	0.2500	s/trx

Figure 5-13. *Numeric CPU forecast for a five CPU (1xM/M/5) configuration*

The first thing I do when using the spreadsheet is to enter the unit of work and unit of time. The units are carried forward throughout the workbook (for example, in cells D5, D6, and D12), which helps reduce data-entry errors. For this exercise, the unit of work is *trx*, short for transactions (cell B26) and the unit of time is *s*, short for seconds (cell B27).

Because a CPU subsystem is being modeled, the number of queues in the system is 1 (cell B3). There are five CPUs, so there are 5 servers per queue (cell B4). Each CPU can service a transaction at an average of 0.250 s. Transactions arrive into the CPU subsystem at 17.75 trx/s (cell B6). No response time tolerance was provided, so just set that to 0. A nicely scaled graph will appear (in the Graph C1 worksheet) when the lambda scale is set to 1.15 (cell B29).

Having entered the data correctly, the forecasted average utilization is 88.8% (cell B11), the queue length is 5.7967 (cell B13), the queue time is 0.3266 s (cell B12), and therefore the response time is 0.5766 s/trx (cell B14).

Figure 5-14 shows the Graph C1 worksheet. This is the classic response time graph and full of information. As we work through more examples, we'll get deeper and deeper. The service time and the queue time have been combined into the response time, and are not shown separately. If you look closely, you will notice that queuing starts when the arrival rate is around 10 trx/s, but starts to significantly degrade response time when it's around 15 trx/s.

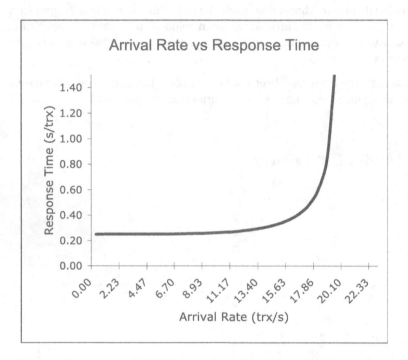

Figure 5-14. *Graphical CPU forecast for a five CPU (1xM/M/5) configuration*

This example states the current arrival rate is 17.75 trx/s and asks to determine when the response time starts to significantly degrade. Looking at the response time curve's horizontal axis—that is, the arrival rate—you'll notice that the current arrival rate is well into the elbow of the curve. So at the current arrival rate, response time has already begun to degrade.

Example 5-14. Performing a "Running Out of Gas" Forecast

We are asked to determine when our company's 32 CPU database server will "run out of gas." Each CPU can service a transaction in 110 ms.

This particular example is meant to get you used to the spreadsheet and to gain some additional queuing theory insight. Later in the chapter, the examples will become more practical and therefore more useful in your work. If you are following along using the spreadsheet, use both Figure 5-15 and this text as a data-entry guide.

	A	B	C	D
1	**Queuing Model Data Entry**			
2	Description	Case 1 Values	Case 2 Values	Unit
3	Queues in system	1	1	#
4	Servers per queue	32	32	#
5	Service time	110.0000	110.0000	ms/trx
6	System Arrival rate	0.10	0.20	trx/ms
7	Response time tolerance	0.00		ms
9	Server Arrival rate	0.10	0.20	trx/ms
10	Traffic Intensity	11.00	22.00	#
11	Utilization	34.4%	68.8%	#
12	Queue time	0.0000	0.3370	ms/trx
13	Queue length	0.0000	0.0674	#
14	Response time expected	110.0000	110.3370	ms/trx

Figure 5-15. *Numeric CPU forecast for a 32 CPU (1xM/M/32) configuration*

The unit of work is trx (cell B26) and the unit of time is ms (cell B27). Because a CPU subsystem is being modeled, the number of queues in the system is 1 (cell B3). There are 32 CPUs, so there are 32 servers per queue (cell B4). Each CPU can service a transaction at an average of 110 ms.

All that is left to enter is the arrival rate, and the spreadsheet will dutifully calculate the desired metrics and generate a nice graph. Unfortunately, we were not given an arrival rate! It is common in forecasting problems for a value to be missing. (This is just one reason why understanding theory is of little value unless you can apply it practically.) We must decide an appropriate arrival rate value and enter it into the spreadsheet (cell B6). Being careful not to type over any formula cells, enter different arrival rates, such as 0.1, 0.2, and 0.3. With the arrival rate of 0.1 trx/ms, the utilization is 34.4% (see Figure 5-15, cell B11). With the arrival rate of 0.2 trx/ms, the utilization is 68.8%. With the arrival rate of 0.3 trx/ms, the utilization is 103.1%, which the system cannot sustain. As shown in Figure 5-16, when the average utilization surpasses 100%, the system is said to become *unstable*, and the queue time, queue length, and expected response time go berserk!

	A	B	C	D
1	**Queuing Model Data Entry**			
2	Description	Case 1 Values	Case 2 Values	Unit
3	Queues in system	1	1	#
4	Servers per queue	32	32	#
5	Service time	110.0000	110.0000	ms/trx
6	System Arrival rate	0.30	0.30	trx/ms
7	Response time tolerance	0.00		ms
9	Server Arrival rate	0.30	0.30	trx/ms
10	Traffic intensity	33.00	33.00	#
11	Utilization	103.1%	103.1%	#
12	Queue time	-134.7818	-134.7818	ms/trx
13	Queue length	-40.4345	-40.4345	#
14	Response time expected	-24.7818	-24.7818	ms/trx

Figure 5-16. *Numeric CPU forecast when utilization surpasses 100% and the system becomes unstable*

Just for the fun of it, let's use our essential queuing theory mathematics to calculate the utilization with the arrival rate at 0.1 trx/ms. It should match our queuing theory spreadsheet exactly! Their utilization calculations are the same, but the queuing theory spreadsheet uses Erlang C mathematics for the queue time calculation. Here's the math:

$$U = \frac{S_t \lambda_q}{m} = \frac{110\,ms/trx * 0.1\,trx/ms}{32} = \frac{11}{32} = 0.344 = 34.4\%$$

Using the spreadsheet, there are two basic ways we can determine when the database servers will run out of gas. We can manually enter in various arrival rates until the utilization reaches into the 80% area or when we notice the response time enters the elbow of the curve. However, since the words "run out of gas" were used rather than an actual response time tolerance, we will assume an exact numeric answer is not required. (Of course, we should double-check this assumption.) We will graphically analyze the system and draw conclusions. A sensible graph (the Graph C1 worksheet, shown in Figure 5-17) is created anytime a stable queuing system is created. A nice graph is created when the lambda scale is set to 1.8. Referencing Figure 5-17, response time begins to significantly degrade—the system is "running out of gas"—when the arrival rate approaches 0.25 trx/ms.

To make an important point, let's create a nearly identical second case. As shown in Figure 5-15, the only difference between Case 1 and Case 2 is their arrival rates. For Case 1, enter an arrival rate of 0.1 trx/ms (cell B6) and for Case 2, enter an arrival rate of 0.2 trx/ms (cell C6). Also enter the graph lambda scale of 1.15 (cell B29). The resulting utilization is what we expect: with an arrival rate of 0.10 trx/ms, the utilization is 34.4%, and with an arrival rate of 0.20 trx/ms, the utilization is 68.8%. Now take a look at the comparison graphs, shown in Figure 5-18.

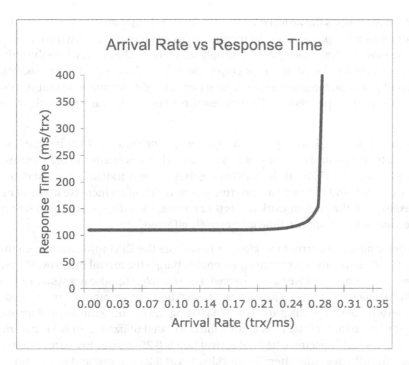

Figure 5-17. *Case 1 graphical CPU forecast for a 0.10 trx/ms arrival rate and 32 CPU (1xM/M/32) configuration*

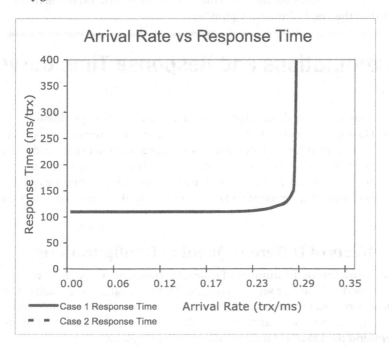

Figure 5-18. *Comparison graphical CPU forecast for a 1xM/M/32 configuration*

The only difference in the cases is the arrival rate. The service time is the same, so when no queuing is involved, the graphs overlap. And since the number of CPUs is the same, when queuing does set in, it is exactly the same for both cases. Case 1 is simply the point on the graph where the arrival rate is 0.1 trx/ms, and Case 2 is the point on the graph when the arrival rate is 0.2 trx/ms. Both cases are just different points on the same response time curve! I highly recommend that you do this exercise yourself using the spreadsheet. The first few times you do this exercise, it will seem very strange.

Back to our original assignment: Looking at either Figure 5-17 or Figure 5-18, it is clear the response time starts to significantly increase when the arrival rate is at around 0.25 trx/ms. But what does 0.25 trx/ms mean? This is the arrival rate; that is, the workload. We must determine the current workload, and then we can determine how much of an increase the system can sustain. For example, if the current workload is 0.12 trx/ms, then the system could sustain a 2X workload increase before response time is negatively effected.

One way we can determine the current workload is to sample the CPU utilization from the production system. Then using the spreadsheet, we could change the arrival rate (row 6) until the utilization (row 11) matches what we have observed. For example, suppose our system is the busiest during a 60-minute period around lunchtime. During this time, we ran the sar -u 3600 1 command and observed the CPU utilization to be 69%. Using the queuing theory spreadsheet, we start changing the system arrival rate (row 6) until the calculated utilization (row 11) became 69%. As Figure 5-15 shows, this occurs when the arrival rate is 0.20 trx/ms. Because response time begins to significantly degrade when the workload is at 0.25 trx/ms, and our system is currently operating at 0.20 trx/ms during peak, the system could possibly sustain a 20% workload increase (20% = 1 − 20 / 25). To communicate this to management, in addition to the numeric analysis, we could also use the graph shown in Figure 5-17.

Queuing Configurations and Response Time Curve Shifts

As a teacher, I long for students to have those "aha!" moments when everything suddenly makes sense and they "get it." Queuing theory is just that—theory. The response time curve is interesting, but is it practical and applicable in daily work? My students seem to begin making the connection between theory, spreadsheets, and the mathematics when they can see how similar queuing configurations dramatically affect the response time and what makes the response time curve shift. Once these can be anticipated and deeply understood, all the theory becomes extremely practical.

Observing the Effects of Different Queuing Configurations

In this section, we will work through a number of examples based on a 4xM/M/1 versus a 1xM/M/4 model. Both models have four servers. The 4xM/M/1 model (Case 2) contains four queues, and each queue is related to one server. The 1xM/M/4 model (Case 1) contains only one queue, and this one queue provides transactions to all four servers. The 4xM/M/1 model is like an IO subsystem, and the 1xM/M/4 model is like a CPU subsystem.

Examples 5-15 through 5-19 focus on contrasting the differences in single queue and multiple queue systems. I find these exercises help to develop an inherent understanding of the difference between CPU and IO subsystems. While the examples use OraPub's queuing theory workbook, you should be able to relate to them based on your own personal experiences. Figures 5-19 and 5-20 show the numeric analysis and graphical analysis worksheets used in these examples.

	A	B	C	D
1	**Queuing Model Data Entry**			
2	Description	Case 1 Values	Case 2 Values	Unit
3	Queues in system	1	4	#
4	Servers per queue	4	1	#
5	Service time	3.0000	3.0000	min/person
6	System Arrival rate	1.00	1.00	person/min
7	Response time tolerance	0.00		min
9	Server Arrival rate	1.00	0.25	person/min
10	Traffic intensity	3.00	0.75	#
11	Utilization	75.0%	75.0%	#
12	Queue time	1.5283	9.0000	min/person
13	Queue length	1.5283	2.2500	#
14	Response time expected	4.5283	12.0000	min/person
19	Queue time stnd dev	2.61	11.62	min/person

Figure 5-19. *A 4xM/M/1 model (IO) and a 1xM/M/4 model (CPU)*

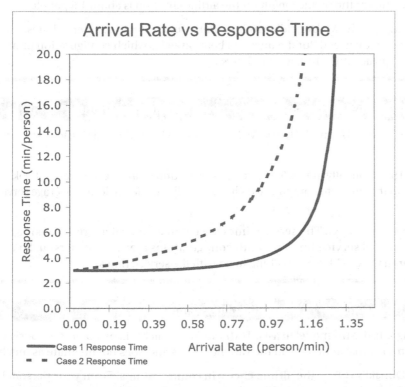

Figure 5-20. *A graphical comparison of a 4xM/M/1 model (IO) and a 1xM/M/4 model (CPU)*

Example 5-15. Forecasting the Lowest Average Queue Time

We are comparing a 1xM/M/4 model to a 4xM/M/1 model. Which will exhibit a lowest average queue time?

Before you look at the spreadsheet or comparison graph, let's think about the question and relate it to real-life experiences. A 1xM/M/4 model is how many airline check-in areas are configured. A single line is serviced by many (well, actually a few) customer service agents. A 4xM/M/1 model is how most McDonald's queuing systems are configured. There are multiple lines, each with an employee taking orders. So, from your personal experience, is it the airline check-in or McDonald's that will provide everyone with the lowest *average* wait time?

At McDonald's, everyone who enters the restaurant must have a line-selection strategy. No one just randomly picks a line. Why? Because if you pick the wrong line, you would be waiting forever (and so would everyone behind you!). Most airline check-in areas have just one line for each class of service, so once you determine the appropriate line, you simply get in that line. There is no strategy necessary because there is only one line.

Look closely at the spreadsheet shown in Figure 5-19, especially rows 12 and 13. These are the average queue time and queue length, respectively. You see a significant difference! Case 1 is the 1xM/M/4 or the airline check-in area. Case 2 is the 4xM/M/1 or the McDonald's configuration. The average queue time for the McDonald's-like configuration is 9.0 minutes, whereas the queue time for the airline check-in is only about 1.5 minutes. They also have significant queue length differences. The average queue length for the McDonald's-like configuration is about 2.3 people, whereas the queue length for the airline check-in is about 1.5 people.

You may be thinking that the McDonald's configuration could result in a better—that is, less—queue time. And you are correct! But the question being asked is which configuration provides the lowest average queue time. The key word is *average*.

Example 5-16. Forecasting the Lowest Average Service Time

We are comparing a 1xM/M/4 model to a 4xM/M/1 model. Which will exhibit a lowest average service time?

Look at Figure 5-19, specifically at row 5, where the service times have been entered. Looking at all the inputs and the forecasted outputs, which model will provide the lowest average service time?

This is a trick question (sorry). The service times are entered, not calculated. Looking at Figure 5-19, the entered service times for both configurations are 3.0 min/person. So the 1xM/M/4 compared to 4xM/M/1 has nothing to do with the service times.

Example 5-17. Providing Consistent Queue Times

We are comparing a 1xM/M/4 model to a 4xM/M/1 model. Which will exhibit more consistent queue times? By more consistent, I mean the variance is less and does not fluctuate as much.

Think about McDonald's versus the airline check-in configurations. From your personal experience, which provides customers with a more consistent wait? This question is not about which configuration provides the ultimate *best case* wait time scenario, but the more *consistent* queue time.

Again, the configuration at McDonald's involves a line-selection strategy. If you choose wisely or get lucky, your wait time could be practically zero! This alone tells us the McDonald's queuing configuration has the potential for highly fluctuating queue times.

Looking at the queue times in row 12 in Figure 5-19, it is clear that Case 1 (1xM/M/4, airline check-in) has a lower average queue time. But that is not what this question is asking. We want to know which configuration provides the most consistent queue time. Take a look at row 19 in Figure 5-19. This is the queue time standard deviation. We know from Chapter 4 that the standard deviation is a measure of dispersion. A low dispersion indicates that the values do not fluctuate much and are more consistent. This is exactly what we are looking for! Clearly, Case 1 has the lowest queue time standard deviation with a value of 2.61 minutes, compared to the Case 2 queue time standard deviation of a massive 11.62. So the 1xM/M/4 (the airline check-in configuration) clearly provides more consistent queue times.

Example 5-18. Providing Best and Worst Queue Times

We are comparing a 1xM/M/4 model to a 4xM/M/1 model. Which will exhibit the best and worst queue times?

We are not interested in the average queue time, but the absolute best and absolute worst queue time possible. Again, anyone walking into a McDonald's has a line-selection strategy. We all know that selecting the right line will provide the absolute best queue time and, conversely, selecting the wrong line will provide the absolute worst queue time. Whereas with the airline check-in configuration, everyone pretty much has the same queue time.

Recall the discussion related to confidence levels and confidence intervals in Chapter 4. One standard deviation represents 68% of our sample or the population. Figure 5-19 shows the average queue time (row 12) and the queue time standard deviation (row 19) for both cases. For Case 1, the average queue time is about 1.5 minutes, plus or minus 2.6 minutes, 68% of the time. This means, statistically, the queue time will range from 0 to 4.1 minutes. For Case 2, the average queue time is 9.0 minutes, plus or minus 11.6 minutes, 68% of the time. This means, statistically speaking, the queue time will range from 0 to 20.6 minutes.

Case 2 clearly provides the worst possible queue times. And this makes sense. We all know that when working with a configuration with one queue *for each server*, you want to pick the right queue! While in this specific example, both cases can have a best case queue time of zero, it is much more likely to find yourself with no wait time if you pick the correct line, which is Case 2, the 4xM/M/1 configuration.

Let's step back for a second and relate the past few exercises to CPU and IO subsystems. Referring to Figure 5-19, Case 1 is like a CPU subsystem, with one queue and four CPUs. Case 2 is like an IO subsystem, with four devices that each has its own queue. Examples 5-15 through 5-18 have demonstrated that queue time fluctuation varies significantly based on the queuing configuration.

To minimize the average queue length and queue time, we obviously want a queuing configuration with one queue. This is possible with CPU subsystems, but not with an IO subsystem. Regardless of a vendor's creative and truly amazing patented optimization algorithms, an IO block is ultimately associated with a specific IO device. As a result, the queuing configuration must have a single queue for each device. While advanced and proprietary algorithms can help minimize the queuing effects, they cannot be eliminated in a real production Oracle system.

There is an important distinction between the *arrival rate* and the *throughput*. The arrival rate is how many transactions arrive into the system within a unit of time. The throughput is how many transactions exit the system within a unit of time. It is common and expected for the arrival rate and the throughput to fluctuate, but for a system to remain operable (sometimes called *stable*), the average arrival rate will equal the average throughput. If the average arrival rate is greater than the average throughput, queuing will eventually become so extreme that the system will essentially shut down. Forecasting professionals sometimes mix up these terms because they are typically the same, but it is always better to be specific to avoid confusion.

The last of the queuing theory comparison examples, Example 5-19, focuses on which configuration provides the most throughput.

Example 5-19. Providing More Throughput

Comparing a 1xM/M/4 model to a 4xM/M/1 model, which will provide more throughput?

Other than the queuing configuration, keep both the service time and the arrival rate the same. Figure 5-21 is a valid example because both service times are set to 3 min/person and both arrival rates are set to 1.0 person/min.

	Description	Case 1 Values	Case 2 Values	Unit
1	**Queuing Model Data Entry**			
3	Queues in system	1	4	#
4	Servers per queue	4	1	#
5	Service time	3.0000	3.0000	min/person
6	System Arrival rate	1.00	1.00	person/min
7	Response time tolerance	0.00		min
9	Server Arrival rate	1.00	0.25	person/min
10	Traffic intensity	3.00	0.75	#
11	Utilization	75.0%	75.0%	#
12	Queue time	1.5283	9.0000	min/person
13	Queue length	1.5283	2.2500	#
14	Response time expected	4.5283	12.0000	min/person

Figure 5-21. *Numeric input for determining which configuration will provide the most throughput*

One of the simplest ways to answer this question is to look at the case comparison graph, shown in Figure 5-22. The graph clearly shows that Case 1 (1xM/M/4) can support a higher average arrival rate than Case 2 (4xM/M/1). How can this be?

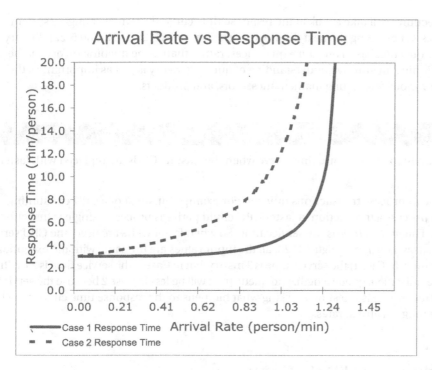

Figure 5-22. *The comparision graph for observing which configuration will provide the most throughput*

Suppose McDonald's allowed two queuing configuration options and the 4xM/M/1 configuration prohibits people from switching lines (known as queue defection). So even if one of the lines was absolutely empty, a person could not defect to that line. A simple graphical simulation would show that sometimes a line would, in fact, be empty (that is, the queue length is zero), even though the server is ready and available to serve. This significantly limits the maximum available arrival rate the system can sustain. With a 1xM/M/4 configuration, as long as there is a queue, all servers will be active.

If you reference Figure 5-21, it's easy to see that with the same service time and arrival rate, Case 1 (1xM/M/4) has the lower queue time (row 12) and lower queue length (row 13). So from both a numeric and graphical perspective, the answer to this question is clearly that the 1xM/M4 (Case 1) will provide more throughput.

Moving the Response Time Curve Around

While understanding the differences between a 1xM/M/4 and a 4xM/M/1 configuration is important as well as useful, I have found that understanding how and why a single case's response time curve shifts provides even more insight. Predicting the general movement of the response time will help you to quickly forecast change and will also help you to communicate basic configuration changes without using a spreadsheet or other forecasting tool.

In this section, we'll take a look at the response time curve *shift* when changing system characteristics. When doing the next three exercises (Examples 5-20, 5-21, and 5-22), first try to answer the question based on your experiences, rather than using queuing theory mathematics. Developing an intuitive understanding of queuing theory is just as important as the ability to use various forecasting mathematics, tools, and products.

Example 5-20. Using Faster CPUs

What will happen to the response time curve when the existing CPUs are replaced with faster CPUs?

Faster CPUs can process transactions quicker. For example, instead of a CPU consuming 3 seconds to process a transaction, a faster CPU could perhaps process a single transaction in 2 seconds. The *process time* is the service time. So when faster CPUs are used, the CPU service time *decreases*. Looking at Figure 5-23, all the input values are the same with the exception of the service time. In Case 1, the service time is 3 ms/trx, but in Case 2, the service time is 2 ms/trx. Obviously the utilization, queue length, and queue time will be less in Case 2 because the service time is less. However, this question is asking what happens to the response time curve, which spans a wide range of arrival rates.

	A	B	C	D
1	**Queuing Model Data Entry**			
2	Description	Case 1 Values	Case 2 Values	Unit
3	Queues in system	1	1	#
4	Servers per queue	4	4	#
5	Service time	3.0000	2.0000	ms/trx
6	System Arrival rate	1.00	1.00	trx/ms
7	Response time tolerance	0.00		ms
9	Server Arrival rate	1.00	1.00	trx/ms
10	Traffic intensity	3.00	2.00	#
11	Utilization	75.0%	50.0%	#
12	Queue time	1.5283	0.1739	ms/trx
13	Queue length	1.5283	0.1739	#
14	Response time expected	4.5283	2.1739	ms/trx

Figure 5-23. *Setup for observing the response time curve shift when using faster CPUs*

Figure 5-24 is the comparison response time graph. The Case 1 response time curve is identified by locating the 3-second response time mark, and the Case 2 response time curve is associated with the curve starting at the 2-second response time mark.

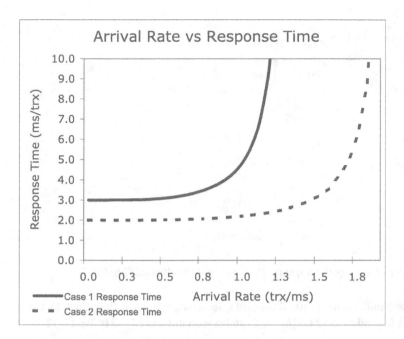

Figure 5-24. *The comparision graph for observing the response time curve shift when using faster CPUs*

The response time curve initially shifted down because the service time dropped from 3 ms/trx to 2 ms/trx. And because the CPUs can process transactions faster, they can now handle a larger transaction load—that is, a larger arrival rate. The result of this ability causes the response time curve to shift to the right. So not only will transactions finish quicker, but the system can handle an increased workload. Graphically speaking, the response time curve will shift down and to the right.

Example 5-21. Adding CPUs

What will happen to the response time curve when additional CPUs are implemented?

Additional CPUs will not process a transaction faster. A transaction that consumes 3.0 ms of CPU will consume 3.0 ms of CPU when additional CPUs are added (or even removed). Figure 5-25 (row 5) shows the service times for both Cases at 3.0 ms/trx. Additional CPUs are modeled as additional servers. Figure 5-25 (row 4) shows Case 1 with 4 CPUs and Case 2 with 8 CPUs (four additional CPUs). The arrival time is set to 1.0 trx/ms for both cases, but any arrival rate that results in a stable system would work fine.

	A	B	C	D
1	**Queuing Model Data Entry**			
2	Description	Case 1 Values	Case 2 Values	Unit
3	Queues in system	1	1	#
4	Servers per queue	4	8	#
5	Service time	3.0000	3.0000	ms/trx
6	System Arrival rate	1.00	1.00	trx/ms
7	Response time tolerance	0.00		ms
9	Server Arrival rate	1.00	1.00	trx/ms
10	Traffic intensity	3.00	3.00	#
11	Utilization	75.0%	37.5%	#
12	Queue time	1.5283	0.0078	ms/trx
13	Queue length	1.5283	0.0078	#
14	Response time expected	4.5283	3.0078	ms/trx

Figure 5-25. *Setup for observing the response time curve shift when adding CPUs*

Obviously, the Case 2 utilization, queue time, and queue length are less than Case 1's values, because Case 2 has four additional CPUs. This can be seen in Figure 5-25 (rows 11, 12, and 13).

Figure 5-26 is the comparison response time graph. Since both cases have a 3-second service time, identifying their respective curves by their response time won't work! As in all of the examples, Case 1 (4 CPUs) has a solid-line curve and Case 2 (8 CPUs) has a dotted-line curve.

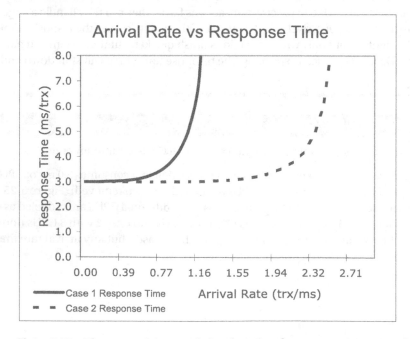

Figure 5-26. *The comparision graph for observing the response time curve shift when adding CPUs*

The response time curve did not shift up or down because there was no service time change. But the four additional CPUs (Case 2) allow the system to comfortably process a greater number of transactions each millisecond, causing the Case 2 graph to shift to the right. This is what we expect: adding more CPUs to an existing computer system will enable it to process more work.

Example 5-22. Increasing the Arrival Rate

What will happen to the response time curve when the arrival rate is increased?

As Examples 5-20 and 5-21 have shown, we can shift the response time curve around by altering the number and speed of the CPUs. But what about altering the arrival rate? What will happen to the response time curve if the arrival rate is increased, for example, from 1 trx/ms to 2 trx/ms?

The exercise setup is shown in Figure 5-27. Notice all entries are the same, with the exception of the system arrival rate (row 6). The Case 1 arrival rate is 1.0 trx/ms, while the Case 2 arrival rate is 2.0 trx/ms.

	A	B	C	D
1	**Queuing Model Data Entry**			
2	Description	Case 1 Values	Case 2 Values	Unit
3	Queues in system	1	1	#
4	Servers per queue	8	8	#
5	Service time	3.0000	3.0000	ms/trx
6	System Arrival rate	1.00	2.00	trx/ms
7	Response time tolerance	0.00		ms
9	Server Arrival rate	1.00	2.00	trx/ms
10	Traffic intensity	3.00	6.00	#
11	Utilization	37.5%	75.0%	#
12	Queue time	0.0078	0.5355	ms/trx
13	Queue length	0.0078	1.0709	#
14	Response time expected	3.0078	3.5355	ms/trx
19	Queue time stnd dev	0.10	1.15	ms/trx
20	Queue length stnd dev	0.13	2.52	#

Figure 5-27. *Setup for observing the response time curve shift when the arrival rate changes*

As you would expect, an increase in the arrival rate results in a higher Case 2 utilization, queue time, and queue length (rows 11, 12, and 13). But the question asks about the change in the response time curve. To answer this question, we will refer to the response time comparison graph, shown in Figure 5-28.

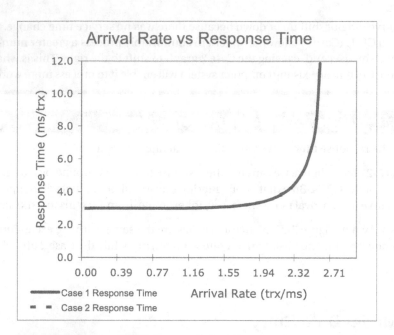

Figure 5-28. *The comparision graph for observing the response time curve shift when the arrival rate changes*

While it may look like a single line plot, both graphs are present in Figure 5-28; they just overlap. In fact, they overlap perfectly. That means there is no response time curve shift when the arrival rate is increased (or even decreased).

If you haven't encountered this before, it probably comes as a shock. So let's think about this for a bit. The only difference between Case 1 and Case 2 is the arrival rate. In Figure 5-28, the arrival rate is shown on the horizontal axis. When the arrival rate is changed, we simply slide either left or right to determine the appropriate response time. No shift in the response time curve occurs when simply sliding left or right on the response time curve (the horizontal axis).

Here's another way to think about this. There is no change in the service time, so the response time curves do not shift up or down. There is no change in the number of CPUs, so the curves do not shift left or right. And because we are changing the arrival rate, the response time curve does not shift. So in a way, this is kind of a trick question, because increasing the arrival rate does not change the response time curve.

Challenges in Queuing Theory Application

While our lives are truly a story, they are rarely lived as described in a textbook. Learning queuing theory is one thing, but using queuing theory in a variety of practical situations is entirely different. When I teach people about queuing theory, the theory part goes pretty quickly, but the application takes a while.

At this point, you should have a solid grasp on the theory and are well on your way in developing a kind of intuition about queuing systems. The next step is to apply the theory to situations that are presented with key pieces missing or in a somewhat confusing way. For example, how would you complete a queuing theory-based exercise when the arrival rate is not provided? Dealing with these types of situations, while uncomfortable at first, will give you the strength and the confidence you will need to be successful in applying the theory in your workplace.

The following exercises in Examples 5-23 through 5-27 each expose at least one common challenge faced when using queuing theory.

Example 5-23. Meeting First National Bank's Commitment

In a high-profile television commercial, the president of First National Bank firmly committed that "Nobody will ever have to wait more than 3 minutes in line!" The chief operations officer (COO) must determine the minimum number of bank tellers required to meet the president's promise. If First National doesn't hire enough tellers, customer service will suffer, which will lead to market share loss. If First National hires too many tellers, the tellers' salaries and benefits will raise the bank's costs, which will reduce the amount of interest the bank can pay its customers, which will also cause market share loss. So it's important to determine the optimum number of bank tellers.

Customers entering the bank line up single file, and the next available friendly teller services a customer at the head of the queue. Lunchtime is the bank's peak operating period and the COO's chief concern. During the lunchtime peak, an average of ten people walk through the door every 5 minutes. It takes a bank teller around 3 minutes to serve a customer. The arrival rate and service rate were confirmed to be exponentially distributed. How many tellers must be working at the bank to meet the president's commitment?

First of all, the president should have never said "never." Mathematically, it will always be possible for a person to wait more than 3 minutes. But we understand what he is communicating: if a customer must wait more than 3 minutes, both the bank and the customer are not happy.

Figure 5-29 shows the exercise setup using the queuing theory workbook. The number of queues in the system is 1 (row 3) because all customers line up single file. The number of servers (row 4) is what we are attempting to determine. It takes a bank teller 3 minutes to service a single customer, so the service time (row 5) is 3.0 min/person. Since ten customers arrive at the bank every 5 minutes, the arrival rate (row 6) is 2.0 person/min.[1] Since the president said no customer will ever have to wait more than 3 minutes, the service time is 3.0 min/person and the maximum allowable queue time is 3.0 min/person, resulting in a response time tolerance of 6.0 min.

---

1. When entering formulas into Excel, you can use the data entry to help reduce entry error and also convey meaning. For example, in this example, I could have entered 2.0, but instead I entered 10/5. Since the units are person/minute, it's easy to see that the problem was presented as 10 people every 5 minutes. This is one of the tricks I do in Excel to help me remember details about the problem.

	A	B	C	D
1	**Queuing Model Data Entry**			
2	Description	Case 1 Values	Case 2 Values	Unit
3	Queues in system	1	1	#
4	Servers per queue	7	8	#
5	Service time	3.0000	3.0000	min/person
6	System Arrival rate	2.00	2.00	person/min
7	Response time tolerance	6.00		min
9	Server Arrival rate	2.00	2.00	person/min
10	Traffic intensity	6.00	6.00	#
11	Utilization	85.7%	75.0%	#
12	Queue time	1.8415	0.5355	min/person
13	Queue length	3.6830	1.0709	#
14	Response time expected	4.8415	3.5355	min/person
19	Queue time stnd dev	2.77	1.15	min/person
20	Queue length stnd dev	5.86	2.52	#

Figure 5-29. *The First National Bank's queuing theory model numeric input*

Let's discuss the numbers a bit before we look at the resulting graph. Look closely at Case 1 in Figure 5-29. The number of servers per queue (cell B4)—that is, bank tellers—is set to 7. If we tried the exercise using 6 as the number of servers (for six tellers), the average utilization would be greater than 100%. That would result in an unstable system, so the queue time and queue length numbers would show as errors. But with seven bank tellers, the system is stable. The queue time (cell B12) is less than 3 minutes and, as you would expect, the forecasted response time (cell B14) is also less then our response time tolerance, with a value of 4.8415 minutes.

On average, seven bank tellers will meet our response time tolerance. However, the president was not talking about *average*. To be more in line with the president's meaning, we need to be more conservative with our forecast. There are many ways to do this, but two broad approaches are to focus on a technical solution and also a business solution.

One way to technically be more conservative is to add a standard deviation of queue time to our forecasted response time, ensuring it still falls below our response time tolerance. Cell B19 shows the value for one standard deviation of queue time, which is 2.77 min. If we sum the forecasted response time and a standard deviation of queue time, our more conservative forecast results in a forecasted response time of 7.61 minutes (7.61 = 4.84 + 2.77). Ouch! That's too high. So if we want to be more conservative, we should do a forecast with more then seven bank tellers.

This brings us to Case 2. Case 2 in Figure 5-29 is configured with 8 bank tellers (cell C4). The resulting Case 2 utilization (row 11), queue time (row 12), queue length (row 13), expected response time (row 14), and the queue time standard deviation (row 19) are all less compared to Case 1. The sum of the expected response time (3.54 min) and one queue time standard deviation (1.15 min) results in a response time forecast of 4.69 minutes. This is well below our response time tolerance of 6 minutes. So while Case 1 will work on average, Case 2 is a more conservative solution.

Figure 5-30 shows graphically the average forecasts for both Case 1 and Case 2. The response time tolerance is the horizontal line at a response time of 6.0, and the arrival rate is shown as a thin vertical line (look at the arrival rate of 2.00 people/min). We must ensure that at the given arrival rate (2.0 person/min) the forecasted response time does not breach the response time tolerance. Clearly, in both Case 1 and Case 2, the response time curve crosses the response time tolerance after an arrival rate of 2.0 people/min. Graphically, as long as the curves intersect the response time tolerance to the right of the vertical line showing the arrival rate, we're in good shape. This graph also easily conveys that Case 1 is a more aggressive solution than Case 2.

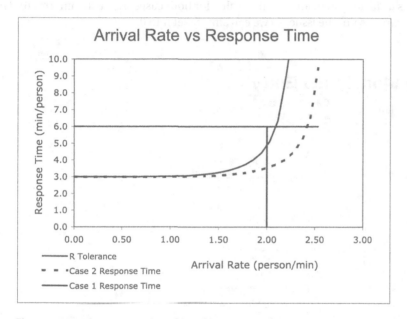

Figure 5-30. *The First National Bank's queuing theory model comparison graph*

I mentioned there are two general ways to be more in line with the president's meaning. The technical approach was just presented. The other approach is more business-focused. Suppose when customers walked into the bank, they were presented with a number and asked to help themselves to a cup of coffee and some snacks, as well as relax in the comfortable surroundings. By the time they got their coffee and snack, and relaxed a bit, 3 or even 5 minutes could have gone by. So the customers' perception is "no excess waiting," yet the reality is that they may have been waiting for 5 minutes. Combining this business-focused approach with the more aggressive Case 1 technical solution could result in a lower labor cost to the bank and happier customers!

Example 5-24. Setting Up Czech-E Czeese Pizza Parlor

Otto is using his family's savings to build a brand-new pizza parlor in downtown Prague. He is calling it Czech-E Czeese Pizza Parlor. He has already hired five people to take customer orders and prepare Czech-E Czeese pizzas. Each server can serve three customers every 5 minutes.

Otto is wondering which will be better for his customers: to have one queue per cash register (like McDonald's) or to have one single queue for all his cash registers (like an economy-class airport check-in counter). Which configuration will best serve his customers?

While there are many values we could enter into the spreadsheet for this example, the fundamental structure of the queuing model is the same. Figure 5-31 is one possible setup. Since Otto has already hired five employees, let's use all five. With one queue in the system, there will be five servers (employees) for the single queue (Case 1, cell B4). With five queues, there will be one server for each queue (Case 2, cell C4). The service times in both cases are the same: 5 minutes per customer, which is 1.6667 min/cust. We are not given the system arrival rate, so we just pick a value that creates a stable system and use that value for both cases: 1.0 cust/min (row 6). The response time tolerance is not the issue, so we can simply set it to 0.

	A	B	C	D
1	**Queuing Model Data Entry**			
2	Description	Case 1 Values	Case 2 Values	Unit
3	Queues in system	1	5	#
4	Servers per queue	5	1	#
5	Service time	1.6667	1.6667	min/cust
6	System Arrival rate	1.00	1.00	cust/min
7	Response time tolerance	0.00		min
9	Server Arrival rate	1.00	0.20	cust/min
10	Traffic intensity	1.67	0.33	#
11	Utilization	33.3%	33.3%	#
12	Queue time	0.0151	0.8334	min/cust
13	Queue length	0.0151	0.1667	#
14	Response time expected	1.6818	2.5001	min/cust
19	Queue time stnd dev	0.12	1.86	min/cust
20	Queue length stnd dev	0.17	0.55	#

Figure 5-31. *Czech-E Czeese's queuing theory model numeric input*

As expected, the average utilization is the same for both cases. But the queue time, queue length, response time, and the queue time standard deviation are significantly different. The single queue configuration (Case 1) results in a lower average queue time and therefore lower average response time. Of course, then the average queue length is also shorter for the single queue configuration. This occurs because when each server has its own queue, sometimes a server's queue is empty yet the other servers have queues. (Otto does not allow queue defection, which allows a person to switch lines.) As discussed earlier in this chapter, one queue per server configurations also cause the queue lengths and queue times to vary more than a single queue solution. This can be seen when comparing the queue time and queue length standard deviations (rows 19 and 20).

While the numbers in Figure 5-31 don't show this, the comparison graph in Figure 5-32 clearly illustrates that the average queue time is always higher in Case 2. But even more interesting is that the single queue configuration (Case 1) can sustain a significantly higher arrival rate! Clearly, the single queue with multiple servers is the better solution for Otto's customers and also for Otto's business!

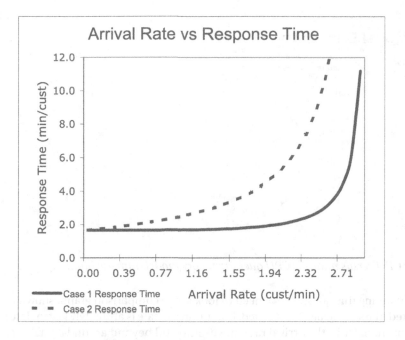

Figure 5-32. *Czech-E Czeese's queuing theory model comparison graph*

Example 5-25. Comparing a Single CPU with Multiple CPUs

Mac is a senior DBA. One of his current responsibilities is to make a computer system recommendation for his company's new IT support system. He has narrowed the search down to two possible scenarios, called Model A and Model B. Model A contains two fast CPUs that are capable of servicing (executing) 45 transactions per second. Model B contains eight CPUs, yet each CPU is capable of servicing only 19 transactions per second. Which computer system should Mac recommend?

This exercise couldn't be more timely! In our industry today, IT is constantly making decisions regarding placing one or two CPU Linux boxes versus larger multiple CPU machines. As we'll see, the best solution is not always clear.

For this example, Mac will compare the two cases. Both cases are shown in Figure 5-33. Case 1 is the faster two CPU configuration (Model A). Case 2 is the slower eight CPU configuration (Model B). The stated service rate for Case 1 is 45 trx/sec, which means the service time is 0.0222 sec/trx (cell B5). The stated service rate for Case 2 is 19 trx/sec, which means the service time is 0.0526 sec/trx (cell C5). The system arrival rate is not stated, so Mac picked 20.0 trx/sec (row 6) to provide plenty of activity.

	A	B	C	D
1	**Queuing Model Data Entry**			
2	Description	Case 1 Values	Case 2 Values	Unit
3	Queues in system	1	1	#
4	Servers per queue	2	8	#
5	Service time	0.0222	0.0526	sec/trx
6	System Arrival rate	20.00	20.00	trx/sec
7	Response time tolerance	0.00		sec
9	Server Arrival rate	20.00	20.00	trx/sec
10	Traffic intensity	0.44	1.05	#
11	Utilization	22.2%	13.2%	#
12	Queue time	0.0012	0.0000	sec/trx
13	Queue length	0.0230	0.0000	#
14	Response time expected	0.0234	0.0526	sec/trx
19	Queue time stnd dev	0.01	0.00	sec/trx
20	Queue length stnd dev	0.19	0.00	#

Figure 5-33. *Single CPU versus multiple CPU queuing theory model numeric input*

To work toward answering this question, we need to look at the comparison graph, shown in Figure 5-34. As noted, the arrival rate is not stated, but the arrival rate is absolutely key to determining the best solution. Once the arrival rate moves into and beyond around 80 trx/sec, the slower yet more CPU box is technically the better solution. Mac also needs to get a good understanding of the potential workload growth, as this will directly relate to the arrival rate. Pricing information and the impact of service-level breaches will also need to be considered. So speaking like a true consultant, Mac's answer is "It depends."

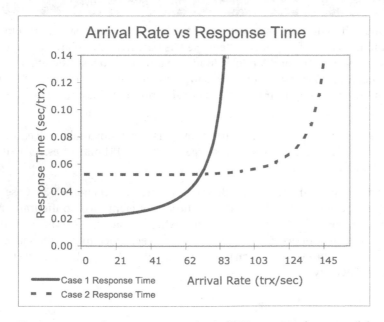

Figure 5-34. *Single CPU versus multiple CPU queuing theory model comparison graph*

Example 5-26. Determining the Throughput Range

Milly has had some strange managers before, but her current boss has brought a whole new meaning to the phrase "one-minute manager." For some unknown reason, Milly's manager decided it was extremely important to determine the company's key web-based OLTP system's transaction throughput during peak processing time.

After Milly instrumented the database server machine, the 16 state-of-the-art CPUs peaked at around 70% utilization. When this occurred, the key service level response time was consistently below 3.0 seconds, with an average of around 1.5 seconds.

To put some structure to her analysis and to help present her findings to her boss, Milly constructed a simple table with the headings Service Time, Arrival Rate, and CPU Utilization. Milly's strategy was to determine a realistic arrival rate range by varying both the service time and the arrival rate, being careful to keep the average CPU utilization at 70%. She observed the response time was consistently below 3.0 seconds. There were times when the response time was above 3.0 seconds, but that was unusual. Since Milly did not want to base a forecast on rare or unlikely data, she knew not to consider service times greater than 3.0 seconds. She also decided to derive the arrival rate when the service time was as low as to 0.5 second to provide a more comprehensive answer to her boss. Table 5-3 shows her result table, and Figure 5-35 shows two of her six forecasts. Case 1 uses a service time of 3.0 sec/trx, and Case 2 uses a service time of 2.5 sec/trx.

Table 5-3. *Result Table for Throughput Forecast*

Service Time (sec/trx)	Arrival Rate (trx/sec)	CPU Utilization
3.0	3.7	70%
2.5	4.5	70%
2.0	5.6	70%
1.5	7.5	70%
1.0	11.2	70%
0.5	22.4	70%

	A	B	C	D
1	**Queuing Model Data Entry**			
2	Description	Case 1 Values	Case 2 Values	Unit
3	Queues in system	1	1	#
4	Servers per queue	16	16	#
5	Service time	3.0000	2.5000	sec/trx
6	System Arrival rate	3.735	4.48	trx/sec
7	Response time tolerance	0.00		sec
9	Server Arrival rate	3.74	4.48	trx/sec
10	Traffic intensity	11.21	11.20	#
11	Utilization	70.0%	70.0%	#
12	Queue time	0.0814	0.0675	sec/trx
13	Queue length	0.3040	0.3026	#
14	Response time expectec	3.0814	2.5675	sec/trx
19	Queue time stnd dev	0.31	0.26	sec/trx
20	Queue length stnd dev	1.28	1.27	#

Figure 5-35. *Two example results while determining the possible throughput range*

Based on the queuing model, Milly expects the arrival rate to vary from around 3.7 trx/sec to around 22 trx/sec. If Milly's service time observations are correct, at 1.5 sec/trx the arrival rate should be centered around 7.5 trx/sec. Summarizing and simplifying, Milly told her manager, "The throughput could be between 4 and 22 transactions per second, but probably closer to around 8 transactions per second."

Most people start by entering a service time and then repeatedly try different arrival rate values until the utilization gets close to 70%. As you might expect, there is a faster way. Actually a much faster way! The Excel Goal Seek tool (accessible from the Tools menu) is a perfect solution. It will significantly speed up this analysis. Figure 5-36 shows the Goal Seek dialog box just before submission.

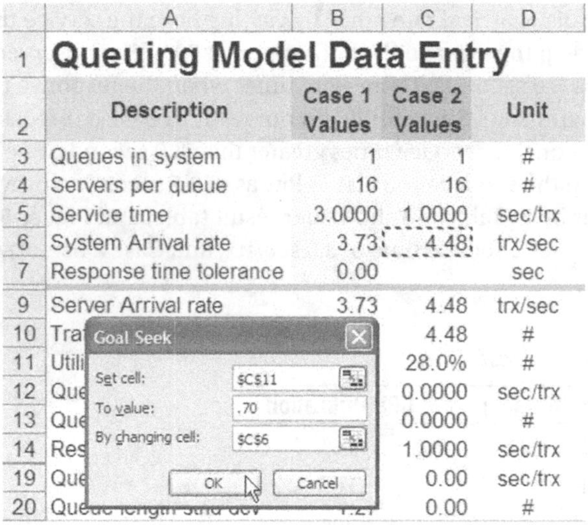

Figure 5-36. *Using Excel's Goal Seek tool can help quickly and accurately solve simple optimization type problems.*

Example 5-27. "Sizing the System" for a Client

Cathy is one of many system architects in a software development company called Zip Zap Ltd. On the company's sales team, the top salesperson is Bodel. He has been working on a deal for months, and it could be the largest deal Zip Zap has ever closed. The prospect is based in Holland and sells flower bulbs to people who call in their orders via telephone.

Through standard salesperson intimidation tactics, Bodel has made it crystal-clear to Cathy that this strategic account is not only the largest telephone seller of flower bulbs in the world, but also a $50 million opportunity. Several members of Zip Zap's executive committee are dedicating their personal attention to this deal. Bodel is insisting that Cathy "size the system" today and has worked with her boss to clear her schedule of less strategically important tasks.

To begin, Cathy asked a few questions. She learned that the client's stated requirements dictate that Zip Zap's software solution be capable of handling 14,000 telephone orders a day. During an interview with the manager of the 20-person order-taking department, Cathy learned the average telephone order takes about 2 minutes. Some preliminary testing has shown the application consumes about 20 seconds of database server CPU time to complete an order. The company assured Cathy that there is not a traditional workload peak, but rather the 14,000 orders are spread evenly throughout the day and night.

After clarifying what Bodel meant by "size the system," it was discovered Bodel must determine the number of database server CPUs so the appropriate computing system can be initially proposed.

Cathy was curious how 20 people could enter 14,000 orders in a system in a single day. So she did some forecasting math to determine how utilized the order-taking people would be:

$$U = \frac{\lambda S_t}{M}$$

$$S_t = 2 \min / order$$

$$M = 20 \, people$$

$$\lambda = 14000 \frac{orders}{day} \times \frac{1 day}{24 hours} \times \frac{1 hour}{60 \min} = 9.722 \, orders / \min$$

$$U = \frac{\lambda S_t}{M} = \frac{9.722 \, orders / \min * 2 \min / order}{20 \, people} = \frac{19.44}{20} = 0.972 = 97.2\%$$

Cathy has been in the consulting business long enough to know it's impossible, not to mention inhuman, for a person to maintain utilization at 97%. And don't forget that people need a lunch break and bathroom breaks. She is also very concerned about the prospect's comments that there are no workload peaks. She has never seen a situation like this before, so she will need to check back with the prospect. Now that her curiosity was piqued, she wanted to determine the average queue length and queue time. To get a more precise forecast, she used Erlang C-based math.

Figure 5-37 shows how she set up the problem using the queuing theory workbook. Any available order-taker can receive the next call, which means there is one queue and each order-taker is, in essence, a server. Based on the prospect and doing a little math, the average order takes an average of 2.0 minutes and 9.722 orders arrive each minute. Case 1 shows the current situation with 20 order-takers, and Case 2 shows the situation with 8 additional workers.

	A	B	C	D
1	**Queuing Model Data Entry**			
2	Description	Case 1 Values	Case 2 Values	Unit
3	Queues in system	1	1	#
4	Servers per queue	20	28	#
5	Service time	2.0000	2.0000	min/order
6	System Arrival rate	9.72	9.72	order/min
7	Response time tolerance	0.00		min
9	Server Arrival rate	9.72	9.72	order/min
10	Traffic intensity	19.44	19.44	#
11	Utilization	97.2%	69.4%	#
12	Queue time	3.0901	0.0109	min/order
13	Queue length	30.0419	0.1061	#
14	Response time expected	5.0901	2.0109	min/order
19	Queue time stnd dev	3.56	0.07	min/order
20	Queue length stnd dev	35.05	0.76	#

Figure 5-37. *Forecasting order-taker utilization resulted in some astonishing discoveries.*

As Cathy expected, the calculated utilization with only 20 workers is 97.2%. What she didn't anticipate was the average queue time—the time a customer waits on the telephone before speaking with an order-taker—is just over 3 minutes (cell B12), and the average number of customers waiting to have their order taken is just over 30 (cell B13)!

Shown in Case 2 in Figure 5-37, Cathy determined that by hiring eight additional workers (for a total of 28), the average worker utilization would drop to 69.4%, the average queue time would be less than 1 minute, and the average queue length would be less than 1.

While Cathy's objective is not to determine how utilized the workers are, she knows that digging a little deeper can help undercover bogus data and assumptions. It's takes only a few minutes to do a few simple checks, and it can reduce the chance of producing an invalid or misleading forecast. So while it may seem "out of scope," it is actually more of a quality assurance activity.

Cathy still needs to "size the system." To increase the forecast precision, she decided to use Erlang C math. She is given the arrival rate and the service time, and must determine the number of servers. She decided to keep all units of time in seconds, and therefore, she needed to convert the number of orders per day into the number of orders per second:

$$\lambda = 14000 \frac{orders}{day} \times \frac{1 day}{24 hours} \times \frac{1 hour}{60 \min} \times \frac{1 \min}{60 s} = 0.162 \, orders/s$$

Figure 5-38 shows how she set up the problem for a 4 CPU (Case 1) and a 5 CPU (Case 2) configuration. Table 5-4 shows the results, along with some of the other cases she ran.

Queuing Model Data Entry

	A	B	C	D
	Description	Case 1 Values	Case 2 Values	Unit
3	Queues in system	1	1	#
4	Servers per queue	4	5	#
5	Service time	20.0000	20.0000	sec/order
6	System Arrival rate	0.16	0.16	order/sec
7	Response time tolerance	0.00		sec
9	Server Arrival rate	0.16	0.16	order/sec
10	Traffic intensity	3.24	3.24	#
11	Utilization	81.0%	64.8%	#
12	Queue time	16.1723	3.4060	sec/order
13	Queue length	2.6199	0.5518	#
14	Response time expected	36.1723	23.4060	sec/order
19	Queue time stnd dev	24.28	8.11	sec/order
20	Queue length stnd dev	4.25	1.51	#

Figure 5-38. *Two configuration options for sizing the system*

Table 5-4. *Results of Various Configurations for Sizing the System*

CPUs	Utilization	Queue Time (sec)	Queue Length
3	108%	Unstable	Unstable
4	81%	16.2	2.6
5	65%	3.4	0.5
6	54%	1.0	0.2
7	46%	0.3	0.0

There is quite a difference between the four and five CPU configurations. The five CPU system's forecasted utilization is a cautious and responsible 65%, but the four CPU system has a risky 81% utilization. As Figure 5-39 shows, with an arrival rate of 0.162 orders per second, the four CPU configuration would be operating well into the elbow of the curve.

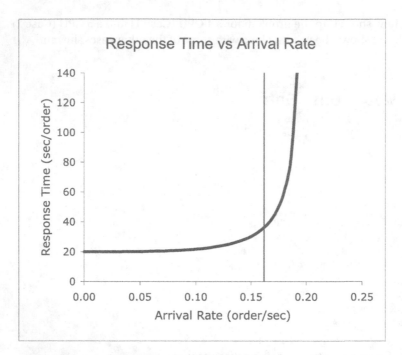

Figure 5-39. *When utilization reaches into the 80% range, the system is operating in the elbow of the curve.*

Cathy told Bodel the data she was given is very suspect. Having no workload peak and having the order-takers working at 97% utilization was virtually impossible. But assuming this is correct, a five CPU configuration should be fine, but a six CPU configuration would provide a more comfortable, low-risk solution (not to mention a bigger sales commission for Bodel's hardware vendor friends).

Summary

From gas stations to post offices, queuing models apply. After reading this chapter, you should be able to quickly, intuitively, and mathematically create useful queuing models. That's what the practical application of queuing theory can do. It's not just about the numbers. It's about solving real-life business questions that are complicated yet still must be answered.

I hope the noncomputing system examples added a bit of humor to what can be a very dry topic. But more important, thinking about noncomputing systems broadens our thinking and forces us to not fixate on simply the CPU and IO subsystem.

One of my objectives in this chapter was to help you develop a kind of queuing intuition. You're probably not going to memorize the essential queuing theory mathematics, have a calculator with you at all times, or always have access to a queuing theory spreadsheet. But what you should have is the ability to discuss freely, confidently, and correctly various queuing theory configuration options. This is something you will have with you the rest of your life.

In addition to this intuition is the ability to solve complex queuing theory problems, even with key pieces of information missing. Knowing how to solve questions that appear to have multiple missing variables is incredibly valuable. You may be amazed how often key pieces of information are not initially available, but that's real life.

Now with the core queuing theory and its practical application solidly in tact, it's time to provide the structure to ensure consistent project success. As your forecasting projects grow in scope, you will be asked about your approach and your method. To help prepare you for these types of questions and to provide a solid framework from which to work, the next chapter is devoted to methodically forecasting Oracle performance.

CHAPTER 6

■ ■ ■

Methodically Forecasting Performance

Forecasting Oracle performance can be just plain fun. The topics covered so far can get forecasters so excited that a kind of frenzy can result. But frenzied forecasting is dangerous and inherently risky, and risk is the very thing forecasting is supposed to help mitigate. No respectable business is going to invest in a person or group of people who are so wild-eyed and pumped on forecasting caffeine that they lack the direction, the structure, the fortitude, and the commitment to carry a serious business task to completion. The goal of this chapter is to allow you to remain wild-eyed while instilling management confidence and to responsibly forecast. It can be done.

The Need for a Method

Even the simplest forecasting exercise naturally follows a method. For example, data must be collected and a model must be selected before a forecast is actually made. This series of events calls out for a method. The challenge with any method is to provide a solid framework that enhances the project's usefulness while not stifling creativity and productivity. In addition, the method must be scalable to accommodate for the varying lengths of Oracle forecasting projects.

Personally, I'm not big on method. I usually find method stifling, smothering, and a productivity-killer. I love to be creative, and methodologies and project plans just don't naturally sit well with me. But over the years, I have learned that even the smallest and simplest forecasting project requires method. And as the projects grow in scope, the method will provide a scalable structure and give everyone a road map to help set expectations. Without a method, business will be reluctant to invest in forecasting, and the underlying technology will always be suspect.

Realizing the need for both method and productivity, I have spent quite a bit of time looking for and testing various forecasting-related methodologies. The method presented in this book is specifically tailored to the realities of forecasting Oracle performance. As you are well aware, forecasting Oracle performance is unique in many ways:

Project duration: Forecasting Oracle performance can take as little as 60 seconds or as long as an ongoing business process. If you have been reading this book from the start, you know that a forecasting project can be very simple and require only a few minutes. But you also know it can be very complex and very volatile, requiring a significant amount of time from a variety of people. The forecasting methodology must support short projects by not over-burdening them, but also supply the structure and direction larger projects require.

Technical complexities: You'll encounter technical complexities in everything from the forecast model to the IT infrastructure. When technological complexity exists, it may take multiple attempts to overcome the challenge. Implementation-type projects are very linear, whereas forecasting projects are very cyclical. The forecasting methodology must embrace this cyclical approach.

Politics: Politically charged environments naturally occur when vendors, users, and IT staff are in the same room. Forecasting not only touches each of these groups, but also must bring them together. Usually a consensus is required. This can be extremely difficult. The forecasting methodology must naturally bring together all parties and build consensus from project inception to completion. Mixing politics and money (which are inherently connected) can bring out the worst in people.[1] A good method, when followed, will make it much more difficult for someone to destroy your credibility.

Money: The financial impact of forecasting is potentially significant to all parties involved. Forecasting is a kind of glue between IT and the business. It responsibly brings together the needs of the business with the services of IT. To service a business, money is required. Sometimes it's in the millions! The methodology must support the IT financial decision-making process by answering questions and supplying information as simply and completely as possible.

Unknowns: Throughout a forecasting project, there are many unknowns. Some of the unknowns will not be answered until the project is completed. Questions about which forecast model to use or which workload peak should be used cannot be answered until the project is underway. This inherently invites risk into all forecasting projects. This is yet another reason why a method is needed to help reduce this risk.

Business questions: Forecasting is about answering staggering business questions. One of the challenges is how to answer a business question that directly involves technology. For example, how does revenue relate to system workload? The methodology must provide steps to help bridge and tie together business and technology.

The need for a forecasting methodology is obvious and significant. Even simple projects touch on each of the items just discussed. Merging together these requirements along with many years of experience has resulted in straightforward six-step method.

---

1. The only time I have been threatened in my career was during a forecasting project. The hardware vendor knew my team's recommendation would affect the hardware sales. And, of course, his quota and potentially his job would be impacted. He made it very obvious that "I had not better screw up this project," which really meant, "I want a big sale and you better not get in my way."

The OraPub Forecasting Method

The OraPub forecasting method is a six-step process that is designed to provide just enough structure to meet the unique forecasting requirements of Oracle projects, as well as provide direction and depth to larger and more complex projects. I introduced this method in Chapter 2, and we used it in a case study in Chapter 3. In this chapter, we will focus on the method. First, here is a recap of the steps:

Step 1: Determine the study question. Every forecasting exercise, no matter how simplistic or complex, is based on a fundamental question or need. Find out what that question is, get everyone involved and agree to it, and don't sway from answering that question.

Step 2: Gather workload data. The study question will give you clues as to what data you need. Gather it, store it, and get ready to use it.

Step 3: Characterize the workload data. Raw data is not all that useful. You will need to transform this raw workload data into a format that is useful for people when forecasting and also appropriate for forecast model input. While characterizing a workload can be very simple, a precise forecast requires a well-characterized workload.

Step 4: Develop and use the appropriate model. You have many modeling options. But your study question, available workload data, and characterization options will lead to an obvious model choice. Part of developing a model is calibration. Calibration is used to slightly adjust the model to increase its precision.

Step 5: Validate the forecast. If possible, you want to verify (that is, validate) the precision and usefulness of your forecasts. A responsible forecast includes a good understanding of precision. It's not enough to say, "This model always yields good precision." You need to measure the precision. Some models inherently do this for you, while others do not. "Professional" capacity planners get irate if you have not validated your forecast, so be prepared.

Step 6: Forecast. As you can see, it takes quite a while before you actually start forecasting. Unless you are using a professional product, you will spend a significant amount of your time doing nonanalysis-related forecasting tasks. When you forecast, you are learning about IT service, risk, and developing strategies to mitigate the risk and to mitigate service-level breaches.

The rest of this chapter details each of these six steps. I've purposely avoided stating specific tasks and deliverables to provide flexibility and allow creativity.

Determine the Study Question

Every forecast answers a question. When you wake up in the morning and look outside to forecast the weather, you need an answer. When you are about to drive into an intersection, you need an answer. If you are tasked with a forecast, yet the question is not crystal-clear, you must get clarification. Attempting to answer a question that is unclear will undoubtedly result in unmet expectations, which is the death of a forecasting project.

Here are some examples of study questions:

- Will the computing system meet SuperFilm's business requirements now and in the future? If not, which technical areas require special attention, and what can SuperFilm specifically do about it?

- Are there are significant technical risks that pose a threat to the QQ project success?

- If business revenue doubles, can the current systems meet service-level requirements?

- What is the impact on IT services if database server capacity is increased?

Our job is to guide others to discover the study question. People not familiar with forecasting will need to be coached. Business-focused people will tend to emphasize the basic business need without a natural connection to IT. For example, a business-focused person's study question could be, "Will this implementation work?" Technology-focused people will tend to emphasize detailed technology specifics. For example, a typical initial IT-focused study question could be, "What will the CPU utilization be if the workload is doubled?" The business people will scratch their heads and ask, "What does utilization have to do with the stock price?"

When formulating the study question, think like a consultant and a coach. Bring both the people and the original purpose together. Keep asking questions that dig into the heart of the matter. You'll need to use very simplistic phrases that everyone can understand.

At some point, there was a very fundamental need that evoked the forecast request. But over time, it may have been muddied by politics, personal defense mechanisms, and budgets. Your job is to work with the key players to uncover the core purpose of the forecast, to rediscover the true study question.

The study question helps keep everyone involved in the project on track. Most people involved in a forecast (business- and technology-focused) tend to want something specific that can be out of scope. For example, the people developing the forecast model may want to try out a new model, or the business people are curious if this "forecasting thing" can save them tons of money. When the project starts to lose focus or direction, or someone wants to stray from the initial intent, bring them back on track by using the study question.

I can remember a project where my team consisted of a number of people who reported directly to me. I was so into trying out a new forecast model on the project that I started to lose focus and burn precious project hours. Fortunately, one of my team members boldly asked me, "Craig, is what we're doing going to help us to answer the study question?" It caused me to step back and think for a bit. The answer was obvious. I had allowed my love for modeling to sway the project too much. What I appreciated was the courage and the way the question was asked. It not only showed me that I had lost focus, but it also showed me that this young man understood the value of the study question and how it could be used.

Keep It Simple

Good study questions are not technical. Speaking as a technology guy, I urge all you technicians to stay away from complex, technically focused study questions. While you may be more easily able to answer them, they will not mean as much to the business. And it is the business that IT serves. It is also difficult for business people to see the connection with terms like *utilization* and *revenue*. When it comes down to it, from a business perspective, revenue, not utilization, is important.

Good study questions are simple. Complexity provides too much wiggle room and can allow for unmet expectations to creep in. Take a look at the study questions listed at the beginning of this section. They are very simple—so simple that both management and technologists can understand them! If the study question is very simple and straightforward, everyone will know if the question has been answered. Now, some people won't like the answer, but it will be answered. And answering the question is the focus, not whether someone likes the answer. Believe me, your forecasting work will be used in ways you can't even imagine. Just focus on your job and let the management folks do what they will.

Specify How the Study Question Will Be Answered

To help ensure everyone understands the study question and to ensure the project scope is understood and respected, state specifically how the study question will be answered. The following is an example.

The study question will be answered as follows:

1. Respond with a direct yes or no as to whether a technical area(s) exists that requires special attention to help ensure the system will be a success now and in the future.

2. List any of these areas that require special attention.

3. Devise solutions to help ensure these area(s) will not thwart a successful production system.

4. Explain how the conclusion was reached.

5. Report the business impact of our findings.

6. Create tools and methods to help empower ZipZap, Inc. to detect technical areas that require special attention now and in the future.

How the study question is answered is presented in the following sections.

Normally, if the project does not identify any significant risk, it will come to a swift and successful end. However, if significant risk has been identified, the project can get intense, and the focus shifts to developing various risk mitigation strategies. A good study question coupled with how it will be answered will provide additional structure and direction if the answer is "we've identified significant risk." Be prepared for this by allocating plenty of project time if complex risk mitigation strategies must be developed.

During the study question development, be thinking about how the workload data will be gathered, what data is required, and which forecast models would work well. If you are not comfortable with these, you will need to be careful how the study question is to be answered. Perhaps an additional study question meeting is warranted, giving you time to do some research. Just don't agree to a study question without a data gathering, workload characterization, and model selection plan. You don't want to get backed into a corner with no way out!

Agree on the Study Question

Get everyone to fully and completely agree to the study question. In email and presentations, restate the study question. I cannot emphasize this enough.

One of the worst things that can happen is at the end of a project, someone says, "Well, I never really agreed with this whole thing." Argh! I promise you this will happen unless you are very aggressive in repeating the study question, thereby giving everyone ample opportunity to voice their opposition. If someone does voice opposition, immediately address the issue. Having key players not fully embrace the study question is one of the best ways to kill a forecast project, not to mention your career.

Once the study question has been agreed upon, it's time to gather the workload data.

Gather the Workload Data

Every forecast requires input. Some of the input will be related to the "what-if" questions, but the bulk of data will most likely be gathered from a production Oracle system. Gathering workload data can be very simple, but it also can be intrusive and impact your systems. Keep the data gathering impact to a minimum, and you may be able to continue the process, which will yield benefits far into the future.

The quality of data is more important than the amount of data. Don't be impressed with a lot of workload data. Gather just what is needed. If your company already has a repository of data, extract just what you need and nothing else. A large amount of data can get confusing, and confusion breeds risk.

Let the study question lead you to how often data should be gathered (that is, the frequency), how many samples are required, and specifically which data is required. It is common for technical people to want to gather a lot of data and as often as possible. Let the study question guide you. Managing a lot of data can be a hassle, so try to keep it to a minimum. A study question that requires a response time-related answer will undoubtedly require more data that is more tightly integrated with the application. In fact, the application may need to be instrumented to get the data you need. But regardless of the workload data requirement, keep it simple and repeatable.

Yes, the data collection should be repeatable. Most forecasting projects will be repeated. In fact, a service-level-minded IT organization will want to continually forecast. Having an automated data collection process in place will reap benefits for both the current project and many to come.

If IT is currently gathering and storing performance data, you may already have access to all the data you need. It is common for IT to already be gathering workload data. Since the operating system administration group is usually gathering data. Usually, some additional workload and application-specific data will need to be gathered, but the mechanisms and process may already have been created. You just have to do a little investigative work.

If there is no automated data collection process occurring at your company, now is your chance to start one! Without workload data, forecasting cannot occur. So it is to your advantage to begin to gather data now. The process does not need to be complicated, but it does need to include data from the operating system, Oracle, and the application. OraPub has a tool kit available for free (`www.orapub.com/tools`), called the OraPub System Monitor (OSM), which contains a module to gather and report not only Oracle data, but also operating system and application data. It's also easily customizable, so you can hook it into specific applications. There is also data gathering information, including code snippets, presented in Chapter 7.

At this point, the study question has been determined and the data is being gathered. Now all that raw data must be made usable.

Characterize the Workload

Raw workload data is worthless. The raw data must be purposefully transformed if it is to become useful. In some cases, this process can be extremely difficult. This is especially true when higher precision forecasts are required.

A computer system model is incomplete when it models only the hardware configuration. Equally important is the workload that all the software programs place on the system. Just as with the hardware, a model is used to simplify a typically extremely complicated workload so it is useful for forecast model input and for our understanding. The end result is a workload picture. The process of creating this picture is commonly called *workload characterization*.

The purpose of characterizing a workload is twofold. First, the data must become useful for forecast model input. Second, the data must be understandable by those who will be using the data (this includes the forecast model users and receivers of the analysis).

Workload characterization is one of the most complicated aspects of forecasting. Forecasting products, like OraPub's HoriZone, have proprietary algorithms to reduce the extremely complex Oracle workload down to a few numbers.

For example, each workload sample or a summary of many samples may produce a single summarization of the system arrival rate, CPU service time, and IO service time. As you can see, the numbers representing a complex workload must be very, very good!

These few numbers represent specific aspects of a complex Oracle-based workload. When an advanced characterization is combined with an advanced forecast model, the forecast precision possibility is staggering. For example, HoriZone's workload characterization and forecast model combination typically produces forecasts with a standard deviation of 0.0%. That's one of the benefits of a commercial product.

Workload characterization is so important to forecasting that I'll devote the next chapter to the topic.

Develop and Use the Appropriate Model

It is rare that you will develop your own forecast models from scratch. So many existing models are available that to start from scratch rarely makes sense. However, it is very common to modify an existing model. During consulting engagements, I always try to use an existing model. It gives me a head start, saves my client money, and reduces the risk of a modeling mistake. Many models are available for free at OraPub's web site (www.orapub.com/tools).

As you know, you can choose from many different model types. Let the study question combined with the available workload data lead you to the obvious model choice. Usually, more than one model will work, so go with them both if possible. Until the forecasts have been validated, you won't really know their precision. So it's a good idea to have two model possibilities in case one doesn't work as well as you would like.

Don't favor a particular model. Especially when you are just starting to forecast, it is natural and common to have an affinity toward a particular model. For example, many people will try to use the queuing spreadsheet at all times. It may work, but it may not work well and perhaps isn't the best model selection. To avoid falling into this trap, learn how to use all the models presented in this book. Practice doing some simple forecasting based on one of your production systems. This will expose you to the "ins and outs" of each model. Once you are comfortable using all the models, you are much more likely to choose the best model as opposed to your favorite model.

Sometimes the forecast models can become quite complicated. When this occurs, it's a good idea to have a person not directly involved with the project double-check the model. Working on and staring at a spreadsheet for a couple weeks is enough to drive anyone nuts! You can be looking at a cell that essentially says "1 + 1 = 3," and you will not even notice. Do yourself, your team, and your career a favor and have someone check your work. Don't let your customer check your work for you, because that's embarrassing, unprofessional, and could change the entire risk analysis.

Some forecast models can be directly calibrated. *Calibrating* a model means to adjust, tweak, and optimize the model to increase its precision. This typically automatically occurs in commercial models. A vendor will calibrate a model based on many workload samples to gain the best precision possible. If calibration is not possible, then the validation phase is even more important.

Now that the study question has been determined, the workload data has been gathered and characterized, and the model has been selected, modified, and used to do some forecasts, it's time to determine just how precise the forecast really is.

Validate the Forecast

A model such as regression analysis is, in a way, self-validating because the confidence interval is naturally a part of using the model. A ratio model has such a low precision that we don't typically bother to validate it. But other models, such as queuing theory, should be validated to establish their precision.

The process of validation does not need to be complicated. In fact, the simpler the process of validation, the better. The more complex the validation process, the easier it becomes to have mistakes or an invalid step find its way into the validation process.

Always be ready to confidently state how your model was validated as well as the resulting precision. Count on being seriously questioned by "the experts" about your validation technique and the results. Traditionally trained capacity planners love to beat up on people who are not prepared with a solid and confident answer. (It's probably because they got beat up when they were learning.) Aside from the challenges you will receive, validation is an important step in the forecasting process and should be taken very seriously.

Some models will be more precise at lower utilizations; others will be more precise at higher utilizations. So it's a good idea to validate the model not only for the complete workload or utilization range, but also for important subsets. For example, most Oracle-related CPU and IO forecasts tend to focus on the elbow of the curve area. This occurs around the 80% utilization area. So an area to specifically validate could be between 75% to 90%.

Whenever I validate a model, I use data that the model has not seen before. For example, if 500 samples were collected, I may randomly choose 400 samples to develop and calibrate my model. I use the remaining 100 samples to validate the model. Because the model has never seen these 100 samples, it can't be influenced by them to make the validation look better than it actually is. If the forecast model was not calibrated using the 100 samples, yet shows high precision in forecasting those 100 samples, then my validation is much more solid. It's always a good idea to randomly select two sets of data: one set for developing and calibrating the model and a second set to validate the model.

When validating a model, I use a simple five-step process:

1. Look for numerical error.

2. Analyze statistical error.

3. Perform a histogram analysis.

4. Perform a residual analysis.

5. Make a go/no-go decision.

Once your model goes through these five steps, you can be confident of the model's precision and know you have satisfied the validation requirement.

If you are not familiar with these steps, they can be daunting at first. The following sections explain each step in more detail.

Look for Numerical Error

Perform a visual check to look for numerical error. The key word here is *look*. As humans, we are incredible pattern matchers. When doing a visual check, look for a break in the pattern. For example, are there negative numbers where there should be only positive numbers? Or when utilization increases, does the workload increase? Look for obvious data errors. If you find an error, then a decision must be made to either remove the data point (which will be discussed in detail in Chapter 9) or to keep the data point.

Table 6-1 shows a snapshot of data taken from a real production Oracle system. To conserve space, only a small portion of the data is shown.

Table 6-1. *Some Data from an Oracle System*

Sample	Actual CPU Util%	Predicted CPU Util%	Predicted Error	Abs (Predicted Error)
1	47.9	35.6	−12.3	12.3
2	47.9	36.1	−11.8	11.8
3	43.2	39.4	−3.8	3.8
4	47.4	35.5	−11.9	11.9
5	47.4	36.0	−11.4	11.4
. . .	. . .	. . .	. . .	. . .
76	39.0	31.6	−7.4	7.4
77	45.1	31.4	−13.7	13.7
		Average	0.9	7.5
		Standard deviation	9.0	
		Skew	0.21	
		Data points	77	

Visually inspect the data in Table 6-1 looking for anything strange or unexpected. Besides all the forecasts being significantly less than the actual utilization, there is nothing outstanding.

Analyze Statistical Error

Analyzing the statistical error enables responsible forecast model confidence. Table 6-1 shows a few of the key statistics needed to gain a basic understanding of the forecast data. If the visual analysis checked out, but the statistical error is poor, the model will need to be recalibrated and then revalidated. If after repeated validation attempts, the model cannot demonstrate the desired precision, you may need to abandon the model.

Table 6-1 shows the average prediction error to be 0.9. This means that, on average, the forecast model overstated the CPU utilization by 0.9%. One way to recalibrate the model would be to subtract 0.9 from all forecasts. This would then reduce the average error to zero! But as you'll see, the average error is just one statistical measure of forecast model usefulness.

Another useful statistic is the average absolute value of the error. As Table 6-1 shows, the absolute value error average is 7.5. This is a much better perspective of the average error. I find this number especially helpful because, for example, an error of −100 and +100 doesn't equal zero! In a way, the average error can disguise the model's error. I try to remind myself that my objective is not to find the most favorable statistics or to have the statistics look good. I'm trying to understand the precision and usefulness of the model. This helps me to maintain a more honest view of the statistics.

The standard deviation shown in Table 6-1 is 9.0, and the standard error is 1.0. If you recall from Chapter 4, this means that 68% of our samples will be between plus and minus one standard deviation. Since the standard deviation is 9.0, we can expect 68% of our sample to be within plus and minus 9.0% utilization of the forecasted utilization.

When forecasting and not referring to our sample, the standard error should be used. For example, if our forecast predicted the CPU utilization to be 65%, then 68% of the time (one standard error), the utilization should be between plus and minus 1.0%, or from 64% to 66%. We can also state that 95% of the time (two standard errors), if the forecasted CPU utilization were 65%, we would expect the actual utilization to be between 63% and 67%. That's good precision.

This statistical analysis assumes our sample data is normally distributed. If it's not, then our analysis is not valid. So the next step is to perform a histogram analysis.

Perform a Histogram Analysis

Chapter 4 drilled into histogram analysis, so if you need a refresher, please refer to that chapter. Here, we'll just take a quick look at the histogram for the sample data in Table 6-1, shown in Figure 6-1.

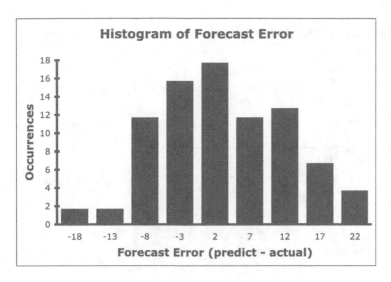

Figure 6-1. *Histogram of forecast CPU utilization error*

While the data is not perfectly normally distributed, it is close. The statistics skew (shown in Table 6-1) is 0.21, which is very good. So while our statistical ranges will not be perfect, they are close.

Perform a Residual Analysis

Residual is error. The analysis of forecast error can highlight areas of good forecasts and areas of bad forecasts. Most forecast models are engineered to minimize the average error. This means that some areas (perhaps lower utilization) will result in very good precision, while other areas (perhaps higher utilization) will result in poor precision. The average error will not highlight these areas of good and bad precision. The statistic skew and our histogram analysis will help, but a residual analysis makes it very easy to understand and to communicate to others the forecast model's precision.

Take a close look at the residual analysis shown in Figure 6-2. A perfect residual graph looks like a long horizontal cylinder with the x-axis going through its middle. Anything other than this requires a close inspection. Since residual analysis is discussed in detail in Chapter 9, I'll just make a few quick points here. First, there are equal blobs of points above and below the zero line, which means the forecasts are just as likely to be high as they are to be low. Second, there is no obvious trend in the data, which means regardless of the utilization (the x-axis), the forecast precision is the same. The only bad news is there is not a wide range of validation data. It would have been better if we had data between 10% and 25% utilization and also data above 50% utilization. Sometimes this is not possible because the system never operates in this area. All in all, this is an acceptable residual analysis.

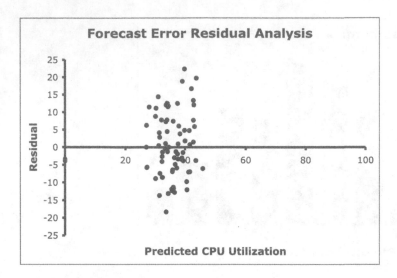

Figure 6-2. *Residual graph of a CPU utilization forecast*

Make a Go/No-Go Decision

After the validation analysis is complete, a decision must be made to use the model, recalibrate the model, or discard the model. Here's a quick summary of each option.

Use the model. If the validation checks out OK and you are satisfied with the precision, then start forecasting! Sometimes when the validation is OK, you may still want to recalibrate to further increase the precision.

Recalibrate the model. If you are not satisfied with the model's precision and there is a chance the precision can be increased, then recalibrating the model can be a good choice. While model recalibration can be a very complicated and intricate process, for many models, it is extremely simple. For example, as I noted earlier, for the data in Table 6-1, the average error is 0.9, and a simple calibration would be to always reduce the raw forecast by 0.9. Then revalidate and make another go/no-go decision. This process can be repeated with the precision continuing to improve. But there is a point of diminishing returns, where the model combined with the workload characterization just won't produce greater precision.

Discard the model. Sometimes the forecast precision is simply not good enough, and the model will have to be discarded. Don't assume the model is at fault. Low precision can also occur because the workload is extremely complicated, and practically any model will not be able to represent (that is, model) the system well. A poor workload characterization could have occurred, or perhaps the workload characterization outputs do not naturally feed into the forecast model. And finally, the precision expectations may simply be above what the model could possible achieve. So don't immediately throw out the modeling technique. Try to determine why the precision is not satisfactory.

Forecast

When learning about forecasting, most people are shocked at all the preparatory work that must occur before actually forecasting. When presentations are made and the focus is on mitigating risk and meeting service levels, all the hard work that went into the forecasts is somehow forgotten. This is especially true when a product is being used. As you now know, the act of forecasting is simply the icing on the cake!

When forecasting occurs, keep your focus on the study question. It is common for more than 100 forecasts to performed, so stay focused and be very organized. Develop some kind of filing system and file-naming convention. Otherwise, you'll spend too much time reorganizing and redoing the forecasts. I typically organize forecasts by scenario. My presentations are usually centered around a scenario, so creating the presentations and answering questions seem to go more smoothly. You can use any system you prefer. Just remember to be focused and organized.

Summary

After spending many years in IT and specifically forecasting Oracle performance, I still don't have any great love for following a method. It just goes against my personality. But like most people, I have recognized that to produce consistent results, a method is required. There is just no way around it. But more than that, others need to understand that what you are doing is a well-planned and well-thought-out process. When your analysis impacts the company's bottom line, it should be taken very seriously.

A considerable part of forecasting is communication and confidence building. Using a very simple yet well-thought-out method will allow your forecasting to go smoothly and also help you to effectively communicate your findings. When you can effectively communicate both the process and the results, confidence is increased. Since potentially millions and millions of dollars are affected by your forecasting work, confidence in what you are doing, how you are doing it, and your results is paramount. Randomness breeds luck, but method breeds confidence. No company wants to risk millions on luck.

CHAPTER 7

■ ■ ■

Characterizing the Workload

Regardless of how amazing a forecast model may be, without quality workload data and an appropriate characterization of the workload, it's totally worthless. That's a pretty strong statement, but it's the truth. Both projects and products fail when the workload is not properly characterized. When raw workload data is transformed into useful information, a model's precision capabilities flourish and the usability of the forecasting system is amazing. A solid and appropriate characterization of the workload is probably the most critical aspect of forecasting.

What brings seasoned capacity planners to their knees? The answer is forecasting Oracle performance. The reason is not because of the mathematics or the queuing theory. It's because an Oracle workload can be harshly complicated, and to a non-Oracle person, where to get the required data is a mystery. We must understand and master complexities like these if we are to understand an Oracle workload.

While characterizing a workload is fundamental, it's also the most difficult part of forecasting Oracle performance. You must be concerned with gathering potentially very intimate Oracle and operating system data without impacting the system. You need to understand where to get the required data, how often to gather data, and how to group the vast amount of data so it is useful. Finally, you need to know how to split the workload apart, modify it based on a forecast scenario, and put it back together appropriately. If it sounds complicated, well, it can be. But the rewards are a very useful and precise forecast.

The Challenge

I'll never forget the day when I was considering switching groups within a large software company. I was on a conference call learning about the specifications and objectives for a new capacity planning product. I was very excited to be part of a team where, finally, a solid Oracle forecasting product would be developed. Knowing that characterizing an Oracle workload is both particularly difficult yet vitally important, during the conference call, I asked the lead product architect how the workload was going to be characterized. There was an uncomfortable silence, and then he said, "What do you mean by characterize the workload?" Needless to say, I did not join the group, and the product never did reach the market. Without an appropriate characterization of the workload, forecasting is futile and, at worst, unethical.

Characterizing an Oracle workload is very unique and extremely difficult. Most capacity planning books speak of gathering data such as the number of disk operations, the number of transactions, and the CPU time associated with a transaction. Many forecasting products gather workload data by using operating system accounting and process-level information. We can do better than this—much better.

Traditional capacity planning workload gathering and characterization techniques immediately cause problems when forecasting Oracle performance. For example, how do you relate a computing transaction to an Oracle transaction, to a user transaction, and to a business transaction? How do you determine just how many IO operations occur when there is IO caching in Oracle's system global area, the operating system's file system buffer cache, and the IO subsystem's cache? And what about Oracle's ability to write many changes in a single IO operation? How about when the IO subsystem says a write has been physically written to disk, but for optimization reasons, this is not true? Appropriately dealing with these questions are the challenges that make forecasting Oracle performance extremely difficult and make seasoned capacity planners wish for the simpler days of well-defined and controlled transactions.

Presented in this chapter are techniques to properly characterize a complex Oracle workload. Multiple techniques are required due to different study questions, different forecast models, varying precision expectations, and varying forecasting needs. But remember that the objective of workload characterization is to transform raw workload data into a form that is useful for model input and so we, as humans, can forecast.

Gathering the Workload

Before any characterization of the workload can occur, data must be gathered. This is not as simple as it may initially appear. When determining how to gather the workload, we must know the intended forecast model(s), how the workload is going to be characterized, and finally, how to gather the information without significantly impacting the system. Balancing these sometimes conflicting requirements can be very difficult.

If you are using a capacity planning product or perhaps only a data collector, your data collection choices may have already been made for you. However, if you are building your own data collection application (that's what it will eventually become), you need to design the system with flexibility and optimization in mind.

How workload is gathered and characterized will also determine the precision possibilities and the usability of a forecast system. For example, if only the number of users and their general business function are gathered and consolidated (that is, characterized), then we cannot expect to produce a high-precision forecast. And if we gathered a mountain of workload data and then grouped by (that is, characterized) transaction service time, we may not be able answer the study question. So both the gathering of workload data and its characterization can limit or enhance the forecast model's precision capabilities and our ability to effectively answer the underlying study question.

Gather only the information you need, and gather it as efficiently and infrequently as possible. It is easy to get carried away and start gathering mountains of workload data. That's good, but it's also bad. Every time a system is probed, the system is impacted. Honestly, just this week, a student of mine said his company had purchased a very expensive SLM product and it takes over 4 minutes to complete the workload gathering cycle![1] This is what can happen when too much information is being gathered, in combination with a poorly optimized approach.

In conjunction with what data to gather, determine how often to gather. If data is gathered only once every few hours, then a significant hit on the system may be acceptable. But surely, taking 60 seconds to gather data at a frequency of once every 5 minutes will be inappropriate.

It is important for IT management and the technical leadership to understand that gathering performance data is a necessary requirement to meet IT's mandate of servicing the business. Without monitoring, collecting, and processing workload data, service levels cannot be managed. No one would purchase a car without the appropriate instrumentation. Why would organizations supported by IT expect to pay millions on hardware without instrumentation? The trick is to find a balance between gathering what you need while minimizing the impact on the system.[2]

Gathering Operating System Data

When I first started forecasting, I tried the classic data gathering techniques: process accounting, process lists, and so on. All of these methods were very operating system-specific, without a direct tie or hook into Oracle. In most cases, I could not find the granularity I needed or the granularity was not meaningful.

When operating system-wide data is required, consider the widely available standard command-line-based tools such as sar, vmstat, and iostat. Whatever tool or script you choose, ensure all of your data sources start and end at the same time. This implies the sample duration will also be the same. A timing mismatch will invalidate the data. If the mismatch is not detected, the forecasts will be misleading, and you probably won't even know it. Using a process scheduler, such as the cron facility, can help reduce the risk of a timing mismatch. A distinct benefit of using a scheduler outside Oracle's control is in the unlikely event that the Oracle system becomes unavailable, the data collection processes will continue operating.

---

1. Let me put this into perspective. Data gathering is usually CPU-intensive (which is generally faster then getting IO involved) because the statistics gathered are usually cached. Suppose data is collected once every 30 minutes, the database server contains 10 CPUs, it takes 4 minutes to gather the data, and the collection process consumes only CPU resources. The collection process would then consume 1.3% of the available CPU resources (4 minutes / (10 CPUs × 15 minutes) = 1.3%). If data were collected every 15 minutes, then the collection process would consume 2.6% of the available CPU. It's difficult to successfully build a case about improving SLM (which includes financial management) when the product itself consumes significant amounts of CPU power. What if the database server had only two CPUs and data were collected every 30 minutes? The CPU usage would be 6.7%.

2. This is also known as the *observer effect* or *observer bias*, described at http://en.wikipedia.org/wiki/Observer_effect.

The following cron entry will run a script named gather_driver.sh every 15 minutes at an interval of 15 minutes. Many collection scripts require the duration as an input variable. Obviously, it is important that the numbers match!

```
0,15,30,45 * * * * /bin/sh /home/oracle/local/book/gather_driver.sh 900  \
>> /tmp/gather_driver.out
```

The following gather_driver.sh data collection script (available at www.orapub.com/tools) is written for Linux, but it can be modified easily for other platforms. If you look closely, you'll discover it not only collects CPU and IO activity, but also a few general Oracle workload statistics. The script creates output files for each collection area: CPU, IO, and Oracle data. Each file is in comma-delimited format, so it can be easily loaded into Oracle or a spreadsheet program for processing and analysis.

```
#!/bin/sh
#
# File: gather_driver.sh
# Desc: Sample workload gathering script for an Oracle Linux system
# Usage: ./gather_driver.sh snapshot_duration
#        Make sure to set the "Must set" variables below!
#
# Output is placed in a comma delimited file by default as follows:
#
#     /tmp/wl_cpu.dat seq, user %, system %, idle %
#     /tmp/wl_io.dat  seq, device, response time, utilization
#     /tmp/wl_app.dat seq, statistic name, value

duration=$1                           # —— Supply on command line

ORACLE_SID="prod3"                    # —— Must set
ORACLE_HOME="/home/oracle/product/10.1"  # —— Must set
LD_LIBRARY_PATH="$ORACLE_HOME/lib"
PATH=$PATH:$ORACLE_HOME/bin

export ORACLE_SID ORACLE_HOME LD_LIBRARY_PATH PATH

ora_access=osmmon/osmmon              # —— Must set
io_device_list="sda sdb sdc"          # —— Must set

seq=`date +%s`

work_file=/tmp/work.dat
sar_file=/tmp/sar_$seq
iostat_file=/tmp/iostat_$seq
cpu_file=/tmp/wl_cpu.dat
io_file=/tmp/wl_io.dat
app_file=/tmp/wl_app.dat
```

```
# Gather initial Oracle workload values
#
sqlplus $ora_access <<EOF
drop table wl_stats;
col value format 9999999999999
set linesize 500
create table wl_stats as
select *
from v\$sysstat
where name in ('redo size','logons cumulative','execute count',
'db block changes');
exit;
EOF


# Start CPU gathering
#
sar -u -o $sar_file $duration 1 &

# Start IO gathering
#
iostat -xdk $duration 2 > $iostat_file &

# Wait for CPU and IO gathering to complete
wait

# print CPU: seq, user, system, idle
#
line=`sar -u -f $sar_file | tail -1`
echo "$seq $line" | awk '{print $1 "," $4+$5 "," $6 "," $7+$8}' >> $cpu_file

# print IO device: seq, device, response time, utilization
#
for dev in $io_device_list
do
  dev_line=`grep "$dev " $iostat_file | tail -1`
  echo "$seq $dev_line" | awk '{print $1 "," $2 "," $14 "," $15}' >> $io_file
done

# Gather final Oracle workload values and calculate delta activity
#
sqlplus $ora_access <<EOF
set heading off feedback off echo off
set linesize 500
col value format 9999999999999
col name  format a20
col the_line format a50
col statistic# format 999
```

```
col xxx format a5
spool $work_file
select '$seq'||','||b.name||',' the_line,
       b.value-a.value value,
       ',good' xxx
from (
     select name,statistic#,value
     from v\$sysstat
     where name in ('redo size','logons cumulative',
           'execute count','db block changes')
     ) b,
     (
     select name,statistic#,value
     from wl_stats
     where name in ('redo size','logons cumulative',
           'execute count','db block changes')
     ) a
where b.statistic# = a.statistic#;
spool off
exit;
EOF

# Print general Oracle workload statistics
#
grep good $work_file | grep -v xxx | awk -F, '{print $1 "," $2 "," $3}' >> $app_file

# Remove work files
#
rm $sar_file
rm $iostat_file
rm $work_file
```

This is about as simple as a data collection script can get. As you can see, even the simplest of workload gathering processes can quickly become complicated.

The gather_driver.sh script gathers only general Oracle workload, not detailed session-level information, for a good reason. When the workload granularity or detail increases to the session level, extreme care must be taken to reduce the probing impact to both the database system and the operating system. Unless you must gather session-level details, don't. You can do a tremendous amount of very useful forecasting while gathering at the system level (for example, using the v$sysstat view data, as described in the next section).

Gathering Oracle Data

Along with the operating system data, you also need to gather software application workload data. You can approach this task in multiple ways. Sometimes, the focus is on the overall workload; other times, the focus is on groups of Oracle activity; and still other times, detailed session-level information is required. Again, if you keep the workload granularity to a minimum, your collection tools will be significantly less complex, more reliable, and have a smaller impact on the system.

Because the Oracle database is well instrumented, you have a virtually endless number of workload-related statistics from which to gather. If you are not familiar with Oracle internals, particularly Oracle's process architecture and virtual performance views, this can be confusing and just plain overwhelming. If you are not familiar with Oracle yet must forecast Oracle performance, I highly recommend you take the time to learn. Oracle is a massive product with a seemingly infinite number of add-ons and extensions. To help minimize your study time, initially focus on the areas of data, memory, and process architecture. The Oracle documentation has plenty of information, and many books are available. You don't need to become an Oracle database administrator or performance specialist, but it does help.

When you start learning about Oracle internals, you'll quickly come across the v$ views, which are the virtual performance views. Table 7-1 lists the key views you will need to know about for workload characterization.

Table 7-1. *Key Oracle Performance Views That Can Be Used When Gathering Workload Data*

View	Description
v$session	Every connected session has a row in this view. It contains detailed information about the session, which can be used to categorize Oracle activity at the session level.
v$sysstat	This view contains system-wide statistics that can be used for performance analysis as well as defining the general Oracle workload, the CPU consumption, and IO activity.
v$sesstat	This view provides many statistics to help categorize a workload, including CPU and IO. These are the same statistics as v$sysstat, but at the Oracle session level.
v$parameter	This view contains the Oracle instance parameters.
v$sess_io	This view contains session-level IO details.
v$mystat	This view also contains session-level statistics.

Let's take a closer look at how each of these views might be useful for gathering Oracle data.

v$session View

The v$session view is useful for gathering data at the session level. For example, you can use the module, action, Oracle username, process, machine, terminal, and program information to create a wide variety of granular workload categories.

v$sysstat View

This v$sysstat view is useful for gathering data at the system level. Common general workload statistics are redo size, logical reads, db block changes, physical reads, physical writes, parse count (total), parse count (hard), sorts (rows|memory|rows), logons cumulative, logons current, execute count, user calls, user commits, and user rollbacks. Any combination of these workload-related statistics may provide for a strong representation of an Oracle workload.

In addition to the workload, CPU and IO information can also be gleaned from this view. The most common CPU consumption statistic is "CPU used by this session." It provides Oracle process CPU user time in centiseconds. Don't be fooled by the word *session*. This statistic contains system-level CPU consumption information.

IO information can be gleaned from a combination of statistics, such as consistent gets, physical gets, db block changes and redo writes.

v$sesstat View

Just like the v$sysstat view, the v$sesstat view provides many statistics to help categorize a workload, including CPU and IO. While the view contains the same statistics as v$sysstat, it provides details at the Oracle session level. This means it can be joined to v$session so the workload, CPU, and IO activity can be related to a specific Oracle session. This allows for a very granular characterization of the workload.

Great care must be taken when gathering from v$sesstat. On large Oracle systems, it could take minutes to gather, process, and store session-level detailed information.

Unlike v$sysstat, v$sesstat does not contain a column with the statistic name (don't ask me why). To get the statistic name, the view must be joined with the v$statname view.

v$parameter View

The v$parameter view contains the Oracle instance parameters. An Oracle *instance* is formally defined as Oracle memory and processes, which do not include the database files. An Oracle database is simply a collection of files. An available Oracle database system contains one or more Oracle instances working in conjunction with a single Oracle database.

For forecasting, the parameters cpu_count and db_block_size can be useful. Be aware that Oracle counts each CPU core as a CPU.

v$sess_io View

The v$sess_io view is a session-level view, which means it can be joined via the sid column with v$sesstat. It contains session-level IO details such as block_gets, consistent_gets, physical_reads, block_changes, and consistent_changes. Some of the statistics are also available from v$sesstat, but for performance reasons, it sometimes can be faster to gather from v$sess_io.

v$mystat View

Just as with v$sesstat, the v$mystat view contains session-level statistics. The difference is you do not need to know the user's SID when querying. Depending on your data-gathering process, this may be useful.

Which View Should You Use?

The question now becomes which view to use. There is no single answer. If you are going to gather at the session level, then v$session will mostly likely be involved. As I have stated many times, if you have a large Oracle system, you can easily impact your system if your collection program is inefficient or run too frequently.

When gathering system-level or simple session counts, v$sysstat will probably meet your needs. And combined with CPU and IO data from the operating system, you will probably have all the data you need. A good way to start would be to modify the gather_driver.sh script shown earlier. Start simple and small with a very well-defined scope. Taking on a company's critical forecasting project without some experience could be one of those "career decisions" I've mentioned before.

Defining Workload Components

Once the raw workload data has been collected, it must be intelligently and meaningfully grouped. The process of meaningfully grouping the raw data is called *workload characterization*. It is one of those capacity planning words that is thrown around all the time. While the definition is simple, the process of defining the workload groups—the categories—can take quite a bit of effort.

The grouping strategy chosen will certainly reflect the study question, the type of forecasting scenarios to be performed, and the desired forecast precision. But the grouping will also reflect the selected forecast model.

Models have distinct input requirements. If the workload is not grouped in a way the model can accept, then, obviously, the model cannot be used. Forcing the data to fit by performing questionable mathematics will certainly reduce the forecast precision. This is one reason for talking about which model to use during study question discussions. If the model selection discussion is postponed until after the data collection process has been determined, it's very possible the required workload data will not have been collected. From the inception of the project, it's important for everyone involved to get together and discuss data collection, precision, and forecast model selection.

As a general rule, keep the workload groupings as simple as possible. We all want to have a full and complete understanding of a system's characteristics. But giving in to this desire can result in a very cumbersome grouping that can reduce forecast precision and make the forecasting activity more complicated and difficult. Using only one general workload category, when done exceptionally well and with an exceptional forecast model, can result in amazing precision.

Once the workload components have been determined, they are combined to develop a model or representation of the workload, as discussed in the next section.

Modeling the Workload

A workload model is an abstraction or representation of workload activity. Just as there are many ways to model an airplane, there are many ways to model a workload. In fact, as you will see, there are many ways to model the same workload. Deciding how to best model a workload depends on the study question, the available workload, the chosen model(s), and the desired precision.

While there are many ways to model a workload, I have found it useful to classify the most widely used Oracle workload models into three groups.

- The *simple* workload model is more application-centric (think number of OLTP users and concurrent batch processes) and used for quick, low-precision forecasts.

- The *single-category* workload model is used when a general workload-centric statistic (think v$sysstat) is used to represent the entire workload.

- The *multiple-category* workload model provides increased precision capabilities and usability flexibility, but gathering the workload can be intrusive.

Each workload model is valuable and effective when used appropriately. Don't be dissuaded by the simplicity of the simple and single-category workload models and jump to the multiple-category workload model. As you'll see, the increased flexibility comes at a price.

The next sections detail each of these three broad workload model types. I have also added some examples to demonstrate how you can use each model in practice.

Simple Workload Model

As the name implies, a simple workload model is extremely simple to create. But don't let the simplicity deter you. Simple workload models are used every day by every IT professional; they just don't know it.

A simple workload model will probably contain multiple workload categories. However, the categories are simple in comparison with the more complex workload models.

For example, suppose you ask someone to talk about his company's Oracle system. While he drones on and on about the system, the moment he says something like, "There are around 500 active users," something happens. Perhaps not even consciously, you immediately begin performing an amazing sizing exercise! While trying to listen to your colleague as he continues to talk, you are figuring out—based on what you know about his application, your experience with similar applications, and your experience with the hardware platform—just how many CPUs his system contains. Why do you do this? Because you want to get an understanding of his system and its complexity. When you perform these mental gymnastics, you are actually creating a simple workload model and applying it to a forecast model. Chapter 8 presents a forecast model that more formally does what you did while listening to your colleague.

As you would expect, collecting and grouping workload data as just described can be very straightforward. Table 7-2 shows some samples I collected from a real production Oracle system. The application workload was characterized into two groups: active OLTP sessions and concurrent batch processes. When combined with the CPU utilization, the result is a simple workload model.

Table 7-2. *Simple Workload Model*

Sample	CPU Util %	Active OLTP Sessions	Concurrent Batch Processes
1	47.9	148	5
2	47.9	154	5
3	43.2	158	7
4	47.4	163	4
5	52.7	169	4
6	52.7	172	7
7	48.2	178	7
8	35.1	180	8
...			
94	39.0	103	4
95	39.0	103	5
96	45.1	101	5

Keep in mind that we are going through a process to ultimately answer the study question. And it's the study question that helps us determine how to best categorize the workload. The simple workload model data shown in Table 7-2 is useful, for example, if the study question is related to changing the number of concurrent users. Perhaps the company is considering acquiring another company, the number of employees is expected to increase, or it is opening a new office.

For Oracle systems, it is very common to categorize the workload with only OLTP sessions and concurrent batch jobs. While that may be surprising at first, especially if you are seasoned capacity planner, it's a very natural way for businesses to think about their Oracle systems. Plus, the forecasting precision is usually acceptable.

Using simple workload models is also common when forecasting using regression analysis. With regression analysis, the objective is to find a strong relationship between, for example, CPU utilization and some business activity. The business activity could be the number of orders entered per hour or the number of orders shipped per hour. In these cases, the categorization of the workload is not the challenge. The challenge is finding the strong relationships and making sure those relationships relate to the study question. This will be presented in more detail in Chapter 9.

The workload categorization shown in Table 7-2 is probably not going to work well with queuing theory. While it can be done and may meet the requirements, you'll typically find the desired precision just isn't good enough. You'll probably need a more advanced workload model, or better said, a multiple-category workload model.

Collecting workload category details such as OLTP users and concurrent batch jobs is relatively simple, so I won't bother to provide a script. In fact, this information is probably already available to you. Most operating system administrators keep detailed CPU utilization history. And most Oracle database administrators store connected session count history. Most applications record when a batch process started and ended, so determining how many are concurrently running is a simple matter.

Be aware that the number of Oracle logons is not the same as the number of *active* Oracle sessions. The number of Oracle sessions can be determined by the simple query: `select count(*) from v$session`. To determine if the session is active, you will need to determine if the session has recently used any CPU time. One way to do this is to check if there has been an increase in the "CPU used by this session" statistic value from the `v$sesstat` view (see Table 7-7, later in this chapter).

If you are looking for more precision than the simple workload model can offer, a single- or multiple-category workload model may be just what you need. While the simple workload model is appropriate in many Oracle situations, there are times when a better understanding of the workload is required to meet both the precision and usability requirements.

Single-Category Workload Model

An Oracle single-category workload model usually focuses on a general workload representation, such as number of commits per hour. In contrast, the multiple-category workload model usually focuses on grouping Oracle activity by, for example, Oracle username, location, terminal, program, or module. This creates some interesting challenges, as discussed in the next section.

With the single-category workload model, the general workload representation will serve as the model's arrival rate and is likely to come from Oracle's `v$sysstat` view. Usually, the workload source will consist of only a single column, but sometimes multiple columns work well. The `gather_driver.sh` shell script presented earlier in this chapter is an example of how the general Oracle workload can be gathered to create a single-category workload model.

Examples 7-1 and 7-2 demonstrate how a single-category workload model can be used appropriately to forecast CPU and IO utilization. Because single-category workload models have wide precision characteristics (that is, sometimes very high and sometimes very low), determining and validating the forecast precision are important.

As both examples demonstrate, it's relatively simple to gather the workload data for a single-category workload model. However, the process of finding meaningful workload statistics that produce satisfactory precision can be challenging. When the workload model is relatively simple, it's common for people to shortcut a proper validation, including a solid statistical analysis. This is unfortunate, because the simpler the workload model, the more likely the forecast precision will be unacceptably low. But I don't want to discourage you from using single-category workload models. They are used all the time and can produce stellar precision.

Example 7-1. Using a Single-Category Workload Model to Forecast CPU Utilization

Mike is the database administrator for a 24 CPU Solaris server, which services up to around 650 active users. IT management expects the number of transactions entering the Oracle system to double in about six months. Mike must determine the risk of not meeting service levels.

For this example, we will focus on only the CPU subsystem, the creation of the workload model, and model precision validation.

Mike gathered 12 workload samples, one every hour during peak quarter-end processing. To answer the study question, Mike must be able to alter both the workload and the CPU hardware configuration. He chose to create a single-category workload model that relates the general Oracle workload to CPU utilization, which will provide inputs into the queuing theory model.

The gather_driver.sh script was used to gather data that was used to derive the service time enabling the response time calculation, as shown in Table 7-3. The essential queuing theory math was used, rather than Erlang C. Keep in mind that M is the number of servers, not the number of servers per queue. (We model a CPU subsystem with a single queue, so the number of servers in the system is the same as the number of servers per queue; for more details, see Chapter 3.) The following is the formula for both CPU and IO utilization:

$$S_t = \frac{UM}{\lambda}$$

Table 7-3. *CPU-Related Results from the gather_driver.sh Script*

Sample	CPU Util % (*U*)	Execute Count/ms (λ)	Derived Service Time (ms)/Execute (*S$_t$*)
1	28.67	3.10	2.23
2	25.08	2.93	2.05
3	44.40	2.71	3.93
4	26.44	2.62	2.42
5	31.97	2.51	3.06
6	32.99	2.36	3.36

Mike determined the average service time to be 2.84, but when weighted by the arrival rate, it is 2.80. Mike now has all the input variables necessary to forecast.

But how well will the number of executions relate to both the CPU utilization and to the business? We can validate the forecasted CPU utilization precision, but how this relates to the business is not well defined. What exactly is "the business"? Is it response time? If so, how can that be measured? Asking these types of questions during the study question phase will remove the ambiguity, allowing the forecast model to be validated directly against what is meant by "the business."

Mike now needs to validate the CPU utilization forecast precision based on the execute count per millisecond. Table 7-4 shows the actual and derived CPU utilization (U) based on the actual execute count (λ), the number of servers ($M = 24$), and the weighted average service time (S_t) of 2.80 ms/trx.

Table 7-4. *Validating the CPU Forecast Model*

Sample	Actual Execute Count/ms (λ)	Actual CPU Util (U)	Pred. CPU Util (U)	CPU Pred. Error	Absolute Value CPU Pred. Error
7	2.18	29.29	25.80%	−3.49	3.49
8	2.13	36.77	25.20%	−11.57	11.57
9	2.08	24.34	24.61%	0.27	0.27
10	1.98	21.34	23.43%	2.09	2.09
11	1.97	26.96	23.31%	−3.65	3.65
12	1.93	19.33	22.84%	3.51	3.51

Based on the numbers, the validation utilization forecasts were, on average, 2.14 below the actual collected values. This means the forecast model is overly optimistic; that is, it predicts the utilization will be lower than it probably will actually be. In addition, the average absolute value error is 4.10, which means the error is typically 4.1%.

However, Mike made some serious mistakes:

- I already mentioned the first mistake, which is that Mike really has no idea if the number of executions relate to "the business." That problem should have been identified while the study question was being discussed.

- Mike used only 12 samples. Using the statistical methods presented in Chapter 4, he needs at least 30 samples. Perhaps he could increase the data-gathering frequency to once every 15 minutes. If he did that, then over a 12-hour period, 48 samples would be available. Regardless of the number of samples used to derive the weighted average service time, using standard statistical analysis, we need at least 30 validation samples.

- To see the third problem, look closely at the CPU utilization figures in Table 7-3 and compare them with the CPU utilization in Table 7-4. The samples used to derive the weighted average service time were taken when the system was busier than it was when the samples used to validate the forecast were taken. It appears the samples may have been simply split based on the time they were gathered. A better strategy would have been to randomly select some samples for service time derivation and others for validation.

So Mike made some common yet significant mistakes, and as a result, his forecasts should not be used.

Assuming Mike's mistakes were not critical, which they are, an average percent utilization error of –2.14 and the average absolute value error of 4.1% are pretty good. The standard deviation is 5.45, and the standard error is 2.23. This means 95% of the samples fall within plus or minus 10.90% of the forecasted utilization, and 95% of his forecasts will fall within plus or minus 4.46% of the forecasted utilization. For this type of analysis, that's not too bad. Should Mike try some other general workload statistics like user calls or user commits? Definitely!

Example 7-2. Using a Single-Category Workload Model to Forecast IO Utilization

Beth is a senior DBA responsible for performance management of a 24 CPU HP server, which peaks at around 800 users. Her manager, who is also the IT director, expects the number of transactions entering the Oracle system to double in about six months. Beth must determine the risk of not meeting service levels.

For this example, we will focus only on the IO subsystem, the creation of the workload model, and the forecast model precision validation.

Beth gathered 15 workload samples during the peak processing times. Only IO devices that were busy more than 5% of the time were considered. Beth knows that when an IO device is not very active, the response times can vary greatly, and yet it doesn't really matter, since the device is not used that often. Usually, not all of the devices are active, but during peak processing times, all 46 IO devices were active.

When CPU data is gathered, the result is a single value, such as the average CPU utilization. When collecting IO data, the situation is very different. Each sample period results in a sample for each active IO device. For Beth, this means instead of 1 value per collection period, there are 46 values.

As customary, Beth calculated the average IO utilization using a simple average based on each individual IO device's utilization. For example, in Table 7-5, the first sample set's average IO utilization was 14%. With the average IO utilization determined, the number of active devices known (46), and the Oracle workload known (1.223 executes/ms), Beth derived the average IO device service time using the essential forecasting formula:

$$S_t = \frac{UM}{\lambda}$$

Because the essential queuing theory math was used, not Erlang C, M is the number of servers, not the number of servers *per queue*. This is important to remember when modeling an IO subsystem, because we model an IO subsystem with one queue per server (for details, see Chapter 3).

Table 7-5. *Summarized IO-Related Results from the gather_driver.sh Script*

Sample	Avg IO Util % (U)	Execute Count/ms (ex/ms=λ)	Service Time (ms)/Execute (ms/ex=S_t)
1	14	1.223	5.266
2	14	0.728	8.846
3	14	0.712	9.045
4	14	1.225	5.257
5	30	0.640	21.563
6	37	0.809	21.038
7	32	0.609	24.171
8	34	0.783	19.974

To enable IO forecasting based on the Oracle execute count, Beth needed to determine the weighted average IO device service time. The average service time is 14.395 milliseconds per execution (ms/ex), and the weighted average service time is 12.920 ms/ex.

Beth now needs to validate the IO utilization forecast precision based on the execute count per millisecond. Table 7-6 shows the actual and predicted average IO utilization (U) based on the actual execute count (λ), the number of servers ($M = 46$), and the weighted average service time (S_t) of 12.920 ms/ex.

Table 7-6. *Validating the IO Forecast Model*

Sample	Actual IO Util % (U)	Actual Execute Count/ms (λ)	Pred. Average IO Util % (U)	IO Pred. Error	Absolute Value IO Pred. Error
9	29	0.612	8.15%	−11.81	11.81
10	23	0.631	6.46%	−5.3	5.3
11	9	0.672	2.53%	9.87	9.87
12	32	0.541	8.99%	−16.83	16.83
13	8	0.602	2.25%	8.9	8.9
14	23	0.361	6.46%	12.86	12.86
15	24	0.358	6.74%	13.94	13.94

Based on the numbers, the forecasted average IO utilization is overly optimistic by 1.66%; that is, the model predicts the utilization will be higher than what actually occurred. In addition, the average absolute value error is 11.36, which means the error is typically around 11%.

Like Mike in Example 7-1, Beth made some mistakes. First, Beth also has no idea if the number of executions relate to "the business." Second, Beth used only 15 samples. For proper statistical analysis using the methods presented in Chapter 4, she needs 30 validation samples to derive the standard deviation. While both Mike and Beth made some serious errors, they both followed the correct process and did attempt a proper validation—something that most people sidestep.

Let's assume that Beth's mistakes were not critical, even though they actually invalidate her forecast model. An average percent utilization error of 1.66% is very good for IO subsystems. Typically, IO subsystem forecasts are not as precise as CPU forecasts. Vendor IO optimization algorithms, combined with IO-related caches, make precise IO forecasts more difficult. The standard deviation turned out to be 12.70, and the standard error was 4.80. This means 95% of the samples fall within plus or minus 25.4% of the forecasted utilization, and 95% of Beth's forecasts will fall within plus or minus 9.60% of the forecasted utilization. While the standard error may perhaps be OK for an IO forecast, the standard deviation is nothing to celebrate. Beth should definitely try some other general workload statistics like user calls, user commits, and user rollbacks. Trying a combination of the general workload statistics would also be a good idea.

Multiple-Category Workload Model

The motivation to create a multiple category workload model is usually the combination of increased usability and higher precision. Businesses are more likely to think in terms of a specific workload category like OLTP users, general ledger users, the Hong Kong office, Building 123 users, or the customer relationship management (CRM) system. While the forecast possibilities are amazing, the ability to create a seemingly infinite number of workload categories can come at a significant cost.

A WARNING

The increased overhead of collecting data to create multiple workload category models is extremely important to consider. Continually probing an Oracle system at the session level can be very intrusive. This is especially true when working with a large Oracle system. If the Oracle performance views were designed for frequent probing, then someone at Oracle messed up. To successfully gather meaningful Oracle session-level data, a potentially advanced and complicated strategy must be developed. It's not only the gathering of the data. Once the data is gathered, it must be processed and stored. This can also impact a system. If your system has only a couple hundred sessions, you may be fine. But if your system has hundreds or thousands of sessions, even the best workload gathering processes can make for a very intrusive workload gathering experience.

I don't want to overly promote anyone's products, including OraPub's. But continually gathering at the session level may require a professional data collection product. The risk occurs because not only is the data gathered, but it also must be processed efficiently, possibly transported, transformed, and stored efficiently. Considering the time and potential impact to your system, it may make more sense to purchase a product.

Another thing to consider is where your time is best spent. Your value to your company is greatest when you're performing risk analysis related to a serious study question. While developing workload gathering systems and advanced forecast models can be fun, your company may prefer your analysis prowess.

Collecting the Data

Whatever your session-level workload gathering tactic, you're sure to have data related to a session's identity (so it can be grouped, or categorized), the amount of work it is generating (that is, its contribution to the overall arrival rate), how much CPU time it is consuming, and how much IO it is consuming. Equipped with this information, along with general operating system information (such as the number and speed of CPU and IO devices), you are presented with a dizzying array of workload characterization and forecasting possibilities.

As an example, the following data shows an extremely small subset of raw session-level data. Note that the session sample includes both identification information and computing resource usage information.

SID	LOGOFF	User	MODULE	PROGRAM	MACHINE	WKLD	CPU_ms	IO_KB
127	12-Jan 14:05	AR	SQL*Plus	perl@sv1.comp.com	sv1.comp.com	46	4200	308000
128	12-Jan 14:05	AR	SQL*Plus	perl@sv2.comp.com	sv2.comp.com	83	4914	302500
129	12-Jan 14:06	AR	SQL*Plus	perl@sv2.comp.com	sv2.comp.com	84	1407	431200
133	12-Jan 14:12	MG	SQL*Plus	perl@sv1.comp.com	sv1.comp.com	1853	7070	0
134	12-Jan 14:14	MG	SQL*Plus	perl@sv1.comp.com	sv1.comp.com	1053	8050	242000
148	12-Jan 14:25	AR	SQL*Plus	perl@sv2.comp.com	sv2.comp.com	98	5054	412500
149	12-Jan 14:26	AR	SQL*Plus	perl@sv2.comp.com	sv2.comp.com	99	1547	618200
143	12-Jan 14:32	MG	SQL*Plus	perl@sv1.comp.com	sv1.comp.com	1763	7070	1100
144	12-Jan 14:34	MG	SQL*Plus	perl@sv1.comp.com	sv1.comp.com	1063	7938	210100
145	12-Jan 14:37	MG	undef	perl@sv1.comp.com	sv1.comp.com	1164	700	122100

Here is the script used to show the preceding session-level workload data:

```
select sid,
       to_char(logoff_time,'DD-Mon HH24:MI') logoff,
       username,
       module,
       program,
       machine,
       workload,
       cpu_ms,
       io_kb
from sess_detail
/
```

The sess_detail table is not a standard Oracle table or view. You must create it and populate it. You, or a DBA, can create the sess_detail table during data collection and use it to store the detailed session-level data. All the data stored in the sess_detail table was gathered from Oracle's v$session and v$sesstat views. The key view columns are described in Table 7-7.

Table 7-7. *Sample Oracle Session-Level Data Source Details*

View	Report Column	View Column	Description
v$session	SID	sid	This is the session ID. Each Oracle session is assigned a session ID. When a session disconnects, the session ID is then available for reuse. It is common for some applications to keep an open connection; that is, the session stays connected. If this is the case, special care in data gathering may be needed to incrementally capture computing resource consumption.
dual	LOGOFF	sysdate	The dual table is a special Oracle table. It contains only one row, with a single column named dummy. But there are many pseudo columns that can be selected from this table, like the sysdate column. For example, a query could be select sysdate from dual. Logon and logoff times can be determined by selecting and storing the sysdate.
v$session	User	username	This is the Oracle logon username. It is common for many applications to have only a few Oracle usernames, although there can be thousands of actual users. But then some applications have an Oracle user for every named user. The application architects make this decision.
v$session	MODULE	module	Application developers can instrument (that is, name) their SQL and PL/SQL code using the DBMS_APPLICATION_INFO package. For example, running dbms_application_info.set_module('PK1', 'Startup') switches the current module to PK1 with an action of Startup.
v$session	Not shown	Action	An application developer can also change the action without changing the module by calling dbms_application_info.set_module('big loop').
v$session	MACHINE	machine	This is the operating system name for the machine. It may show as the machine's domain name.
v$session	Not shown	terminal	This is the terminal name of the client machine. For example, in a client/server environment, the terminal name could be the name of a Windows PC.
v$sesstat	WLKD		Any workload-related column can be used, but not all will result in precise forecasts. The "v$sesstat View" section earlier in this chapter lists some common workload columns. This view will need to be joined to v$session via the sid column.
v$sesstat	CPU_ms	CPU used by this session	This column is the most common CPU consumption source. The default unit of time is centiseconds.

View	Report Column	View Column	Description
v$sesstat	IO_KB		There are a number of possible choices to gather session IO information. But unlike CPU time consumed, because of batch writes and multiple levels of system caching, it is not possible to get a perfect number. Even so, the precision capabilities are astonishing. The "v$sesstat View" section earlier in this chapter lists the common IO-related columns. This view will need to be joined to v$session via the sid column.

Combining Oracle and Operating System Data

With the raw data collected, transferred, and stored (for example, loaded into an Oracle database), it must be transformed to become useful. A successful raw data transformation combined with a solid mathematical model can result in a brilliant representation of the database server. If the model and workload establish a realistic link between the Oracle system and the operating system, the model becomes more useful because it responds more like the real system.

We have created this link between Oracle and the operating system many times in the previous chapters, and will continue to do so in subsequent chapters. Establishing the Oracle and operating system relationship is fairly straightforward when working at the system level (think v$sysstat). However, when working with a multiple-category workload model, the data will probably be collected at the session level, and establishing the link can be difficult.

One way to establish this link is for the mathematical equations to use both Oracle and operating system data. Once this relationship has been established, changing one aspect of the model's equation or coefficients will affect the other aspects. A simplistic example is when the arrival rate data source is from Oracle (or an Oracle software application), the utilization and number of CPUs is from the operating system, and the service time is derived. When this occurs, a link between Oracle and the operating system is established.

There are many other methods (most of them proprietary) for establishing the Oracle and operating system link working with session-level data. Regardless of how it is accomplished, the relationship between variables must hold true to both queuing theory principles and reality. Here, I'll present one way to establish this link. This method is simple and it works. First, I'll focus on the CPU subsystem, and then on the IO subsystem.

The CPU Subsystem

When working with the CPU subsystem, the utilization formula is helpful:

$$U = \frac{S_t \lambda}{M}$$

As with any formula, if we can collect all but one of the variables, we can derive the missing variable. Data from both Oracle and the CPU subsystems provides the necessary information to derive the service time. Oracle provides the CPU consumption (CPU used by this session) and the number of transactions (for example, user calls). This enables the service time calculation, S_t (for example, 10 ms/trx). Oracle also provides the number of CPUs via the instance parameter cpu_count. The operating system provides the average CPU utilization (for example, using sar -u). The only missing variable is the arrival rate (λ). Since the arrival rate is the only missing variable, we can derive it. By combining the available and appropriate Oracle and operating system data, we not only have all the necessary variables, but we have also established a link between Oracle and the operating system.

There is a very convincing argument that the reported Oracle CPU consumption is more closely aligned with response time than with service time. Oracle CPU consumption is based on the duration of running a piece of Oracle kernel code. Oracle does not know if the request for CPU power resulted in queuing. It simply knows how long it took the code to run. How long code takes to run—that is, its duration—is more closely aligned with response time than with service time.

This will result in lower precision forecasts only if data was collected and used when CPU queuing was occurring. Typically, CPU subsystem data collection and its use in forecast models occur when queuing is limited. For example, it is rare for someone to ask if the system is at risk of poor performance when the CPU utilization is currently at 85% utilization. The answer is probably yes. (An exception would be if application activity was expected to decrease as opposed to remaining the same or increasing.) However, if you are going for maximum precision, it is better to treat Oracle CPU consumption as response time rather than as service time.

Example 7-3 demonstrates one way to fit the pieces appropriately together for a CPU subsystem. The results of this exercise will be used in Examples 7-4, 7-5, and 7-6.

Example 7-3. Constructing the CPU Baseline

Katrina needs to construct a peak CPU usage baseline to enable her forecasts. She has been collecting session-level workload data for the past six months. The data has been loaded into the sess_detail table she created. She performed an analysis and determined peak application activity normally occurs over a 30-minute period, between 2:00 p.m. and 2:30 p.m. every Friday. The actual day for the data she selected was January 12.

The following is the script Katrina used to determine the CPU service time (35.611 ms/trx). Notice the service time is calculated from what appears to be a pure Oracle data source (v$sesstat view, CPU used by this session column). However, Oracle gathers the CPU time from the operating system. As a result, what first appears to be a purely Oracle-derived service time is actually a combination of both Oracle activity (that is, the workload) and the operating system CPU time. So right from the start, she has established a link between Oracle and the operating system!

We do not know how Katrina defines a transaction, as it is hidden within the sess_detail table's workload column. This is not a problem if this definition is used consistently throughout the forecast model. Never assume a transaction is an official Oracle transaction or a business transaction. If you need to know, ask.

```
select avg(cpu_ms/workload) avg_cpu_ms_trx
from  sess_detail
where logoff_time between
      to_date('12-Jan-07 14:00','DD-Mon-YY HH24:MI') and
      to_date('12-Jan-07 14:30','DD-Mon-YY HH24:MI')
/
```

$$\frac{\text{AVG\_CPU\_MS\_TRX}}{35.611}$$

Katrina issued the SQL command select value from v\$parameter where name = 'cpu_count' to determine that the database server contains 64 CPUs. She also referenced the operating system activity repository and determined that during the same peak day and time period, the average CPU utilization was 65%.

Katrina now has the following queuing-related variables:

$$S_t = 35.611\,ms/trx$$
$$M = 64$$
$$U = 65\%$$

To establish the baseline metrics, only the arrival rate is missing, which she calculated using the following standard queuing theory formula:

$$\lambda = \frac{UM}{S_t} = \frac{0.65*64}{35.611\,ms/trx} = \frac{41.600}{35.611\,ms/trx} = 1.168\,trx/ms$$

Katrina now has all the baseline information needed to begin validating her CPU forecast model.

The IO Subsystem

When working with the IO subsystem, the utilization formula is also helpful.

$$U = \frac{S_t \lambda}{M}$$

Data from both Oracle and the IO subsystems provides the necessary information to determine all but one variable, the service time. Fortunately, we do have data to derive the time required to service all the IO transactions within a period of time. This result is more closely aligned with response time than with service time. While Oracle knows how long it takes the IO subsystem to complete a transaction, Oracle does not know the response time breakdown; that is, it does not know how much is true service time and how much is queue time. Unlike with CPU subsystems, significant queuing occurs in IO subsystems even at a low utilization (for example, 10%). Therefore, based solely on Oracle data, we cannot responsibly derive the service time.

Oracle provides IO consumption over the sample period (see Table 7-1 for possible sources). This enables the arrival rate calculation (kb/ms). The IO units may seem strange, as we are used to "transactions." However, an arrival rate represents how much work enters the system within a specified period of time. Since we know how many bytes of IO data entered the system and we know the duration, the arrival rate can be calculated.

If you are uncomfortable with the arrival rate format, realize that you will undoubtedly validate the forecast model's precision, and so you will know if there is a low-precision problem.

This method is relatively simple and straightforward. And finally, if the arrival rate doubled, then the IO per unit of time (for example, mb/s) should also double, and it does. So while this arrival rate may seem strange at first, it can be used very effectively. And, of course, this is just one of many IO forecasting models and methods.

The operating system provides both the average IO device utilization and the number of active devices (for example, using, `sar -d` or `iostat`). Based on the utilization formula, service time is the only missing variable. Therefore, we can derive it. By combining the available Oracle and operating system detail, we have all the variables necessary.

Example 7-4 demonstrates one way to fit the pieces appropriately together for an IO subsystem forecast. The results of this exercise will be used in Examples 7-5 and 7-6.

Example 7-4. Constructing the IO Baseline

Zia needs to construct a peak IO usage baseline to enable forecasting. She has been collecting session-level workload data for the past six months. The format of the data is similar to what is shown on the prior pages. She decided to use the peak activity, which occurred over a 30-minute period on January 12, between 2:00 p.m. and 2:30 p.m. Here is the script she used to extract the data, along with the results:

```
select sum(io_kb/((to_date('12-Jan-07 14:30','DD-Mon-YY HH24:MI')-
                    to_date('12-Jan-07 14:00','DD-Mon-YY HH24:MI')
                )*24*60*60*1000)) io_kb_ms
from   sess_detail
where  logoff_time between
       to_date('12-Jan-07 14:00','DD-Mon-YY HH24:MI') and
       to_date('12-Jan-07 14:30','DD-Mon-YY HH24:MI')
/

  IO_KB_MS
  ────────
   3.784
```

Operating system IO activity was gathered using the `iostat` command. Referencing this information during the chosen peak day and time, the 50 active IO devices (which are actually RAID arrays) had an average IO utilization of 65%.

At this point, Zia had the following variables.

$$\lambda = 3.784\,kb/ms$$
$$M = 50$$
$$U = 65\%$$

To establish the baseline, only the average IO service time was missing, which she calculated using the following standard queuing theory formula.

$$S_t = \frac{UM}{\lambda} = \frac{0.65*50}{3.784\,kb/ms} = \frac{32.500}{3.784\,kb/ms} = 8.590\,ms/kb$$

Zia now has all the baseline information needed to begin validating her IO forecast model.

Creating a Useful Workload Model

So far in this chapter, I've tried to draw a clear distinction between a system-level and session-level workload model. In addition, I've tried to responsibly combine Oracle and operating system data to enable a more realistic Oracle-based system forecast model. Now I want to move on by using this foundation to develop diverse multiple-category workload models. By creating multiple-category workload models, it becomes possible to answer a wide variety of study questions.

Examples 7-5 and 7-6 demonstrate how to develop a usable session-level Oracle-based multiple-category workload model. As you'll quickly come to understand, creating a multiple-category workload model can be very difficult. We could simply create a model based solely on operating system information, but then we would lose the realities of an Oracle workload. The increased precision occurs when we correctly combine Oracle activity with the operating system's activity. This also increases the complexity.

Just because a session-level multiple-category workload model exists does not mean that general workload-related questions will not be asked. Example 7-5 demonstrates how to answer questions about general workload changes when using a multiple-category workload model.

Example 7-5. Increasing the Overall Workload

Management wants to know if the system will be at risk of overutilized resources and a significant response time change if the overall system workload increases by 50%.

The workload data is the same as in Examples 7-3 and 7-4. Based on these two exercises, the following variables are known. For the CPU subsystem, the arrival rate is 1.168 trx/s, the average utilization is 65%, the number of CPUs is 64, and the average service time is 35.611 ms/trx. For the IO subsystem, the arrival rate is 3.784 kb/ms, the average IO device utilization is 65%, the number of active IO devices is 50, and the average service time is 8.590 ms/kb. Assume the forecast model has been validated and is within an acceptable precision tolerance. Based on these numbers, which we'll call the baseline numbers, and using our essential forecasting mathematics, the baseline response times are as follows.

$$R_{t-cpu} = \frac{S_t}{1-U^M} = \frac{35.611\,ms/trx}{1-0.650^{64}} = \frac{35.611\,ms/trx}{1-0.000} = \frac{35.611\,ms/trx}{1.000} = 35.611\,ms/trx$$

$$R_{t-io} = \frac{S_t}{1-U} = \frac{8.590\,ms/kb}{1-0.650} = \frac{8.590\,ms/kb}{0.350} = 24.543\,ms/kb$$

A 50% CPU subsystem arrival rate increase results in an adjusted arrival rate of 1.752 trx/s ($1.168 \times 1.5 = 1.752$). A 50% IO subsystem arrival rate increase results in an adjusted arrival rate of 5.676 kb/ms ($3.784 \times 1.5 = 5.676$). The utilization and response math for both the CPU and IO subsystems are as follows.

For the CPU subsystem with a 50% arrival rate increase:

$$U_{cpu} = \frac{\lambda S_t}{M} = \frac{1.752\,trx/ms * 35.611\,ms/trx}{64} = \frac{62.390}{64} = 0.975 = 97.5\%$$

$$R_{t-cpu} = \frac{S_t}{1-U^M} = \frac{35.611\,ms/trx}{1-0.975^{64}} = \frac{35.611\,ms/trx}{1-0.198} = \frac{35.611\,ms/trx}{0.802} = 44.403\,ms/trx$$

For the IO subsystem with a 50% arrival rate increase:

$$U_{io} = \frac{\lambda S_t}{M} = \frac{5.676\,kb/ms * 8.590\,ms/kb}{50} = \frac{48.757}{50} = 0.975 = 97.5\%$$

$$R_{t-io} = \frac{S_t}{1-U} = \frac{8.590\,ms/kb}{1-0.975} = \frac{8.590\,ms/kb}{0.025} = 343.600\,ms/kb$$

With a 50% increase in the arrival rate, both the CPU and IO utilizations increased to 97.5%. The IO subsystem response time is about to hit infinity at 343.600 ms/kb! The CPU subsystem response time increased from 35.611 ms/trx to 44.403 ms/trx. The reason the CPU response time has not quite skyrocketed, even with a utilization of 97.5%, is that the server has 64 CPUs. Figure 7-1 shows the response time is flat until the end. And then it skyrockets!

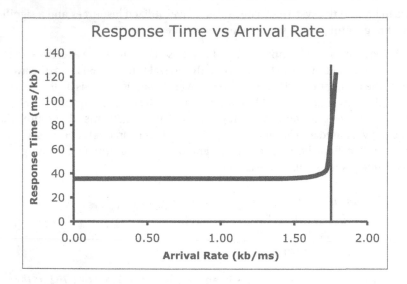

Figure 7-1. *The extreme sloping response time curve with 64 CPUs*

Given that the average CPU utilization is 97.5%, you might be surprised that the CPU response time is not higher. If we were to use Erlang C math for the CPU response time, with the 50% workload increase, the new response time would be 52.753 ms/trx. That is an incredible difference between the essential forecasting math and Erlang C. This is another example of why you should always use Erlang C math.

A direct answer to the study question could be, "With a 50% workload increase, the system is expected to be at significant risk of overutilized resources and significant response time change. Both the CPU and IO subsystems' utilization is expected to be near 100%."

Workload Characterization

Armed with raw session-level workload data, many different characterizations of the workload can occur. The following are three workload groupings based on the same session-level data. Only their characterization is different.

User	AVG_CPU_MS_TRX	IO_KB_MS
AR	59.340	3.172
MG	3.972	0.612

MODULE	AVG_CPU_MS_TRX	IO_KB_MS
SQL*Plus	41.444	3.582
undef	0.614	0.202

MACHINE	AVG_CPU_MS_TRX	IO_KB_MS
sv1.comp.com	35.692	2.268
sv2.comp.com	35.409	1.516

The following code snippet was the base code used to quickly create each of the preceding three characterizations of the workload. The only difference is the word `username` was switched to `module` and then `machine`.

```
select username,
       avg(cpu_ms/workload) avg_cpu_ms_trx,
       sum(io_kb/((to_date('12-Jan-07 14:30','DD-Mon-YY HH24:MI')-
                   to_date('12-Jan-07 14:00','DD-Mon-YY HH24:MI')
               )*24*60*60*1000)) io_kb_ms
from  sess_detail
where logoff_time between
      to_date('12-Jan-07 14:00','DD-Mon-YY HH24:MI') and
      to_date('12-Jan-07 14:30','DD-Mon-YY HH24:MI')
group by username
/
```

You probably are thinking what I'm thinking. How about if we ask some forecast questions such as, "Will the system be at risk if we double the number of AR users?" or "Will the system be at risk if we double the SQL*Plus sessions, remove the `undef` workload, and use 20% faster CPUs?" The possibilities are endless, and the forecasting freedom is intoxicating (to some of us anyway).

One of the most trivial yet useful concepts to keep in mind is that the total arrival rate equals the sum of all the workload category arrival rates.

$$\lambda_{tot} = \lambda_{cat-1} + \lambda_{cat-2} + \ldots + \lambda_{cat-n}$$

For example, if there are three workloads—OLTP, Batch, and DSS—the total transaction arrival rate equals the arrival rates of all three workload categories.

$$\lambda_{tot} = \lambda_{OLTP} + \lambda_{Batch} + \lambda_{DSS}$$

If the OLTP workload were doubled, the adjusted total arrival rate would look like this:

$$\lambda_{tot-adj} = 2 * \lambda_{OLTP} + \lambda_{Batch} + \lambda_{DSS}$$

So when segmenting, modifying, and recombining workloads, the sum of all the arrival rates will equal the newly adjusted total arrival rate. This new arrival rate will then most likely be reentered into our forecasting models to derive the adjusted utilization, response time, and so on.

Example 7-6 is one of the most difficult exercises in this book. It demonstrates how useful yet rigorous it can be to manually work (without the aid of a product or even a spreadsheet) with a multiple category workload model.

Example 7-6. Increasing a Workload Component's Arrival Rate

John is a system architect responsible for capacity planning. One of his largest database servers contains two major applications: the MG application and the AR application. Three months from now, management expects the MG application users to triple, while the AR application's activity will remain the same. John needs to know if the system will be at risk of significantly increased response times and high utilization.

The raw workload data is the same as in Examples 7-3, 7-4, and 7-5. In these examples, the following baseline information was either observed or derived. For the CPU subsystem, the arrival rate is 1.168 trx/s, the average utilization is 65%, the number of CPUs is 64, the average service time is 35.611 ms/trx, and the response time is 35.611 ms/trx. For the IO subsystem, the arrival rate is 3.784 kb/ms, the average IO device utilization is 65%, the number of active IO devices is 50, the average service time is 8.590 ms/kb, and the response time is 24.543 ms/kb. John has validated the forecast model and it is within an acceptable precision tolerance.

The sum of all the category arrivals equals the total arrival rate.

$$\lambda_{tot} = \lambda_{AR} + \lambda_{MG}$$

Since the workload is changing only for the MG application, its workload must be separated from the total workload, appropriately increased, and then added back into what will become the newly adjusted total workload rate. Since the MG workload is increasing three times, the formula is as follows:

$$\lambda_{tot-adj} = \lambda_{AR} + \left(3 * \lambda_{MG}\right)$$

The adjusted workload must be derived for both the CPU and IO subsystems.

The Oracle username can be used to identify the application. In this case, the Oracle username MG represents all MG application users. To help with John's analysis, he ran the following SQL script.

```
select username,
       sum(workload),
       avg(cpu_ms/workload) avg_cpu_ms_trx,
       sum(io_kb/((to_date('12-Jan-07 14:30','DD-Mon-YY HH24:MI')-
                   to_date('12-Jan-07 14:00','DD-Mon-YY HH24:MI')
                  )*24*60*60*1000)) io_kb_ms
from  sess_detail
where logoff_time between
      to_date('12-Jan-07 14:00','DD-Mon-YY HH24:MI') and
      to_date('12-Jan-07 14:30','DD-Mon-YY HH24:MI')
group by username
/
```

User	SUM(WORKLOAD)	AVG_CPU_MS_TRX	IO_KB_MS
AR	878	59.340	3.172
MG	12480	3.972	0.612

As the output shows, it was easy for John to derive the IO subsystem arrival rate directly from the Oracle activity (see Example 7-3 for details). However, the CPU subsystem arrival rate will take some work (see Example 7-4 for details), especially since he must derive the CPU arrival rate by application; that is, the Oracle username.

John started with the IO subsystem first. Since the MG application users are expected to triple, he simply multiplied the current MG arrival rate by three, resulting in an adjusted MG arrival rate of 1.836 kb/ms. Adding the increased MG arrival rate (1.836 kb/ms) to the existing AR arrival rate (3.172 kb/ms) brings the newly adjusted total arrival rate to 5.008 kb/ms. Mathematically, it looks like this:

$$\lambda_{io-adj} = \left(3 * \lambda_{io-MG}\right) + \lambda_{io-AR} = \left(3 * 0.612\,kb/ms\right) + 3.172\,kb/ms$$
$$\lambda_{io-adj} = 1.836\,kb/ms + 3.172\,kb/ms = 5.008\,kb/ms$$

Placing the adjusted IO arrival rate into the utilization and response time formulas, John quickly discovered the predicted utilization was over 100%!

$$U_{io} = \frac{\lambda S_t}{M} = \frac{5.008\,kb/ms * 8.590\,ms/kb}{50} = \frac{43.019}{50} = 0.860 = 86.0\%$$
$$R_{t-io} = \frac{S_t}{1-U} = \frac{8.590\,ms/kb}{1-0.860} = \frac{8.590\,ms/kb}{0.140} = 61.357\,ms/kb$$

The IO utilization increased from 65% to 86% and the response time more than doubled from 25 ms/kb to 61ms/kb. While we don't know for certain, there is high likelihood the users will not be pleased with the response time, regardless of what changes the CPU subsystem undergoes.

With the IO subsystem forecast complete, John now turns his attention squarely on the CPU forecast. He needs to categorize the CPU arrival rates by application. This is a bit tricky. As the preceding SQL report shows, John easily calculated the CPU service times for each application (MG and AR) using the Oracle workload and Oracle CPU consumption information. He also knows the number of CPUs (64) and the average CPU utilization (65%). Now he must calculate each application's CPU subsystem arrival rates.

Back in Example 7-3, the total CPU arrival rate was derived to be 1.168 trx/ms. The SQL output shows the AR workload is 878 trx (this is out of a total workload of 13358 trx). Therefore, the AR workload is 6.573% of the total workload or 0.077 trx/ms. The MG workload is 12480 trx out of a total workload of 13358 trx, which is 93.427% of the workload, or 1.091 trx/ms. Shown in a more mathematical way; it looks like this:

$$\lambda_{tot-cpu} = \lambda_{cpu-AR} + \lambda_{cpu-MG} = 1.168 \, trx/ms$$

$$\lambda_{cpu-AR} = \left(\frac{878}{878+12480}\right) * 1.168 \, trx/ms = 0.066 * 1.168 \, trx/ms = 0.077 \, trx/ms$$

$$\lambda_{cpu-MG} = \left(\frac{12480}{878+12480}\right) * 1.168 \, trx/ms = 0.934 * 1.168 \, trx/ms = 1.091 \, trx/ms$$

As verification, the total arrival rate should equal the sum of the individual (separated) arrival rates.

$$\lambda_{tot-cpu} = \lambda_{cpu-AR} + \lambda_{cpu-MG} = 0.077 \, trx/ms + 1.091 \, trx/ms = 1.168 \, trx/ms$$

Now with the CPU subsystem arrival rates separated by application, John can apply the specific MG workload increase and add the pieces together to determine the newly adjusted CPU arrival rate. Here is the math:

$$\lambda_{cpu-adj} = \left(3 * \lambda_{cpu-MG}\right) + \lambda_{cpu-AR} = \left(3 * 1.091 \, trx/ms\right) + 0.077 \, trx/ms$$

$$\lambda_{cpu-adj} = 3.273 \, trx/ms + 0.077 \, trx/ms = 3.350 \, trx/ms$$

The newly adjust CPU arrival rate is 3.350 trx/ms. Placing this into the utilization formula, the results show a predicted utilization of 186.4%.

$$U_{cpu} = \frac{\lambda S_t}{M} = \frac{3.350 \, trx/ms * 35.611 \, ms/trx}{64} = \frac{119.297}{64} = 1.864 = 186.4\%$$

Obviously, there will be CPU utilization issues! With the CPU utilization greater than 100%, the system becomes unstable and unable to process the workload. Mathematically, the response time will be a negative number.

John can now confidently discuss the upcoming situation with his manager. He also has some serious risk mitigation strategy work to do. As the forecasts clearly show, based on management's expectation of a 3X MG application workload increase, the CPU subsystem closely followed by the IO subsystem are at a substantial risk of high utilization and poor response time.

Selecting the Peak

So far in this chapter, I have casually made statements about the workload peak. The focus was on creating the baseline and the workload model. But now the focus needs to shift a bit toward understanding, determining, and selecting the peak. Selecting the correct peak, or peaks, is important because it becomes the forecast reference point—that is, the baseline.

Most forecasting questions center around some scenario related to peak activity. The question then becomes, "Well, what is the peak?" This single question can cause hours of discussion and become very frustrating. One solution is to not select a single peak, but perform identical forecasting scenarios using the most likely peaks.

When selecting the peak, you have two basic choices: you can select a group of the workload samples and summarize them to create a single workload representation, or you can pick a single workload sample. If you are gathering at the session level, your peak will surely constitute multiple samples (as in Examples 7-1 and 7-2), but that window of time chosen to represent the peak may be very narrow. Gathering at the system level truly forces the question, "Should we use one sample or summarize multiple samples?"

In addition to deciding which workload samples to include in the peak, the definition of *the peak* must also be determined. Deciding exactly what constitutes the peak workload is not always as easy as it seems. Oracle workloads are constantly changing. What may appear to be a similar peak from one perspective (for example, CPU utilization) may actually contain a very different workload mix.

How the peak is defined makes all the difference. For example, referring to Table 7-8, if the peak were defined to be the maximum CPU activity, then sample 1320 and sample 1978 would be the peak. But even then, they both have a radically different workload mix and could result in significantly different forecasts. Suppose the peak were defined to be the maximum workload. But what is the workload? Is it one of our workload categories, such as OLTP activity, or a combination of two, three, or four workload categories? As you can see, defining a single sample to be the obvious peak is not to be taken lightly.

Table 7-8. *Identifying Peak Activity Is Not Always a Simple Matter*

Sample	CPU Util %	OLTP Activity (trx/s)	Concurrent Batch Processes
1320	95	50	15
1978	95	225	6
2232	93	218	5
6573	92	75	8
1098	88	116	11
0897	84	263	4
1907	84	198	8
2057	84	112	6
1870	83	85	13

It may be useful to plot various relationships to help understand and determine peak activity. Figure 7-2 shows a graph of system activity taken from a large Oracle production system. There are five possible CPU peaks, but many transactional activity peaks. Even more challenging is one of the CPU peaks (close to activity sample 21 in Figure 7-2) is clearly not the transactional activity peak. The definition and selection of a single peak can be extremely difficult and frustrating.

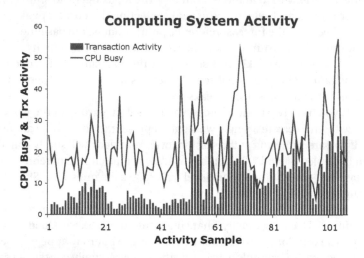

Figure 7-2. *Graphically selecting peak activity*

The solution to this problem is to perform the same set of forecasts (that is, scenario) using various workload peaks. This will result in many forecasts, which must be organized and stored for easy retrieval and analysis. When many forecasts are run using the same scenario but with different workload mixes, a range of probable outcomes will begin to emerge. This probable range will represent the best and worst case scenarios, or what many like to call the pessimistic and optimistic scenarios. Presenting the range of likely outcomes and discussing their associated risks is exactly the kind of information management needs to help manage service levels.

Table 7-9 is an example of running three identical scenarios while selecting three different peaks. If each scenario is considered to be just as likely to occur, then the forecasted CPU requirement range is from 10 to 22 CPUs. That's quite a range! Also notice peak 1 always results in the highest CPU requirement. These results would then force serious discussions around the likelihood of scenario 1 and peak 1 occurring.

Many people believe that forecasting results in a single best answer. But in reality, many possible answers arise. Only after combining forecasting analysis, computing system technical architectural analysis, business activity analysis, and financial analysis does the best answer start to rise above the rest. When forecasting, our role is to create the raw data and transform it into useful information so the best possible decisions can be made. Based on any number of nontechnical constraints, what may appear to be a risky solution may actually be the best solution for the company.

Table 7-9. *Emerging Capacity Requirements Occur When Performing the Same Scenario with Multiple Peaks*

Scenario #	Peak #	CPU Required
1	1	22
1	2	16
1	3	18
2	1	16
2	2	10
2	3	11
3	1	20
3	2	17
3	3	17

Selecting a Single Sample

You can't get around the fact that any time data is summarized, precision is lost. So if possible, try to select a single workload sample. And make sure it is a good representation of your system's peak workload.

Deciding to select a single sample is really only an issue when collecting workload at the system level. When workload is gathered at the session level, some type of summarization or consolidation always occurs.

Be aware that a single workload sample may not represent your entire system appropriately. This is important: The more frequently workload is gathered, the less likely a single workload sample will be appropriate. For example, if the system workload is gathered every 15 seconds, the workload variations will be massive. Because CPUs are either on or off, you can bet at least a few of the CPU sample peaks will hit 100%. That is probably not a good representation of the system, however. If you were to select the peak activity sample, it's unlikely that would represent the true peak. In fact, forecasting based on the absolute peak workload sample may result in a startling high utilization forecast, which may be financially and practically unrealistic.

When using a single workload sample, use a larger data-gathering frequency, such as 30 minutes, 60 minutes, or perhaps even 2 hours. A good place to start is with 60-minute samples. After you gain some experience, you can modify as you are led. With larger gathering frequencies, such as 1 hour, a truer peak is likely to emerge and can be more easily selected.

However, just as gathering frequently can create workload peak selection problems, gathering infrequently can also flatten out or smooth over important workload peaks. If many data samples are averaged, the peak may not be apparent. Even more problematic is the smoothed peak will result in an overly optimistic forecast. For example, suppose you have the following information: when gathering every minute, the peak utilization is 95%; when gathering every 15 minutes, the peak utilization is 75%; and when gathering every 30 minutes, the peak utilization is 55%. Which peak should be selected for forecasting? I cannot answer this question for you. But you and your colleagues, when faced with this decision, will need to find an answer.

Don't forget that you can always run the same scenario using different peaks.

Summarizing Workload Samples

When gathering at the session level, summarization naturally occurs. The focus then will be on how to define the workload peak. However, when gathering at the system level, it is common to summarize perhaps many workload samples into a single summarized sample.

If workload samples are gathered frequently or the samples naturally belong together from a business perspective (for example, around the morning activity peak or between 12 p.m. and 1 p.m. each day), then use great care. Use the statistical analysis techniques presented in Chapter 4 to get an understanding of the mean, variations, and skew of your data. To be conservative, it may make sense to use the ninetieth percentile instead of the mean. And don't forget about using a weighted average and validating the model's precision. Summarizing data without validating the forecasts is simply irresponsible.

Summary

This chapter may be the most complex one, but it is certainly needed and presents some of the most unique and powerful material in the entire book. If you have read other capacity planning books, you know that they fall short—pitifully short—in their coverage of how to gather, characterize, and forecast Oracle-based systems. How many times have you been told to simply "count the application's IOs" and enter the information into a queuing theory model? Arrgh! That is simply not realistic.

But with realism comes some additional complexity. The complexity is due to our desire to create a workload that combines the characteristics of Oracle, the application, and the operating system. If our workload model can embrace their uniqueness and their interaction, then we have truly succeeded in something wonderful and very useful.

While I wouldn't have written this at the beginning of the chapter, consider all the topics presented here:

- Selecting a workload peak

- Gathering workload from both the operating system and Oracle

- Creating a workload link between Oracle and the operating system

- Grouping workload data so it is useful for forecasting and forecast model input

- Considering whether to gather system-level or session-level data

- Finding the data you need to collect

- Using a simple workload gathering script

That's a lot to cover. But it all falls under the very necessary, yet sometimes messy, topic of workload characterization.

CHAPTER 8

■■■

Ratio Modeling

In some cases, a low-precision forecast is not only useful and appropriate, but also vitally necessary. Imagine the following four situations:

- You just arrived at the office and your boss informs you the budget for next year's hardware purchases is due today, by close of business.

- While you are in the meeting, a hardware vendor recommends that you purchase the vendor's newest and most powerful server. While it sounds great, you want to quickly do a "sanity check" just to make sure the vendor's claims are reasonable.

- You are a CRM software development company that must quickly "size the system" for your prospects. This occurs as part of the sales cycle, and you don't have a lot of time. But you must somehow responsibly recommend a hardware solution and also validate the hardware vendor's counter-recommendation.

- You are creating a number of alternative technical architectures for a very large and technically complex application servicing thousands of users around the world. Your task is to recommend three technical architectures with their associated costs, risks, and benefits. The combination of the number of users, the number of batch processes, the number of interfaces, and the number of geographies served thrusts this project into an area of extremely high risk with a very high project failure impact.

If you are used to laboratory-style capacity planning, situations like these may be distasteful and undesirable. Yet these are real situations faced by many people in IT. We can't just hope they go away, because they occur every day. So we had better come up with a way to address the challenge. This chapter covers one solution, called the ratio modeling technique.

Ratio modeling is not very scientific, and it's not pretty. It's messy, and it's cluttered with imprecision and unknowns, yet it is entirely realistic. This technique has been in use for many years now, and has proven itself effective in dealing with quick, low-precision forecasts.

What Is Ratio Modeling?

I bet that you have mentally determined the general size of computer system while listening to someone quickly describing his system. For example, suppose someone says, "Our order entry system has 500 concurrent users," Don't you start thinking, "Well, our system has about 250 concurrent users and we have 10 CPUs, so they must have around 20 CPUs"? What you are doing is equating a computing system resource (think CPU) to a workload category (think concurrent user). This is the essence of ratio modeling.

Dave Cook, Ellen Dudar, and I first developed the ratio modeling technique in the mid-1990s. We constantly found ourselves needing to provide an initial CPU sizing assessment within only a few hours or days. We discovered was that by sacrificing precision, we could provide an assessment within the time, budget, and precision constraints. We presented the original technical paper about our technique at an Oracle conference held in 1995. Since that time, the ratio modeling technique has been used by consulting groups, at least one hardware company, and many DBAs around the world. It has certainly proven itself over the years.

A formal method was developed so we could teach others and help ensure that its inherent low precision was not misused. That's the downside: low precision. It is easy to be overly optimistic and aggressive. You must not forget that this technique is truly a "back-of-the-envelope" forecasting technique for quickly producing low-precision forecasts.

The essence of ratio modeling is equating a computing system resource to a workload. For example, one CPU may be able to handle 150 OLTP users. Once determined, this ratio, called the *OLTP-to-CPU ratio*, allows us to responsibly forecast. Determining and using these ratios are actually quite simple.

The Ratio Modeling Formula

The core ratio modeling technique is deceptively simple.

$$P = \frac{C_1}{R_1} + \ldots + \frac{C_n}{R_n}$$

where:

- P is the number of fully utilized CPUs.

- C is the number of workload category occurrences. For example, the number of OLTP users or the number of concurrently running batch jobs.

- R is the ratio linking a single workload category occurrence to a CPU.

Also important is understanding that if ten CPUs are 50% utilized, then effectively there are five CPUs working at 100% utilization. So mathematically, this is:

$$P = UM$$

where:

- U is the CPU utilization.

- M is the number of servers; that is, CPUs.

Putting this all together, we have the following:

$$UM = \frac{C_1}{R_1} + \ldots + \frac{C_n}{R_n}$$

Example 8-1 demonstrates how ratio modeling can be used in practice. Notice how fast the method can be employed.

Example 8-1. Doing a Quick Forecast

Gabrielle was asked if 25 additional GL users would significantly impact response time. Oh, and her boss was standing there waiting for the answer. Gabrielle repeatedly observed the 18 CPU database server peaks at around 41% utilization. When this occurs, there are around 250 concurrent OLTP users and around 12 concurrent batch jobs running. Gabrielle is a ratio modeling practitioner and knows her system's OLTP-to-CPU ratio is 125 and the batch-to-CPU ratio is 2.

She simply plugged the numbers into the equation like this:

$$P = \frac{C_{oltp}}{R_{oltp}} + \frac{C_{batch}}{R_{batch}} = \frac{(250+25)}{125} + \frac{12}{2} = \frac{275}{125} + 6 = 2.2 + 6 = 8.2$$

This means that 8.2 CPUs will be 100% utilized. Now she needed to know the expected utilization on her 18 CPU system.

$$P = UM; \ U = \frac{P}{M} = \frac{8.2}{18} = .46 = 46\%$$

The expected utilization is 46%. She knows her ratios are very conservative, so it would be very unlikely that the forecasted utilization error would be more than 10%. So she turned to her boss and said, "Twenty-five more users? If nothing else changes, we should be OK." That is the power of ratio modeling!

Gathering and Characterizing the Workload

Before you can forecast using ratio modeling, you must know the ratios. You have two basic options for getting the necessary ratios: derive the ratios yourself on your production system or find a similar system and use its ratios. Obviously, the best option is to derive the ratios from your current production system. This is usually not a problem unless you are implementing a new application. In that case, you must find a similar system and derive the ratios.

If you need to use another system to determine ratios, try to match your system's operating system, number of CPUs, Oracle release, application, industry, and so on. The more similar the computing environment, the better the ratios will be.

When I worked for Oracle, everyone in my group was involved with installing, upgrading, tuning, and forecasting for large Oracle E-Business Suite systems. As a result, we collected ratios from various vendors, CPU types, number of CPUs, and applications. We kept each other up-to-date on the latest ratios. (This is one reason why ratio modeling can be a very good fit for a packaged application vendor.) With everyone in the group gathering ratio data, we continued to build and refine our ratio repository. This allowed anyone in the group to very quickly do an initial sizing assessment based on very little information.

Deriving ratios for your environment is a relatively painless process, but it is a process and can be automated and repeated. When some change affects system performance, consider updating the ratios. Such changes include a database upgrade; an applications upgrade; or patches on the operating system, Oracle, or the application. Other examples are when the business experiences changes with the number of users, the types of users, location of users, and so on. Essentially, any change that affects performance is grounds for updating the ratios.

When you need to derive ratios for your environment, remember to keep things simple. Because ratio modeling is inherently a low-precision forecasting technique, don't get fancy. A perfect illustration of this is in selecting the workload categories. Make them obvious, simple, and useful. The classic workload categories are concurrent OLTP users and concurrent batch processes. On most Oracle systems, this information is easily collected.

To gather the number of concurrent OLTP sessions, you could do a count from Oracle's v$session view. Make sure to exclude background processes, and don't forget to subtract the number of batch processes. The following code snippet will exclude the background processes but include the running batch processes.

```
select count(sid)
from v$session
where username is not null
```

To determine the number of concurrently *active* users, count only sessions that have used some CPU time within the sample period. This will require a more complex script, but it will probably be worth the effort.

Gathering the number of concurrent batch processes is highly application-dependent. For example, Oracle's E-Business Suite has a table called fnd_concurrent_requests that has a status column. All running batch processes will have a status of R, for running. To determine the number of concurrently running E-Business Suite batch jobs, a query like this will work fine:

```
select count(*)
from fnd_concurrent_requests
where status = 'R'
```

You must know the number of database server CPUs, as well as the CPU utilization. You can use the sar -u command to determine the CPU utilization.

Gather as many samples as you can. Having a few samples will allow you to determine the ratios, but it is much better to have hundreds or thousands of samples. Table 8-1 shows some samples taken from a production Oracle application categorized by concurrent OLTP users and concurrent batch processes.

Table 8-1. *Partial Listing of the Information Required to Determine the Ratios*

CPU Util %	OLTP Users	Batch Processes
19	60	11
20	175	10
21	0	14
17	10	10
13	20	15
23	15	12
39	685	7
42	680	8
34	650	8
33	965	7
52	910	10
...	...	...

While not obvious from the partial listing in Table 8-1, during peak OLTP processing, there are between 700 to 900 concurrent OLTP users. During peak batch processing, there are between 10 to 15 concurrent jobs running.

Deriving the Ratios

After you've gathered all your samples, you're ready to derive the ratios. Continuing with the example of using the workload categories of concurrent OLTP users and concurrent batch processes, you need to determine the batch-to-CPU ratio and the OLTP-to-CPU ratio.

Deriving the Batch-to-CPU Ratio

It is usually easiest to start with the batch-to-CPU ratio. Consider a typical ratio modeling formula with no ratios derived:

$$UM = \frac{C_{oltp}}{R_{oltp}} + \frac{C_{batch}}{R_{batch}}$$

While we can supply the number of workload category occurrences (for example, C_{oltp}), the number of CPUs, and the average CPU utilization, we are still missing both ratios. That's two unknowns! However, this is usually not a problem.

On most Oracle-based systems, there is a time when the number of concurrent OLTP users is so low that the impact on the system is negligible. On most Oracle systems, even ten OLTP users will not significantly stress the system. If the number of concurrent OLTP users is for all practical purposes zero, then the formula becomes:

$$UM = \frac{0}{R_{oltp}} + \frac{C_{batch}}{R_{batch}} = \frac{C_{batch}}{R_{batch}}$$

Now the only missing variable is the batch-to-CPU ratio. Solving for the batch-to-CPU ratio, the formula becomes:

$$R_{batch} = \frac{C_{batch}}{UM}$$

The next step is to remove all data points where less than three batch processes are running. Since such a low batch workload will probably never occur during peak time, and peak is our concern, don't let it skew the results. The lower the number of concurrent batch processes, the more significant the overhead from the operating system, the Oracle database system, and the application. Thus, if the ratios are calculated with only a few concurrent batch processes, the ratios will be inappropriately low. This means the forecasts will be overly pessimistic and conservative. For example, our forecast may show that with ten concurrent batch jobs, the CPU utilization will be 75%, when it really would be closer to 65%.

Using only the data points with less than 25 concurrent OLTP processes (with fast CPUs, 25 OLTP users may not significantly impact performance), calculate the batch-to-CPU ratio. There are 28 CPUs in our example system, and the batch-to-CPU ratios are derived only when there are more than three batch processes running and the number of concurrent OLTP users is relatively low. The results, based on Table 8-1, are shown in Table 8-2.

Table 8-2. *Using Some Sample Data to Calculate the Batch-to-CPU Ratios*

CPU Util %	OLTP Users	Batch Processes	Batch-to-CPU Ratio
21	0	14	$R_{batch} = \dfrac{C_{batch}}{UM} = \dfrac{14}{0.21*28} = \dfrac{14}{5.88} = 2.38$
17	10	10	$R_{batch} = \dfrac{C_{batch}}{UM} = \dfrac{10}{0.17*28} = \dfrac{10}{4.76} = 2.10$
13	20	15	$R_{batch} = \dfrac{C_{batch}}{UM} = \dfrac{15}{0.13*28} = \dfrac{15}{3.64} = 4.12$
23	15	12	$R_{batch} = \dfrac{C_{batch}}{UM} = \dfrac{12}{0.23*28} = \dfrac{12}{6.44} = 1.86$
...	...	...	...

Plotting the Batch-to-CPU Ratios

Now that we have calculated potentially hundreds of batch-to-CPU ratios, we must determine the best ratio for our purposes. You may wonder why we don't simply take the average ratio and use that as "the ratio." The reason is that we can glean information by visually inspecting the data. Plus if we simply mathematically calculated the "best ratio," it may include outliers and data points that do not represent sensible ratios.

For example, looking at Figure 8-1, notice that we have a clear outlier when there are 15 concurrent batch jobs running. Also notice that when there are only a few concurrent batch jobs (for example, less than five), the ratio is strangely very low. You may also notice a general trend, or flow, of the data points. These characteristics can be spotted very quickly when visually inspecting the ratios.

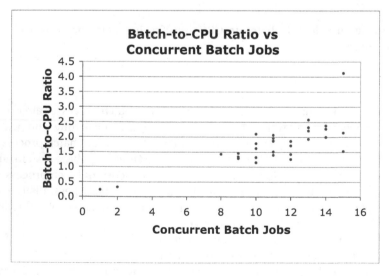

Figure 8-1. *Plotting the ratios allows the ratios to be chosen based on the visual data, risk, and other factors, as opposed to straight mathematics.*

Once you have viewed the initial plot, it's time to give the data a good scrubbing. I have never seen perfect ratio data. If we were to calculate the ratios without closely examining the data and removing bogus data points, our ratios would be skewed and our predictions hopelessly flawed.

I'll be blunt. Remove the outlier data points. Outliers are data points that fall outside the data point cluster or trend. In real scientific studies, outliers are where discovery lives and Nobel Prizes are achieved. But that's not what we are trying to do. We are trying to answer difficult questions very quickly, not win a Nobel Prize. So get rid of the outliers and don't feel guilty about it. However, never hide the fact that you removed an outlier. Keep the original data and document the criteria for removing outliers.

Also remove data points where other significant nonpeak-related computing activity was occurring. For example, if a backup was running or if massive data loads or data extraction were occurring, then the data will be skewed. While gathering ratio data points, it is common to periodically run the Unix ps command, log the output, and review it for unexpected and significant system resource consumers. Figure 8-2 shows the data plot after the ratio data has been scrubbed.

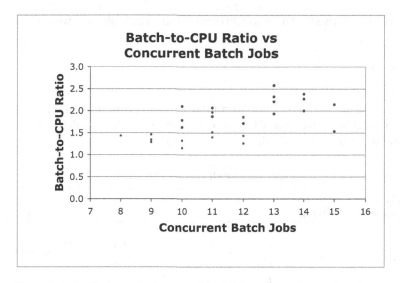

Figure 8-2. *With the ratio data scrubbed, it's easier to determine the most appropriate ratio.*

Selecting the Batch-to-CPU Ratio

Once the raw batch-to-CPU ratios have been scrubbed and plotted, it's time to pick the most appropriate ratio. It's always best to pick the ratio with other people present. If you're having a great day, you will naturally tend to pick a more aggressive ratio, and that's bad. A lively discussion is a good thing and will naturally touch on topics like risk, the impact of the risk event occurring, and the quality of the data. All these topics will fuse together and birth the most appropriate ratio. When the ratio is determined, document the meeting and the results. Later, if there is a disagreement about the ratio decision, whoever documented the meeting wins.

Looking at Figure 8-2, a more aggressive batch-to-CPU ratio would be 2.5, whereas a very conservative ratio would be 1.0. Notice the natural trend: as the number of batch processes increases, the slope of the batch-to-CPU line decreases. A ratio between 1.5 and 2.0 would be fine. Anything above 2.0 is getting a little too aggressive. Because of the inherently low precision of ratio modeling, aggressive ratios will surely produce very optimistic sizing scenarios, so be as conservative as you can. I personally would choose a ratio of say, 1.5 to 1.75. For our purposes, a batch-to-CPU ratio of 1.75 will be used.

If the group cannot agree on a single ratio, then use two ratios. Simply run the same set of scenarios using both ratios. There could be a more conservative (low-risk) scenario and a more aggressive (higher-risk) scenario. Don't feel like a single best ratio must always be determined.

Once the batch-to-CPU ratio has been determined, we can move on and determine the OLTP-to-CPU ratio.

Deriving the OLTP-to-CPU Ratio

Referring back to our ratio modeling formula, notice all but the OLTP-to-CPU ratio is now known.

$$UM = \frac{C_{oltp}}{R_{oltp}} + \frac{C_{batch}}{R_{batch}}$$

This allows us to easily derive the OLTP-to-CPU ratio. Using a little algebra, we get this:

$$R_{oltp} = \frac{C_{oltp}}{UM - \dfrac{C_{batch}}{R_{batch}}}$$

Table 8-3 shows some of the sample data from Table 8-1 along with the OLTP-to-CPU ratio math. Keep in mind that the batch-to-CPU ratio of 1.75 has already been derived (in the previous section) and there are 28 CPUs in the database server.

Table 8-3. *Using Some Sample Data to Calculate the OLTP-to-CPU Ratios*

CPU Util	OLTP Users	Batch Processes	OLTP-to-CPU Ratio
19	60	11	$R_{oltp} = \dfrac{C_{oltp}}{UM - \dfrac{C_{batch}}{R_{batch}}} = \dfrac{60}{0.19*28 - \dfrac{11}{1.75}} = \dfrac{60}{5.32 - 6.29} = \dfrac{60}{-0.97} = -61.86$
34	650	8	$R_{oltp} = \dfrac{C_{oltp}}{UM - \dfrac{C_{batch}}{R_{batch}}} = \dfrac{650}{0.34*28 - \dfrac{8}{1.75}} = \dfrac{650}{9.52 - 4.57} = \dfrac{650}{4.95} = 131.31$
33	965	7	$R_{oltp} = \dfrac{C_{oltp}}{UM - \dfrac{C_{batch}}{R_{batch}}} = \dfrac{965}{0.33*28 - \dfrac{7}{1.75}} = \dfrac{965}{9.24 - 4.00} = \dfrac{965}{5.24} = 184.16$
52	910	10	$R_{oltp} = \dfrac{C_{oltp}}{UM - \dfrac{C_{batch}}{R_{batch}}} = \dfrac{910}{0.52*28 - \dfrac{10}{1.75}} = \dfrac{910}{14.56 - 5.71} = \dfrac{910}{8.85} = 102.82$
...	...	...	...

You probably immediately noticed two things:

- There is a negative ratio. Expect to see negative ratios when there is relatively little OLTP activity. When determining the OLTP-to-CPU ratio, we are interested in data only when the system is very active with both batch and OLTP activity. When the workload is lopsided toward batch activity (and more than a couple batch concurrent processes are significant), the ratios simply are not useful.

- The OLTP-to-CPU ratio variance is large. This is normal and also to be expected. The combination of complex Oracle workloads and the inherent low precision of ratio modeling will create a wide ratio variance.

Just as with the batch-to-CPU ratio, plot the ratio data. Plotting will reveal aspects that the pure numbers can't show. Figure 8-3 shows a cluster of data at the graph's origin and also a point with a negative ratio. Because these data points will not be considered when determining the chosen ratio, remove the distraction by removing those data points.

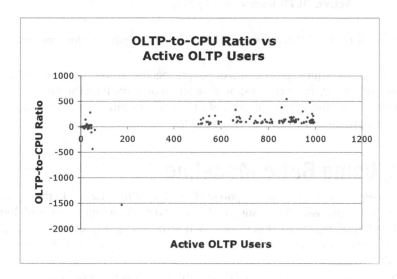

Figure 8-3. *The raw OLTP-to-CPU ratio plot, including outliers and negative ratios*

Figure 8-4 shows the scrubbed OLTP-to-CPU data points. Notice the scaling vertically stretches the plot and makes it easier to get a good view of the flow of the data. Looking at Figure 8-4, an OTLP-to-CPU ratio of greater than 300 would be very optimistic, producing high-risk forecasts. A ratio of less than 50 would clearly be overly pessimistic. A ratio between 75 to 200 would be acceptable. For our example, I'll select an OLTP-to-CPU ratio of 100.

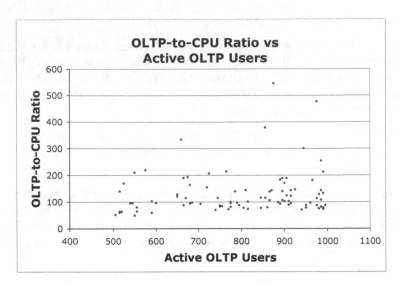

Figure 8-4. *The scrubbed OLTP-to-CPU ratio plot, with outliers and negative ratios removed*

As I mentioned earlier, you should get a group of people together when selecting the best one or two ratios. Remember that the decision should be based on more than the pure mathematics and the data plot. Issues like risk, the impact of a risk event occurring, and the quality of the data also need to be discussed and taken into consideration.

Forecasting Using Ratio Modeling

Once you are in possession of some good ratios, you're all set! I want to stress again that ratio modeling is inherently a low-precision forecasting technique, so don't be aggressive. And don't let people talk you into being aggressive. If in the future it turns out your forecast was overly aggressive, people will come back *to you*, not the person or group of people who were pressuring you to be aggressive.

The best way to teach people how to forecast using ratio modeling is to practice. The next best thing is working through some examples. So I'm going to take you through a series of three examples demonstrating some of the common ratio modeling situations. Example 8-2 focuses on how someone working in a pre-sales role would typically use ratio modeling. Example 8-3 shows how to perform an initial sizing and risk assessment using ratio modeling. Finally, Example 8-4 shows how to use ratio modeling to check if a hardware vendor is using its sizing recommendation to close a deal, as opposed to adding real sizing value.

Example 8-2. Closing the Deal

Sally is a top-notch pre-sales associate for a large enterprise resource planning (ERP) vendor. Her company is about to close a large deal and needs to make a general hardware sizing recommendation. The prospect is expecting to have a maximum of 750 concurrently active OLTP users. (Companies implementing a new application typically do not have a clue as to how many concurrent batch processes will be necessary.) Based on Sally's experience, she expects no more than 15 concurrent batch jobs will be running.

She put a call into the consulting staff to get the latest ratios. The closest similar system was a 20 CPU box with an OLTP-to-CPU ratio of 100 and a batch-to-CPU ratio of 1.75. Knowing the reference site's number of CPUs is important when considering scalability. Since the ratio data was gathered and the ratios derived from a 20 CPU box, 20 CPU scalability is naturally included in the ratios. One of the benefits of ratio modeling is scalability is built into the ratios. However, if the number of forecasted CPUs is different from the number at the reference site, scalability will need to be considered. For example, if the forecast calls for more than 20 CPUs, the forecast will be optimistic and the actual number of CPUs will be greater than the forecast. However, if the forecast calls for less than 20 CPUs, the forecast will be pessimistic and the actual number will be less than the forecast. (For more information about scalability, refer to Chapter 10.)

Sally wants to produce an aggressive, moderate, and low-risk forecast. The aggressive forecast will set the CPU utilization to 75%, the moderate forecast will set the CPU utilization to 65%, and the low-risk forecast will set it to 50%.

To start, Sally simply plugged the numbers into the core ratio modeling equation as follows:

$$P = \frac{C_{oltp}}{R_{oltp}} + \frac{C_{batch}}{R_{batch}} = \frac{750}{100} + \frac{15}{1.75} = 7.50 + 8.57 = 16.07$$

This means that 16 CPUs will be 100% utilized. But Sally wants to see a variety of risk possibilities, hence her desire to see a high-risk, moderate-risk, and low-risk forecast. The low-risk forecast is set up as follows:

$$P = UM; \ M = \frac{P}{U} = \frac{16.07}{0.50} = 32.14$$

The low-risk solution would need to contain at least 33 CPUs. And because of the scalability performance loss, more than 33 CPUs are desirable.

The moderate-risk (65% CPU utilization) forecast is set up as follows:

$$M = \frac{P}{U} = \frac{16.07}{0.65} = 24.72$$

The moderate-risk solution requires at least 25 CPUs. Again, scalability would need to be taken into consideration. But the difference from 20 CPUs (that's how many CPUs exist on the site where the ratios were gathered and derived) to a 25 CPU machine will not be that significant. Perhaps an extra CPU or two would be adequate.

For the high-risk solution (75% CPU utilization), the calculation is as follows:

$$M = \frac{P}{U} = \frac{16.07}{0.75} = 21.43$$

The high-risk solution would need to contain at least 22 CPUs. Because the reference ratios came from a 20 CPU machine, scalability is not significant. However, recommending a solution at 75% utilization is significant and probably reckless. At 75% utilization, the arrival rate is already well into the elbow of the curve. It would be extremely rare to recommend a solution at 75% utilization.

Equipped with multiple risk-ranging forecasts, Sally is better prepared to make a responsible sizing recommendation.

Example 8-3. Adding a New Branch Office

Annalisa is a technical architect who needs to determine if adding a new company branch office will significantly impact performance. The new branch office will reside in Istanbul. The management expects 25 additional concurrently active users, and the experienced application users expect two additional concurrent batch processes will be required.

Annalisa is smart. Before she embarks on a high-precision, time-consuming, and more costly forecasting study, she is going to perform a quick, low-precision forecast. If the forecast indicates the risk of poor performance is low, then she will conclude performance will not be negatively impacted. However, if there is reason to believe (even a slight reason to believe) performance will be impacted, she will perform a more detailed and higher-precision forecast.

She decided to perform the initial risk assessment using ratio modeling. Annalisa has been collecting ratio data over the past year and is very confident with the OLTP-to-CPU ratio of 125 and a batch-to-CPU ratio of 1.35. Currently, the 16 CPU database server peaks at 61% CPU utilization during month-end activities, when there are 250 active concurrent OLTP users and 10 concurrent batch jobs.

Just to double-check her ratios, she plugged the current peak numbers into the ratio modeling equation. Here is the setup:

$$P = \frac{C_{oltp}}{R_{oltp}} + \frac{C_{batch}}{R_{batch}} = \frac{250}{125} + \frac{10}{1.35} = 2.00 + 7.41 = 9.41$$

$$P = UM; \quad U = \frac{P}{M} = \frac{9.41}{16} = 0.588 = 59\%$$

Annalisa observed a peak utilization of 61%, so a forecasted 59% utilization is very close, especially considering she used ratio modeling. If this validation did not check out (for example, the forecasted utilization was 70%), she would need to update her ratios.

Adding in the expected 25 additional OLTP users and the 2 additional batch jobs, she started with the core ratio modeling formula, and then solved for the utilization (U). Here's what she did:

$$UM = \frac{C_{oltp}}{R_{oltp}} + \frac{C_{batch}}{R_{batch}}$$

$$U = \frac{\frac{C_{oltp}}{R_{oltp}} + \frac{C_{batch}}{R_{batch}}}{M} = \frac{\frac{(250+25)}{125} + \frac{(10+2)}{1.35}}{16} = \frac{\frac{275}{125} + \frac{12}{1.35}}{16} = \frac{2.20 + 8.89}{16} = \frac{11.09}{16} = 0.693 = 69\%$$

With the current system peaking at 61% and the forecast calling for a 69% peak utilization, Annalisa knows the system's workload is starting to enter the elbow of the response time curve. With a forecasted peak utilization at 69%, she feels there is enough risk to justify performing a more precise forecast. So her work is just beginning.

Example 8-4. Performing a Vendor Sanity Check

Guido is a pre-sales associate for a large hardware vendor. Part of his responsibilities is to perform initial sizing assessments for prospective clients. During a conference call with the prospect, Guido recommended the prospect purchase the vendor's 18 CPU server. When the prospect's lead DBA, Willy, asked how Guido determined that 18 CPUs were required, Guido casually said that based on similar customers, the 18 CPU solution had worked very well. Guido thought he was safe, but then Willy asked how he characterized the workload. All Willy and his colleagues heard on the other end of the phone was the sound of papers being shuffled. Finally, Guido spoke. In a panicked voice, he said something like, "I can't seem to find the specifics." From there, it went downhill for Guido.

The reason Willy asked these questions was to ensure the vendor's recommendations were reasonable. Based on the company's expected workload and vendor's recommendations, Willy quickly performed a "sanity check" using ratio modeling. The question about characterizing the workload would also provide insights as to how well the vendor understood the prospect's expected application usage and how Guido performed his forecast. Willy quickly exposed that the vendor did a minimal sizing assessment simply to close the deal.

Here's what Willy did during the phone call. Willy's company expects there to be 2,250 concurrent OLTP users and 23 concurrent batch jobs. Using the highly optimistic ratios of 400 for the OLTP-to-CPU ratio and 4 for the batch-to-CPU ratio, Willy determined the number of CPUs required for the database server to run at 65% CPU utilization. Here's how he set up the problem.

$$P = \frac{C_{oltp}}{R_{oltp}} + \frac{C_{batch}}{R_{batch}} = \frac{2250}{300} + \frac{23}{4.00} = 7.50 + 5.75 = 13.25$$

That shows 13.25 CPUs at 100% utilization. To bring that down to a lower-risk utilization, like 65%, Willy did this:

$$M = \frac{P}{U} = \frac{13.25}{0.65} = 20.38$$

So using highly optimistic and aggressive ratios, at a forecasted CPU utilization of 65%, the forecast requires at least 21 CPUs. The vendor's recommendation of an 18 CPU box is clearly unrealistic.

When Guido said 18 CPUs were required, Willy quickly knew something was up. Perhaps Guido simply messed up. Perhaps the sales team wanted to close the deal and later "be surprised" at how poor the performance turned out to be. And, of course, the hardware vendor could then sell Willy's company more hardware (at a higher price). Or perhaps Guido performed a high-precision forecast and forgot to bring his notes. Regardless of what actually happened, Willy earned his pay that day and Guido will have to earn his!

These examples are just a small sampling of the many situations in which ratio modeling can be employed. Ratio modeling is so easy to use, so flexible, and so understandable that there is little reason not to be prepared with your production system's ratios. Since we do ratio modeling in our heads all the time anyway, we might as well have some real-life production ratios ready when needed.

Summary

I like to say that ratio modeling is a "poor man's" regression analysis. There is a lot of truth to this because regression analysis is similar in many ways. The benefit of ratio modeling over regression analysis is that it can be performed literally on the back of an envelope at a meeting or at lunch. The other benefit, as I hope the exercises demonstrated, is ratio modeling can be used in a wide variety of real-life situations. But, of course, there are many drawbacks to ratio modeling as well. Two important issues are the low precision and unvalidated forecasts. Another issue is that because of its simplicity, it can be easily misused to create overly optimistic forecasts. In my view, this is *the* risk when using ratio modeling. You'll do yourself, your group, and your IT department a favor by being very conservative.

However, with all the drawbacks, ratio modeling is an indispensable tool that every DBA and architect needs to be equipped to use. There are occasions when we simply must answer a capacity planning question without having the time to produce a more "respectable" forecast. When a quick, low-precision forecast is required, ratio modeling shines.

■ ■ ■
Linear Regression Modeling

When used appropriately, linear regression is a fantastic modeling technique. As with all regression analyses, the idea is to establish and enumerate the relationship of one or more independent values to a single dependent value. For example, we may want to investigate if there is a strong relationship between CPU utilization (the dependent value) and the number of orders entered per hour (the independent value). If the relationship is indeed linear and strong, we can forecast.

Linear regression is one of my personal favorites. It's a fantastic way to forecast because it pushes you to automate data collection and provides industry-accepted statistical validation. It can produce very precise forecasts and is very simple to use. While most forecasting mathematics is based around changing the physical hardware configuration, linear regression is typically used to determine how much of some *business activity* can occur before the existing system "runs out of gas." For example, suppose you have a production system and are asked to determine the maximum number of orders the system can be expected to process within a single hour. This is a perfect fit for linear regression.

Avoiding Nonlinear Areas

As with any forecast model, linear regression can be abused. This is one reason why it's not used or talked about much in the capacity planning community. The abuse is centered on two themes. One abuse occurs when applying linear regression to nonlinear areas, and we'll talk about that here. The other is failing to methodically determine and establish if an appropriate relationship exists between the dependent and independent variables, which we'll look at in the next section.

Everyone knows performance is not linear. So it follows that forecasting in the nonlinear areas is inappropriate. This calls for self-control. You simply cannot push the envelope with linear regression, or your forecasts will certainly be too aggressive and overly optimistic.

If you want to forecast in the nonlinear areas, nonlinear regression analysis is a possibility, but be very careful. An assumption is being made that application activity will follow a simple nonlinear pattern that the regression formula will capture (model). This could be true, but there is a high probability it is not true. Personally, I never forecast in the nonlinear areas when using regression analysis and therefore have no need to use nonlinear regression. This low-risk posture has served me well over the years.

Take a look at Figure 9-1. Linear regression will always determine a linear equation, and the resulting line can be seen easily. However, when the number of orders per hour increases, as does the CPU utilization, CPU queuing eventually sets in, and the number of orders per hour cannot remain linear. The area above the dashed line (area A) would be an inappropriate and irresponsible area to forecast. When dealing with CPU subsystems, as we know from queuing theory and practical experience, once the CPU utilization reaches around 75%, queuing becomes significant and the relationship is clearly not linear.

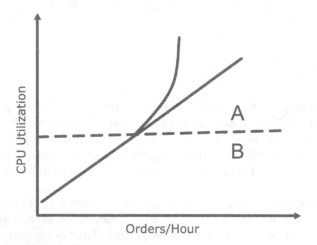

Figure 9-1. *Linear regression works wonderfully until the linear relationship breaks down. In the area below the dashed line (B), the relationship is linear, but in the area above the dashed line, (A) the relationship is nonlinear.*

The solution is to never forecast in the nonlinear areas, and to reduce the effect of the nonlinear behavior, remove the nonlinear-related samples (as described in the "Dealing with Outliers" section later in the chapter). Again, as a general rule of thumb, for CPU subsystems, the danger area lies above 75% utilization. For modern IO subsystems, the danger area is above 65% utilization.

Finding the Relationships

Linear regression is all about relationships. The trick with successfully using linear regression is to quickly discover strong and useful relationships.

First, find a business relationship between the study question and one or more key business functions. Second, the key business functions must have an established linear relationship with an operating system resource (like the CPU subsystem).

For example, suppose the study question is, "Can the system handle 25% growth?" Suppose we are focusing on the CPU subsystem and growth can be expressed as a 25% increase in customer calls, orders taken, order lines, and orders shipped. Now we must establish if there is a strong linear relationship between one or more of these key business activities and the CPU subsystem. If we can establish the strong link between the study question and a key business activity, and then also establish a strong linear relationship between a key business activity and CPU utilization, we can forecast using linear regression. As you might imagine, establishing these relationships can be difficult.

Sometimes there is another business-related step involved. Suppose the study question is "If the business grows 25%, will the database server response time significantly increase?" The next question is to determine what a 25% increase in business growth means to the company. For example, it could mean a 25% stock price increase or a 25% revenue increase. Once this question is answered, then we must determine how that relates to business activity. For example, if a 25% business growth means a 25% revenue increase, then we must ruminate about the business activities that clearly relate to revenue. After some brainstorming, the possibilities could include the number of invoices entered, orders entered, orders shipped, and so on. The final step is to determine if there is a strong linear relationship between any of these business activities and, for example, CPU utilization.

Establishing these relationships can be very difficult, and at times, extremely frustrating. To help work through this process, break the process into four distinct steps:

1. Determine the study question.

2. Define how the study question relates to the business.

3. Brainstorm many possible business activities or functions that relate directly to the business.

4. Determine if a strong linear relationship exists between any of the business activities and, for example, CPU utilization.

Example 9-1 shows how this four-step process might work in a real production environment. Notice the brainstorming step (sometimes called *discovery*) is key to this entire process.

Example 9-1. Relationship Brainstorming

William is a database administrator who is responsible for routinely analyzing the risk of the CPU subsystem "running out of gas" three to six months into the future. William checked with the planning department and learned that the business is expected to grow about 15% each quarter for the next year.

Since this analysis does not entail physically changing the computing architecture or the hardware configuration, but directly relates to business activities, William is thinking linear regression may be a good modeling possibility. But before linear regression can be used, he needs to establish relationships between the study question, the business activities, and the CPU subsystem. Following the four-step process, here is how William worked through the process:

- **Determine the study question.** The study question is very straightforward: "What is the risk of the CPU subsystem becoming overutilized in three to six months?" This is a relatively technical study question. In this case, it works fine because the focus is on the CPU subsystem. But in many cases, a better study question could be, "Can the system sustain our business over the next three to six months?"

- **Define how the study question relates to the business.** Talking with the planning department, William found management looks at business growth in terms of sales revenue. After discussing the study question with representatives from management, application users, and technical leads, a more business-centric study question becomes, "What is the risk of the CPU subsystem becoming overutilized when the revenue increases 15% to 30%?"

- **Brainstorm possible business activities that relate directly to the business.** To begin the independent value(s) discovery process, William called a meeting. He asked for two representatives from the technical team and also two representatives from the application team. The group brainstormed and bounced ideas off each other about what business activities or processes related closely to revenue. After a lively discussion, they came up with customer calls, orders taken, order lines, order amount, average line item amount, and orders shipped.

- **Determine if a strong linear relationship exists between any of the business activities and CPU utilization.** Next comes the process of establishing the strength of the linear relationship between the business activities and CPU utilization. If a strong linear relationship is confirmed, then William can do the forecasts.

Brainstorming, which tends to generate potentially good predictors of system processes related to the study question, and analyzing the potential predictors can be very frustrating. Initially, the frustration occurs because so much time can be spent brainstorming potential independent variables. No one really knows which one or ones will be good predictors. So there is tension between, "We have enough candidate independent variables, so let's move on!" and "We don't want to go through this process again, so let's come up with some more possibilities." No one wants to start another round of discovery meetings after the analysis did not yield any good independent variables.

The other question lurking in the back of everyone's mind is, "What if we cannot find a good predictor that relates to the study question?" This is entirely possible, and you won't know if this is the case until you go through the entire analysis process. This is why it is good to come up with a dozen or so candidate independent variables. Usually, at least one will provide adequate precision.

I don't want to discourage you from trying regression analysis, but there will be times when you just can't find a good predictor. When this happens, you'll need to use a different modeling technique. This isn't unique to linear regression though. Every time you embark on a forecasting project, you don't know what the precision will be until the validation occurs. And as you know, the validation doesn't occur until after a significant amount of time has already been expended. I think the frustration occurs with linear regression because, until you are proficient at quickly finding good predictors, the process can be somewhat overwhelming.

The process of quickly finding good predictors is important. Once potential independent variables have been decided, the data collected, and finally placed into a spreadsheet, your speed at quickly determining the relationships between the dependent variable (for example, CPU utilization) and one or more independent variables (for example, invoices entered per hour) will make all the difference. If you use a good linear regression spreadsheet (such as the linear regression analysis template available for free from OraPub at www.orapub.com/tools), after a few cycles, you will become familiar with the process, and each cycle will go very quickly.

While quickly determining if an independent variable is a good predictor is important, rushing through the process can introduce errors. Staring at a spreadsheet for hours and repeatedly performing the same steps will cause anyone to make mistakes. I always recommend that people have a colleague check their work. To review the work, simply repeat the same linear-relationship-determining steps presented in the next section. As you'll learn, the review process can be performed very quickly, and will add a deep level of confidence in your work.

Determining a Linear Relationship

Speed and quality are essential in determining a linear relationship. As with most things in life, a desire to move quickly can result in errors. The way to mitigate this risk is to follow a practical methodology. Over the years, I have settled on a seven-step methodology, which has proven invaluable. Since the trick to linear regression is discovering and enumerating a strong linear relationship, all but the last step focus directly on ensuring the relationship is appropriate.

While the number of steps may seem excessive, forecasting using a weak relationship will typically provide a very optimistic forecast, which could be disastrous to your credibility and the future stability of the system being analyzed. And besides, once you get used to the process, it can be performed confidently and effectively in minutes.

The method relies on visual and mathematical analysis. You'll quickly discover that relying completely on mathematical analysis is incomplete. The mathematics may indicate a very strong linear relationship, while the other steps clearly show the relationship to be otherwise. If you are a "math person," this may come as a shock. But relying completely on the math results gives you an incomplete analysis. Sometimes we can visually detect a nonlinear relationship that the numerical analysis did not detect.

Here is a brief outline of the seven-step method:

1. View the raw data. Look for obvious numeric problems.

2. View the raw data graph. Look for outliers, nonlinearity, and a weak linear relationship.

3. View the residual data. Look for obvious numeric problems.

4. View the residual data graph. Look for patterns indicating nonlinearity.

5. View the regression formula. Quickly check the formula to ensure it makes sense.

6. View the correlation strength. Check the strength of the linear relationship to ensure it is strong enough to be useful.

7. If everything is OK, then forecast. If all the six previous steps are OK, then the relationship is indeed a strong linear relationship, and you can do the forecast.

To summarize, the first two steps focus on the raw data. The next two steps focus on what is known as residual data. And then the next two steps focus on the mathematics. If all six steps show a strong linear relationship, you can feel confident with proceeding to the final step: forecasting!

Now we'll walk through each step in the method.

View the Raw Data

The first step to ensuring a strong linear relationship is a thorough visual inspection. Numerical analysis is great, but your eyes can easily and quickly spot bad, strange, and just plain unusual data.

If an inappropriate value is discovered, it should be removed. But you should never indiscriminately remove data. Document the data removed, and if possible, understand how the data occurred. While a few bogus data points are typical of a dynamic Oracle system, a significant number (say, more than 5%) or a pattern of bogus data is an indication of a faulty data collection system.

Take a look at Table 9-1, which shows some samples gathered from a real production Oracle site. Of the total 61 samples, the first 17 are shown in the table.

Table 9-1. *Partial List of Gathered Samples*

Sample	CPU Util %	Order/Hr
1	15	71.00
2	27	159.00
3	28	167.00
4	–3	157.00
5	31	188.00
6	30	192.00
7	32	198.00
8	40	266.00
9	44	309.00
10	43	316.00
11	49	377.00
12	110	210.00
13	53	386.00
14	21	74.00
15	13	20.00
16	64	2431.00
17	16	19.00

In the data shown in Table 9-1, we can spot three data errors:

- Notice sample 4 has a CPU utilization of –3%! Whoops. The data obviously is incorrect, so remove it. But you may want to find out how it was possible that a CPU utilization sample of –3 was collected.

- Sample 12 has a CPU utilization of 110%. This is a little more difficult to visually spot. However, being in IT, we should know that triple-digit CPU utilization numbers (other than 100%) can't occur. Just as with sample 4, the data is obviously incorrect, so remove it and determine why and how the sample could have been gathered.

- Sample 16 is a little trickier. This data point could be possible, but it is much higher than the others, so it should catch our attention. When a number like this is discovered, do not immediately remove it. Double-check the number. For example, in this case we could probably run a SQL query to verify the number, ask end users if it's possible to enter nearly 2,500 orders in a single hour, or check with a business manager about the unusual amount of order activity. If the data is confirmed, it should probably stay (outliers are discussed later in the chapter). However, if you discover it's bogus, understand how it was collected and then remove it.

It is rare, but if enough visual data errors are discovered, the entire data set may have to be scrapped. If this occurs, it is likely the core data collection process is flawed.

Once the sample data has been visually inspected, the bogus samples removed (and noted), and a consensus is reached to move forward, it's time to plot and view the graph.

View the Raw Data Graph

Plotting and viewing the sample data is a very common linear regression analysis step. But do not rely just on this step. Ensure all the other steps are also followed. Sometimes what appears to be a linear relationship will be proved to be otherwise. If more than a single independent variable is involved, then a simple two-dimensional graph is not possible. You could create a fancy three-dimensional graph, but I would just skip this step and move directly to the residual steps.

For example, suppose you are trying to predict the maximum sustained IO throughput using web hits per hour and concurrent batch jobs. Those are two independent variables (web hits and batch jobs), so a simple two-dimensional graph is not possible.

Continuing with the example presented in Table 9-1, Figure 9-2 contains all 61 samples. The data appears to be fairly linear. But notice that there is a slight oscillation above and below the line. This is OK, since the samples wrap around the linear line.

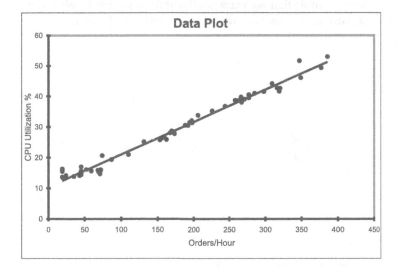

Figure 9-2. *With all samples plotted, our eyes can be very effective in spotting nonlinearity.*

Another common relationship is shown in Figure 9-3. Clearly, considering all samples, the relationship between CPU utilization and orders per hour is not linear. But the data is also not surprising. As we would expect, when there are fewer orders, there may significant initial overhead creating an initial surge in CPU utilization. But once the order rate increases, the system settles down and a linear relationship is established. A solution to this seemingly nonlinear relationship is to remove the initial nonlinear lines.

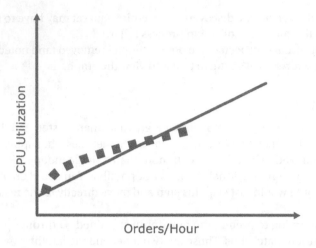

Figure 9-3. *The actual data point trend implies the system can indefinitely increase the number of orders each hour without increasing CPU utilization. This is not possible. However, by scrubbing the data, a linear relationship may be found.*

Figure 9-4 shows another example that is clearly nonlinear from start to finish and very strange indeed. If you see a pattern like this, start working on another independent variable, because this one is not going to make it!

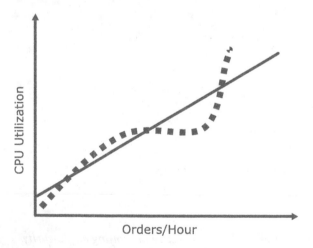

Figure 9-4. *A clear nonlinear relationshp between CPU utilization and orders per hour*

If after plotting and viewing the sample data, the relationship appears to be linear, then continue with the residual analysis.

View the Residual Data

It shouldn't surprise you that forecasts are not perfect. Analyzing this imperfection is a powerful data analysis technique. The difference between the forecasted value and the actual historical data value is the forecast error.

For example, if the actual CPU utilization is 65% but the regression formula forecasted the CPU utilization to be 68%, there is a difference of 3%. This 3% difference is commonly called the *residual*, or simply the *error*.

I have found residual analysis to be one of the most simple, powerful, and versatile data analysis techniques available. If you are not familiar with residual analysis, pay close attention. I think you'll discover it can be extremely useful.

Residual analysis can be used to spot nonlinearity that our simple data plots can't easily capture, and even more shocking, that regression mathematics (that is, the correlation coefficient) also may not capture. In addition, residual analysis is commonly used when validating and determining forecast model precision.

Table 9-2 is a partial residual display of our sample data. Scan both the residual and the residual squared. Because the residual squared will result only in ballooned positive numbers, the error is more easily distinguishable. For example, sample 48 has a residual of 4.5, which may not seem all that bad. But a residual squared of 20.3 stands out and is easily seen. In fact, sample 48 may be considered an outlier and removed! As you'll see in the upcoming "Dealing with Outliers" section, the residual squared is one of the easiest ways to spot outliers.

Table 9-2. *Partial Residual Display of Sample Data*

Sample	CPU Util %	Orders/Hr	Predicted CPU Util %	Residual	Residual Squared
1	15	71.00	17.9	–3.2	10.3
2	27	159.00	27.2	–0.5	0.3
3	28	167.00	28.1	0.0	0.0
4	31	188.00	30.3	0.2	0.0
5	30	192.00	30.7	–0.2	0.1
6	32	198.00	31.4	0.2	0.0
7	40	266.00	38.6	1.2	1.4
8	44	309.00	43.1	1.0	1.1
9	43	316.00	43.9	–1.1	1.3
...	...	...	...	...	...
48	52	347.00	47.1	4.5	20.3
...	...	...	...	...	...
Sum				**0.0**	
Avg.	27.6	162.6	27.6	0.0	2.4

Most regression systems determine the best linear line by iteratively changing the line's equation until the sum of all the residuals equals zero. This means there will be just as much error above the linear line (positive residuals) as there is below the line (negative residuals). We can use this fact to ensure all of our data points are actually being included in the regression mathematics. If some of our data points are not being considered when the regression formula is created then the sum of the residuals will not equal to zero. This is a problem.

Here's an example of how this can happen. Suppose rows 85 thru 89 are appended to a spreadsheet, yet the regression formula considers only rows 1 through 84! The spreadsheet may look like the additional lines are being considered. However, this may not be the case. To reduce the chances of this occurring, in OraPub's linear regression spreadsheets, the number of data points is always shown on the Analysis worksheet, and the sum of the residuals (which should always equal zero) is shown at the bottom of the Data worksheet. The sum line in Table 9-2 is an example of this and indicates that the sum of all the residuals is zero. If this is not the case, then one or more of the samples are not being included when the spreadsheet program (for example, Microsoft Excel) determines the best-fit regression formula. If the sum of the residuals is not zero, then an investigation to fix the problem must occur before continuing.

Once the residuals have been calculated and visually reviewed, it's time to perform a graphical residual analysis.

View the Residual Data Graph

Another approach to discovering the error of a forecast is by plotting the residuals in a residual graph. A residual graph has the horizontal axis set to the predicted values and the vertical axis set to the residual values. The end result is a visual of the error. While viewing residual values is an important aspect of our methodology, plotting the residuals is where the value is quickly realized. The residual graph flattens the linear line and visually stretches the residual values— that is, the error. With this effect, our eyes are less likely to be fooled into thinking the relationships are linear.

In a way, the residual plot is more important than the data plot! Because residuals are simply the predicted value minus the actual value, they can be two-dimensionally plotted, regardless of the number of independent values. For example, if we are investigating the relationship of the combination of orders per hour and concurrent batch jobs to CPU utilization, we can create a simple graph displaying the residuals.

Figure 9-5 shows a residual plot using the sample data from Table 9-2. Earlier, Figure 9-2 showed the data wasn't perfectly linear but oscillated around the linear line. The residual analysis took the residual (the error), and effectively stretched it out so now it can be easily seen. If you are following the residual plot trend, you can see this cyclical nonlinearity.

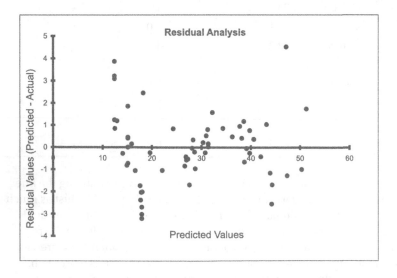

Figure 9-5. *The residual plot is a powerful tool to spot nonlinearity.*

Using residual analysis, a dangerous nonlinear pattern can be seen when there is a single swoop of the data. By *dangerous*, I mean the independent variable(s) should not be used for prediction, even if the other steps pass with flying colors. Notice that the residual data graph in Figure 9-5 has multiple swoops. This is fine, because the data cycles back toward the zero line.

Now look at Figure 9-6, which shows another example of a residual plot (using different real-life data). You can see that the data does not swoop back to the centerline, indicating an unsatisfactory relationship. Notice the data starts at the upper left and trends down to the bottom right. A residual plot that indicates a satisfactory relationship will either have a pattern that *repeatedly* swoops back toward the centerline (for example, in Figure 9-5) or have a horizontally rectangular shape, as shown in Figure 9-7.

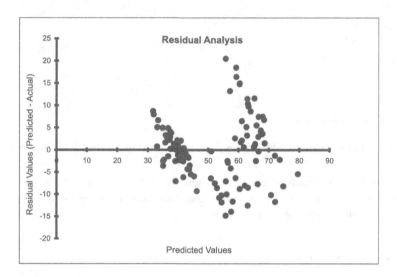

Figure 9-6. *Notice the pattern from upper left to bottom right. This is a classic nonlinear residual pattern indicating it would be unwise to forecast using this data.*

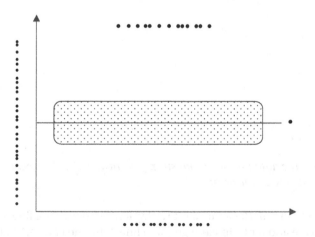

Figure 9-7. *This is what we are hoping to see: a consistently horizontal band that is tightly wrapped around the centerline.*

Let's look at a few more problematic residual plots. Figure 9-8 shows a common nonlinear pattern where the data flows from one corner of the graph to the other. Consider the residual analysis a "no-go" when you see this pattern.

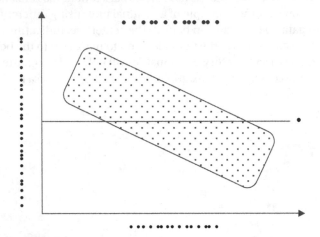

Figure 9-8. *A nonlinear pattern where the data flows from one corner of the graph to the other.*

Figure 9-9 shows another very common pattern, where the data plot starts out steeply vertical below the linear line, turns horizontal, and crosses the linear line again. Clearly, forecasting with this residual pattern would be irresponsible.

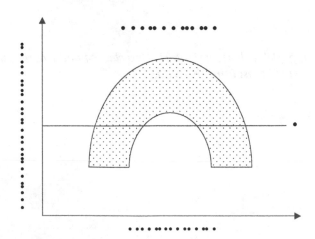

Figure 9-9. *A common pattern where the data plot starts out steeply vertical below the linear line, turns horizontal, and crosses the linear line again.*

The type of pattern shown in Figure 9-10 can be a bit tricky. Remember that a linear regression program will always create and plot a linear regression line. It has no choice! While there is no swoop or nonlinear pattern, there is also no obvious linear pattern. It's like the linear line could go in any direction through the data! Fortunately, the numerical analysis will show a low correlation, indicating the formula is not to be used for forecasting.

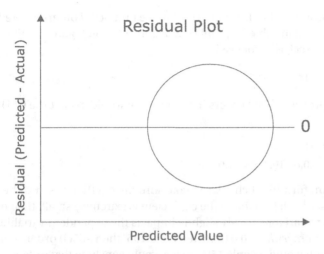

Figure 9-10. *Although there is a linear line, there is no obvious linear pattern.*

I hope you see residual analysis is fast, easy, and extremely useful. I stumbled upon it one day while browsing in a bookstore, and it has proven useful year after year![1] Once the residual analysis is complete, it's time to move on and look closely at the mathematics.

View the Regression Formula

By the time you get to look at the regression formula, you probably will be able to guess if a strong linear relationship exists, but you might be surprised. Sometimes the data looks good, but the math says "NO!" This can happen when the residual plot looks somewhat like Figure 9-10, but is horizontally stretched, disguising a large data variance.

You might wonder why I don't look at the mathematics first. Well, I'm human, and if the math looks good, it will influence me and I'll tend to think the data and residual analysis look better than they really are. I'm much more objective if I can view the data and visuals first, and then finally look at the mathematics. In fact, I try to guess the correlation coefficient (discussed in the next section) before I actually take a look at the mathematical results!

The regression formula is actually quite simple. Here's an example of the general single independent value regression formula:

$$y = m_1 x_1 + b$$

And here's the multiple regression formula.

$$y = m_1 x_1 + ... + m_n x_n + b$$

---

1. A wonderful regression analysis book is entitled *Regression Analysis by Example*, by Samprit Chatterjee and Ali S. Hadi (Wiley, 2006).

Suppose we are trying to forecast CPU utilization based on the number of orders entered per hour. Using the actual data shown in Table 9-1, Table 9-2, Figure 9-2, and Figure 9-3, the regression formula, as derived by Excel, is as follows:

$$CPU\% = 0.106 * orders/hr + 10.414$$

For example, if the system processed 200 orders in an hour, we would expect the CPU utilization to be around 31%.

$$CPU\% = 0.106 * orders/hr + 10.414$$
$$CPU\% = 0.106 * 200 + 10.414 = 20.6 + 10.414 = 31.01\%$$

When I review the regression formula, I check to make sure the coefficients and the y-intercept (that is, *b*) make sense. You'll find that if the coefficient is extremely small, then no matter the size of the independent variable, it only slightly impacts the dependent variable. For example, if the coefficient for *orders/hr* is 0.010 instead of 0.106, then at 500 orders per hour, the forecasted CPU utilization would be only 15%. So we would conclude that orders do not have a large influence on the CPU utilization and therefore are not a very good predictor. I have also seen situations where, according to the regression formula, increasing the number of orders per hour *decreases* CPU utilization! So just by making a few quick checks, you can determine if there is a significant problem with using the formula.

Regression mathematics can also determine a confidence interval for a given confidence level! This provides another usability test. As discussed in Chapter 4, an average by itself does not communicate nearly enough information. We need to understand *dispersion*; that is, the plus and minus at a given percentage. With the preceding CPU utilization forecast formula, Excel calculated the confidence interval to be ±2.02 at a 90% confidence level. This means, according to the regression mathematics, if the system is processing 200 orders per hour, we can expect the average CPU utilization to be 31.01%, ±2.0%, 90% of the time.

I can look back and laugh now, but while trying desperately to find a good CPU utilization predictor, I've seen at a 90% confidence level, a utilization confidence interval was ±30%! So if the CPU utilization forecast is 40%, then 90% of the time I can expect the actual CPU utilization to be between 10% and 75%. Or the times when I've wanted to forecast megabytes of IO per second and the regression formula indicated an IO device could provide an average IO throughput of 12 MB/s ±10MB, 90% of the time! It sounds funny now, but at the time it was very disappointing.

Once the regression formula and the confidence level/interval have been reviewed, it's time to check how mathematically strong the relationship is between the dependent variable and the independent variable(s).

View the Correlation Strength

The correlation strength is a measure of how strong the relationship is between the dependent variable and the independent variable(s). It is one of the most important aspects in determining if a strong linear relationship exists. Of course, the previous steps must indicate a strong linear relationship as well, but even if they do, if the correlation strength does not indicate a strong relationship, then we can't responsibly forecast.

The statistic for correlation strength is called the *correlation coefficient* and is symbolized by a lowercase *r*. The larger the absolute value of *r*, the stronger the correlation. The correlation coefficient can range from a –1 to a +1. The sign designates the correlation direction. For example, a positive correlation indicates an increase in the dependent variable will cause an increase in the independent variable. A correlation coefficient of –0.8 is just as strong as a +0.8. Remember that the absolute value is what matters.

Sure, a correlation of 1.0 is good and 0.0 is bad, but it's difficult to find a published statistical reference for the in-between values. Table 9-3 is taken from Derek Rowntree's *Statistics Without Tears* (Allyn & Bacon, 2003). Personally, unless the correlation coefficient is at least 0.70, I won't use the regression formula to forecast.

Table 9-3. *A Practical Interpretation of the Correlation Coefficent Strength*

Correlation Coefficient (*r*)	Practical Meaning
0.0 to 0.2	Very weak, negligible
0.2 to 0.4	Weak, low
0.4 to 0.7	Moderate
0.7 to 0.9	Strong, high, marked
0.9 to 1.0	Very strong, very high

To most people, the correlation coefficient is just a number. But it is immensely practical and can be used to increase communication and understanding about a forecast's precision. The square of the correlation coefficient (that is, r^2) indicates how much the independent variables explain the dependent variable's output. For example, if r^2 is 0.64, we can say that 64% of the dependent data (for example, CPU utilization) can be explained by the independent variables (for example, *orders/hr*). This is why a seemingly high correlation coefficient of 0.8 (that is, $r^2 = 0.64$) in reality leaves a lot to be desired. So while we can explain 64% of the dependent variable, the remaining 36% is not attributed to our independent variables, but to some other variable(s). This is why we want the highest correlation coefficient possible.

A correlation coefficient of only 0.70 may seem easy to come upon, but you might be surprised just how difficult it can be to find a strong numeric correlation. One way to responsibly increase the correlation is to responsibly remove outliers, as they tend to skew the regression line and reduce precision. (Removing outliers is addressed soon, right after the final step in the methodology.)

If our data has passed all six steps, we're ready to forecast! Some people may feel that these six steps are overly burdensome, but I hope you can appreciate the risk you will take by forecasting using a weak linear relationship. It is always best to be conservative and perform a thorough and methodical analysis.

If Everything Is OK, Forecast

If you've made it this far, it's truly time to celebrate! Finding a strong and useful linear relationship can be a long process, but the rewards can last the life of the application. You will find that once you have discovered a good linear relationship, it can be repeatedly used. So while the up-front work can take a while and be frustrating, the payoff continues year after year.

While the process of forecasting using linear regression is very simple, restraint must be exercised. Just because the formula says the system can process 50,000 orders each minute at 250% average CPU utilization does not mean it's going to happen! Remember way back to Figure 9-1? Queuing happens. As a result, I never, ever forecast letting the CPU utilization exceed 75%, and for IO subsystems, never, ever over 65% utilization. For older IO subsystems, without the large caches and advanced optimization algorithms, the limit is around 35% utilization.

The reason for the difference between CPU and IO utilization limits is that queuing immediately sets in with an IO subsystem (one queue for each server), whereas with CPU subsystems (one queue for all servers), queuing does not become significant until the mid-70%. If you look back to Chapter 5, you can use Figure 5-20 and Figure 5-30 as examples to support this assertion.

Before I take you through a few case studies, a discussion about outliers is necessary. Outliers can be troublesome, but they also present us with an opportunity to increase forecast precision.

Dealing with Outliers

Outliers are those nagging data points that don't flow with the main data trend. While irritating at times, investigating outliers and seemingly odd behavior is what leads to scientific discoveries. In the scientific community, removing outliers is a very, very serious matter. While I take forecasting seriously, I also am not hoping for a Nobel Prize! So I'm much more likely to remove a bunch of outliers that are clearly skewing the regression line.

While I routinely remove outliers, I also document what is removed. Do not remove data points without documentation. And never try to hide the fact that data points were removed. You've got to ask yourself, "Can I stand up in front of a group of people and justify removing these data points?" If the answer is a confident yes, then go ahead and remove the points. But remember to document their removal, because you will surely be asked about outliers later. The outlier removal process I'll present makes it very easy to document and explain outlier removal.

In an active production Oracle system, outliers can be caused by a number of things, such as backups, large file copies, and any upgrade or patch process. Think of any process that is not part of the standard workload and you have an outlier-causing candidate. You can argue that these are part of the normal workload and therefore are not true outliers. However, outliers can significantly skew linear regression formulas and cause the resulting forecasts to be less precise.

Without a doubt, outliers skew data, forcing a sometimes obviously less useful linear formula. Take a close look at Figure 9-11. You'll notice the regression line does not follow the main data trend. This is because the outliers must be mathematically accounted for and therefore essentially *pull* the linear line toward themselves. In fact, the initial correlation coefficient is only 0.47. Figure 9-12 is the same data set, but with the outliers removed![2] Not only is the linear line following the data trend, the correlation coefficient is an amazing 0.94.

---

2. If you look at the vertical axes in Figures 9-11 and 9-12 you'll notice that Excel changed the scale. If the vertical axes were set to be the same (which can be done), then either Figure 9-11 would be ten times taller or Figure 9-12 would occupy a small fraction of the graph's space. The point I'm trying to make is that with the outliers removed, the linear behavior is now both visually and numerically evident.

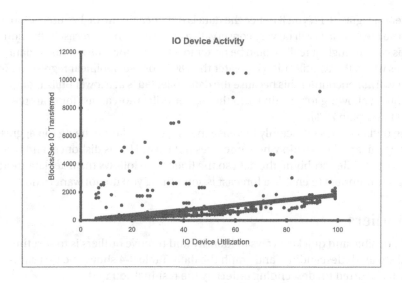

Figure 9-11. *Notice how the outliers are essentially pulling the linear regression line up and away from the main data set.*

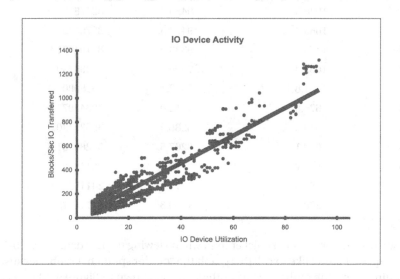

Figure 9-12. *With the outliers removed, the linear regression line is much more in line with the data.*

If you look closely at Figure 9-12, you'll notice the data is not linear at the higher utilization, but that is OK, because the forecasts will be very conservative and we will not forecast in the non-linear portion. In this case, though, it really would be better to either remove the nonlinear data (for example, samples where the IO utilization is greater than 80%) or use nonlinear regression. In most situations, you will *not* encounter this because the data collected is at a lower utilization (for example, less than 50%), allowing forecasting into the higher utilization areas (for example, greater than 50% yet lower than 75%).

While removing outliers can significantly increase the linear correlation, being too aggressive can force a strong linear relationship where one does not exist. That is dishonest and will result in bogus forecasts. While scrubbing the data so the linear line follows the true data trend is reasonable, fixing the numbers to enable a forecast is something you do not want to do.

Identifying Outliers

One of the most responsible and quickest ways to identify and remove outliers is to sort the data by the residual squared (descending) and graph the data. Table 9-4 shows the first samples used in Figure 9-11, sorted (in descending order) by the residual squared.

Table 9-4. *First Rows After Sorting by Residual Squared, Descending*

Blks/Sec	IO Util %	Predicted Blks/Sec	Residual	Residual Squared
10485.6	57	1026.3	9459.3	89478385.9
10485.6	59	1063.3	9422.3	88780239.8
10488.7	64	1155.7	9333.0	87104691.9
8763.0	59	1063.3	7699.7	59285790.7
9193.9	93	1691.8	7502.1	56280807.4
6987.0	38	675.0	6312.0	39840877.0
6906.5	35	619.6	6286.9	39525430.3
6905.6	36	638.1	6267.5	39282031.3
5548.4	25	434.7	5113.7	26149925.6
5197.8	17	286.8	4911.0	24117914.6
4928.6	16	268.3	4660.3	21718273.0

Our eyes can visually spot trends much quicker than when viewing the raw data. Figure 9-13 is the initial residual-squared plot. I like to call this graph the "outlier spotlight graph" because it shines a spotlight directly on the outliers. The spotlight graph shown in Figure 9-13 is very typical for the first round of identifying and removing outliers. Most of the data points are squished at the bottom of the graph, but the outliers are clearly shown on the far left. When removing outliers, I am careful not to remove data from the main trend. By focusing on the data with relatively massive residual-squared values, I reduce the risk of removing the core trend data.

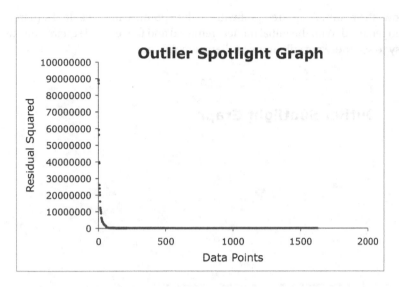

Figure 9-13. *The initial residual-squared plot based on data from Figure 9-11*

Looking closely at Figure 9-13, suppose a decision was made to remove all the samples with a residual squared larger than 20 million. With those samples removed, the correlation coefficient increased from 0.47 to 0.63. The resulting data plot is shown in Figure 9-14.

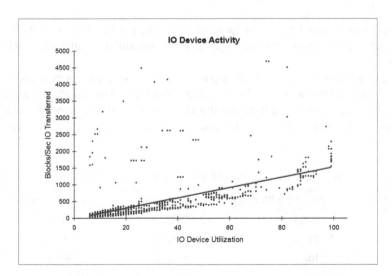

Figure 9-14. *The data plot with samples having a residual-squared value great than 20 million removed*

Compare the original data plot (Figure 9-11) to the initially scrubbed data plot (Figure 9-14). Figure 9-14 looks better, but we can still clearly see many outliers and also that the linear regression line is being pulled up toward those outliers. This is an indicator that we need to repeat the process to identify and remove (once again) additional outliers.

Figure 9-15 shows the residual-squared plot with all data points with a residual squared of larger than 20 million removed. With the initial outliers removed and the residual squared plotted once again, it is easy to see there are still many outliers remaining.

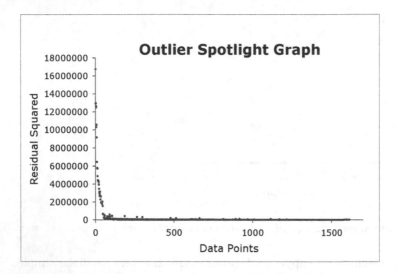

Figure 9-15. *Modifed residual-squared plot based on data from Figure 9-11 but with samples removed if their residual-squared values are greater than 20 million*

As you repeat this process, look for gaps in the residual-squared values. For example, in Figure 9-15, there is a clear gap between the main trending data set and the outliers just below a residual squared of 2 million.

Looking for residual-squared gaps is typically a good method to separate the outliers from the main data. Table 9-5 provides a subset of the actual samples around the residual-squared 2 million value. Notice the significant gap between the 1553110.0 and the 679876.8 residual-squared values. This is a natural break between the outliers and what appears to be the main data trend.

Table 9-5. *Rows Sorted by the Residual Squared, Descending, Centered Around 2M Residual Squared*

Blks/Sec	IO Util %	Predicted Blks/Sec	Residual	Residual Squared
1725.8	24	362.1	1363.7	1859694.3
1725.7	26	393.1	1332.6	1775812.1
1726.9	27	408.6	1318.3	1737891.1
2740.2	97	1494.0	1246.2	1553110.0
1062.6	16	238.1	824.5	679876.8
1062.6	16	238.1	824.5	679876.8
1062.1	16	238.1	824.0	679052.5
919.5	10	145.0	774.5	599814.0
919.5	10	145.0	774.5	599814.0

With the samples having a residual squared of greater than 1.5 million removed, the data is plotted once again, as shown in Figure 9-16.

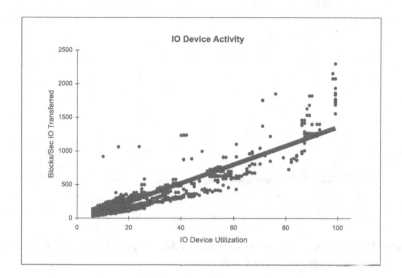

Figure 9-16. *The data plot with samples removed having a residual-squared value great than 1.5 million*

Not only does the linear regression line better follow the main data trend, but the correlation coefficient has now increased to 0.90. But notice there are still some points that are outside the main bulk of data. At this point, a delicate team decision must be made to either stop the outlier removal process or repeat the cycle again.

Determining When to Stop

One of the key factors in determining when to stop removing outliers is knowing which forecasts will be performed. The data set used in our examples was based on a relatively old IO subsystem where significant queuing occurs when the utilization reaches only 35%. Looking closely at Figure 9-16, while the linear regression line passes close to the center of the main data trend at 35% utilization, it's not perfect. This is a sign that it is OK to remove additional data points.

In fact, the team did decide to continue. After one or two more cycles, it was agreed to remove data points with a residual squared greater than 85000. The resulting correlation coefficient was 0.94. The outlier spotlight graph is shown in Figure 9-17, the residual graph is shown in Figure 9-18, and the final data plot is shown earlier in Figure 9-12.

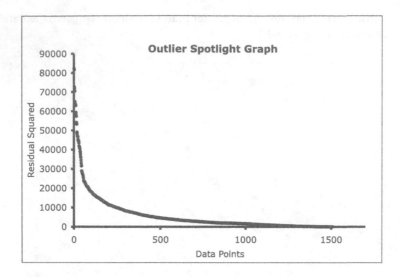

Figure 9-17. *The modifed residual-squared plot based on data from Figure 9-11 but with samples with their residual-squared values greater than 85000 removed*

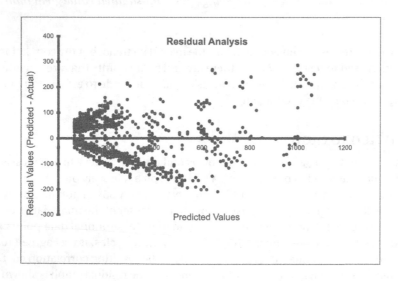

Figure 9-18. *The residual graph after samples have been removed that had a residual-squared value great than 85000*

It's worth mentioning this unique residual analysis data spread. It's like someone is spraying water! Notice how the residual line goes nearly straight through the middle of the residual data and there is no alarming trend. This residual trend is similar to the trend shown in Figure 9-7. However, the graph in Figure 9-18 has a group of data points in the upper-right corner that are not balanced out by a group in the lower-right corner. But this is not alarming enough to disqualify forecasting, especially considering the quality of both the correlation coefficient and the data plot.

Removing outliers has always been a controversial topic. I find that mathematical purists tend to wince even at the discussion. However, after realizing how outliers clearly skew the linear regression line, reduce the correlation coefficient, and prohibit the use of a truly good set of data, even purists seem to relax a bit. When faced with the daunting task of forecasting Oracle performance, this kind of elitist attitude quickly fades. But please don't misunderstand me. I am not recommending a free-for-all sample data removal to fit my purposes.

Outlier removal must be methodical, documented, and decided upon in a team environment. Be prepared to confidently present why you removed data points. If you cannot do this, then the data points should probably remain.

Regression Analysis Case Studies

I have found the best way to teach people how to use linear regression is for them to view many actual data sets. The next best thing is to review case studies. Examples 9-2 and 9-3 are such case studies, which I hope will pull together all that has been presented so far and will leave you with the confidence to effectively use linear regression.

Example 9-2. Analyzing Memory Utilization vs. Forms Sessions

Otto is responsible for ensuring the forms server has adequate memory. Every quarter, he has the opportunity to present requests for additional memory to his management. When he stands in front of management, he wants to know that he has done his homework and is thoroughly prepared.

The study question is quite straightforward: "Will the forms server have enough memory to support the expected growth over the next six months?" Otto has been gathering forms session activity for quite some time and also knows who to talk to about user growth. After performing some basic trend analysis and consulting with the business managers, everyone felt comfortable that the number of forms sessions would not exceed 600 within the next six months. To account for unexpected bursts of required memory, Otto will limit the forecasted memory utilization to a maximum of 85%. Otto converted the initial study question into a more technical question, "Can the forms server support 600 concurrent forms sessions while keeping memory utilization at or below 85%?"

While Otto has literally thousands of data points, he wisely wants to use data only from the previous month. Older data points may not include the latest memory technology, forms memory requirements, and recent workload activity changes. As a result, only 120 samples were chosen.

Otto needs to decide what the dependent (think Y) and independent (think X) variables should be. Because he wants to limit the memory utilization and wants to predict how many concurrent forms sessions could be supported, he decided the dependent variable would be forms sessions and the independent variable would be memory utilization.

While there are many Microsoft Excel regression analysis spreadsheets available for download, Otto went to OraPub's web site and downloaded the latest single independent variable linear regression spreadsheet. He then pasted the 120 data points into the spreadsheet.

Using the six-step process presented in this book, Otto conducted his analysis.

- **View the raw data.** Otto checked to ensure the spreadsheet considered all 120 data points. While reviewing the raw data, he noticed there were a few samples in which memory was being utilized but there were no forms sessions. At this point, he couldn't justify removing the data points, so he left them in the spreadsheet. No other strange-looking samples caught his eye, so he moved on to the next step.

- **Plot and view the graph.** The initial data plot containing all 120 samples is shown in Figure 9-19. Otto immediately was drawn to the data points on the horizontal axis. These are the samples where memory was being utilized while there were no forms sessions. Looking at the data, he couldn't see how the samples were obviously skewing the linear line, so from this perspective, he did not feel justified in removing them.

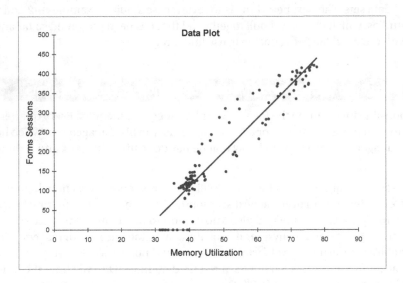

Figure 9-19. *The initial data plot containing all 120 samples*

- **View the residual data.** Otto reviewed the residual data and nothing caught his eye. He checked to ensure the spreadsheet was using all 120 data points when creating the regression formula. Otto also checked to ensure the sum of the residuals was indeed zero and found that it was. So he continued to the fourth step.

- **View the residual graph.** Figure 9-20 is the initial residual graph containing all of the original 120 samples. The residual graph clearly shows some nonlinear behavior. Similar to Figure 9-8, there is clearly a trend from upper left to lower right. There also a cluster of samples on the left above the zero line, with only a few points below the zero line. The lack of balance is a sign of nonlinearity. And finally, near the bottom left, a strange dotted line exists from the results of those "zero forms sessions." One possible way to minimize the first two problems is to remove the zero forms sessions so they don't skew the regression line.

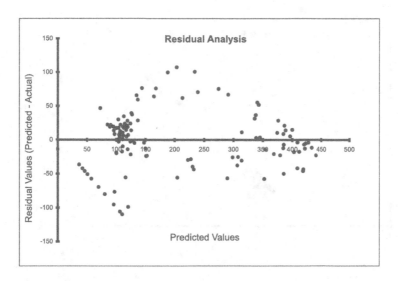

Figure 9-20. *The initial residual plot containing all 120 samples*

Otto considered the residual analysis a failure and decided the model cannot be used in its current form. He decided to continue on to view the regression formula, with the intention of removing the zero forms sessions later.

- **View the regression formula.** Otto reviewed the linear regression formula, and it looked fine. One common check he performed was to ensure that if the number of sessions increased, so would the memory utilization. The regression formula is sessions = 8.710 × memory utilization – 236.664. Otto now moved on to reviewing the regression strength.

- **View the regression strength.** Interestingly, the regression correlation coefficient is 0.95. That's an amazing correlation coefficient and typically justification for a party! However, even though the mathematics show the correlation strength is exceptional strong, Otto knows forecasting with a failed residual analysis will produce bogus forecasts.

At this point, Otto will not continue to the next step and forecast. Instead, he will remove the zero forms sessions samples and restart at the second step:

- **Plot and view the graph.** Figure 9-21 is the data plot with the ten zero forms sessions samples removed. After Otto removed these samples, the data plot looks much better, yet contains two interesting occurrences. First, the data does not follow the regression line, but rather goes around it on both sides, which is strange. The trend does appear to be strong, and the mathematics will surely derive the appropriate confidence interval to reflect data surrounding the regression line. Second, a couple of data points are related to around 20 forms sessions, yet the memory is 40% utilized. These points could most likely be removed, as they are not part of the true trend and skew the regression line slightly. For this example, the data points will remain.

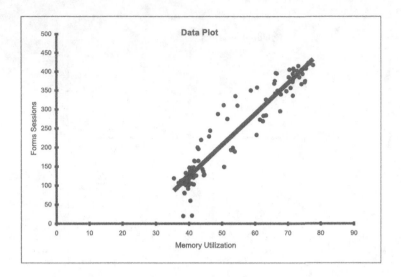

Figure 9-21. *The data plot with the zero forms sessions samples removed*

- **View the residual data.** Otto reviewed the residual data, checked that the sum of the residuals is zero, and there appeared to be no issues.

- **Plot and view the residual graph.** The residual graph is shown in Figure 9-22. With the zero forms sessions samples removed, the residual graph looks much better. You can see the two outliers near the bottom left, but as mentioned earlier, for this example, they will remain. With the residual graph being acceptable, Otto moved on to the next step.

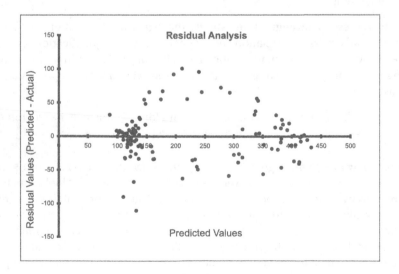

Figure 9-22. *The modified residual plot with the zero forms sessions samples removed*

- **View the regression formula.** Otto reviewed the linear regression formula and, just as before, it looked fine. The formula has changed though. The memory utilization coefficient dropped from 8.710 to 8.203. The means the memory utilization has less impact on the number of forms sessions. The new formula is: sessions = 8.203 × memory utilization – 203.914. Otto moved on to reviewing the regression strength.

- **View the regression strength.** Strange as it seems, the regression correlation coefficient is once again 0.95. As before, this signifies a very strong relationship between the number of forms sessions and memory utilization. With all the steps OK, Otto can move to forecast to answer the study question.

- **Forecast.** Near the beginning of his analysis, Otto restated the business-focused study question into a more technical-focused study question: "Can the forms server support 600 concurrent form sessions while keeping memory utilization at or below 85%?" Placing 85% memory utilization into the regression formula:

$$sessions = 8.203 * util - 203.914 = 8.203 * 85 - 203.914$$
$$= 697.255 - 203.914 = 493.341$$

At a 90% confidence level, the confidence interval is ± 46.40 sessions. This means Otto can expect the system to support 493 sessions, ± 46, 90% of the time; that is, between 447 and 540 sessions, 90% of the time. If Otto allows memory utilization up to 90%, the average number of sessions increases to 534, with a worst case 488 to 581, 90% of the time.

Based on Otto's forecast, there is little chance the system will support 600 concurrent forms sessions. While this may be bad news, Otto is now prepared to confidently speak to his management about a true risk IT will be facing. As with many forecasting situations, when the answer to the study question is something like, "We will be at risk," Otto now will need to determine when the system will be at risk and what can be done to mitigate the identified risk.

Example 9-3. Running Out of Gas at Harry's Hubcaps

Harry's Hubcaps specializes in—you guessed it—hubcaps. The company has thousands of different hubcaps picked up from roads all over the world. The business receives 100% of its sales from the Internet. People browse the company's web site looking at hubcaps, pick how many they want (usually one or four), and then place their order. Customers sometimes order by telephone, but not very often, because the web site is simple yet comprehensive. It's a great business model, and it's combined with great business systems and great people. The combination has been working well over the past five years.

With more and more people shopping on the Internet, business has been good and is expected to continue to grow over the next few years. The CIO has helped executives to understand that if the business grows, the company's current systems may not be able to handle the increased workload. While they understand this, no one in the company knows how long their systems will last before response time degradation begins to impact their business. IT has started an SLM initiative. There are many aspects to this initiative and many different systems involved. Samira has been specifically given the responsibility of determining when the company's Oracle database server's CPU subsystem will "run out of gas."

One of Samira's first tasks is to find a good predictor or predictors for the CPU subsystem. She met with business managers, end users, and IT to help determine how the growth of the business is measured and discussed. After quite a few meetings, she found they routinely refer to the growth when they mention web site visitors/hour, average order amount/hour, customer logins/hour, sales/hour, orders/hour, order lines/hour, orders shipped/hour, support calls/hour, and employees on payroll. Samira also managed to acquire *historical* data for each of these aspects of the business. For the independent variables that appear to be good predictors of CPU utilization, she will get their respective activity *forecasts* from business managers and use them during forecasts. For example, the web site visitors per hour number is expected to grow January, February, and March to 29500, 32750, and 42500.

Then for each good predictor, using the business forecasts, she will determine which month the CPUs will start to "run out of gas." Samira is going to use 75% CPU utilization as the run-out-of-gas figure. For example, suppose the linear regression formula combined with the business forecast indicate that when customer logins/hour reach 35000/hour, the CPU utilization will reach 75%. And since the business people told Samira customer logins/hour is expected to reach 35000/hour this coming July, she will expect the CPUs to become a bottleneck in July.

Because there were many independent variable possibilities, Samira created a matrix to keep track of her analysis. Table 9-6 is the result of her efforts. As typical, while many independent variables did not pass all the tests, multiple variables did pass. Many people think that only the best predictor can be used. But this is not true and limits the predictive information we can gain. For example, forecasting based on web site visitors per hour may indicate the current system can handle the load for the next six months, while logins per hour may indicate the system will be OK for the next seven months. This is like having multiple seasoned advisors—sure, they don't all agree, but the consensus can be used to deepen the analysis, resulting in a very robust recommendation.

Table 9-6. *Organizing Prospective Independent Variables*

Independent Variable	Data OK?	Data Plot OK?	Residual Data OK?	Residual Plot OK?	Formula OK?	Correlation Strength	OK to Forecast?
Web site visitors/hr	Y	Y	Y	Y	Y	0.84	Y
Avg order amount/hr	N	N	N	N	Y	0.23	N
Logins/hr	Y	Y/N	Y	Y/N	Y	0.71	Y
Employees	Y	Y/N	Y	Y/N	Y	0.67	N
Orders/hr	Y	Y/N	Y	Y	Y	0.82	Y
Sales/hr	Y	Y	Y	Y	Y	0.77	Y
Support calls/hr	Y	N	Y	N	Y	0.45	N

After reviewing the contents of Table 9-6, Samira decided to forecast using web site visitors/hour and orders/hour. (She could have also used logins/hour and sales/hour, but for this example, only the top two predictors will be used.) Samira then talked with business managers to create the activity forecasts for both of these variables. The resulting graphs are shown in Figures 9-23 and 9-24.

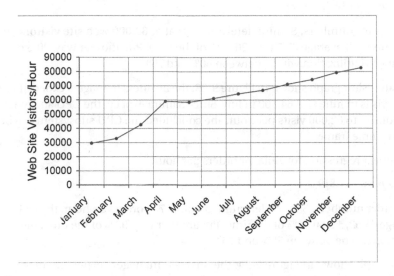

Figure 9-23. *The graph of anticipated web site visitors per hour*

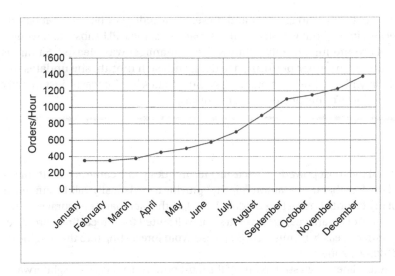

Figure 9-24. *The graph of anticipated orders per hour*

Based on the linear regression analysis, the resulting regression formulas, Samira's desire to limit CPU forecasting to 75% CPU utilization, and the anticipated business activity, Samira is able forecast which month the database server will run out of gas. She started with the web site visitors per hour forecast first, followed by the orders per hour forecast.

The following is the linear regression formula for web site visitors per hour:

$$Util = 0.000858 * visitors + 14.334$$

After trying various visitor numbers, Samira determined that at 62,000 web site visitors an hour, the CPU utilization will average 67.54, ±7.26 90% of the time. Put another way, 90% of the time, the forecast CPU utilization will be between 60% and 75%.

Looking at the web site visitor graph shown in Figure 9-23, the business managers expect there to be 61,000 web site visits in June and 64,300 in July. Since Samira expects the CPU subsystem can responsibly handle up to 62,000 visits per hour, she concluded the CPU subsystem will be fine until the June/July time frame.

The following is the linear regression formula for orders per hour:

$$Util = 0.074585 * orders + 11.819$$

After trying various order numbers, Samira determined that at 720 orders an hour, the CPU utilization will average 65.52, ±9.60 90% of the time. Put another way, 90% of the time, the forecast CPU utilization will be between 56% and 75%.

Looking at the order graph shown in Figure 9-24, the business managers expect there to be 700 orders an hour by July. Since Samira expects the CPU subsystem can responsibly handle up to 720 orders per hour, she concluded the CPU subsystem will be fine until the July time frame.

Samira is now ready to meet with management and present her findings. She said that based on the forecast model and input from various business managers, the CPU subsystem would not run out of gas until around June or July. While Samira's manager was pleased, Samira is also a realist. She continues to gather performance data, and each month, she updates the forecast model, checks in with the business managers, and updates her forecasts, just to make sure the CPU subsystem doesn't unexpectedly run out of gas.

Summary

Linear regression is one of the most powerful forecasting techniques you'll come across. Its natural business focus and the fact that it can "automatically" provide a statistically valid confidence interval make it one of my favorite forecasting models. I also like the fact that it encourages automatic data collection. It is not a panacea, however. It's not well suited for forecasting hardware configuration changes and can easily be misused. So please avoid forecasting into the nonlinear areas—what I call the "danger zone."

With all this considered, linear regression is one of the most powerful, precise, straightforward, and business-centric forecasting models available. When coupled with self-discipline and a lot of samples, I think you will find it to be an invaluable modeling technique.

CHAPTER 10

■■■

Scalability

Scalability can be defined in many ways and from many different perspectives. However, from a capacity planning perspective, a solid definition is that scalability is a function that represents the relationship between workload and throughput. The workload is essentially the arrival rate, and the throughput is the rate of work being completed. If a system scales perfectly, then a linear relationship exists between an increasing workload and the resulting throughput. But we all know that doesn't happen in real-life production Oracle systems. As I'll present in this chapter, even with very ingenious and creative approaches, there are a number of very real reasons why systems don't scale linearly.

Scalability limitations create a challenge when forecasting Oracle performance because most of our forecasting models do not consider the realities of scalability. The solution, which is much easier said than done, is to create a scalability model of your system and combine that with your forecasting model (such as Erlang C queuing theory and the essential forecasting mathematics). How to create a good scalability model of your Oracle system and combine that with your validated forecast model is what this chapter is all about.

The Relationship Between Physical CPUs and Effective CPUs

Scalability is more than a function representing the relationship between workload and throughput. When more broadly applied, scalability helps us understand the relationship between physical CPUs and their *effective application processing power* (sometimes referred to as *effective CPU power*, *effective CPUs*, or simply *power*).

As you might imagine, just as there are various ways to model transaction queuing, there are also multiple ways to model scalability. Figure 10-1 shows the graphical result of four different scalability models relating physical CPUs to effective CPUs. We will study each of these four scalability models in this chapter: Amdahl scaling, geometric scaling, quadratic scaling, and super-serial scaling. Each of these models takes as input the number of physical CPUs, along with a parameter or two, and outputs the number of effective CPUs.

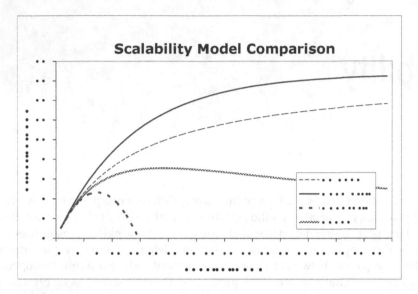

Figure 10-1. *The four scalability models (serialization parameter set to 0.06; super-serial model's additional parameter set to 0.003). The relationship between physical CPUs and effective CPUs is clearly not linear.*

Let me be a little more practical. Suppose database servers scaled linearly. Then for every additional CPU added, an additional full CPU of application processing power would be available. But you're probably not surprised that a 32 CPU database server really doesn't provide 32 CPUs of effective application processing power, nor twice as much effective application processing power as a 16 CPU system.

As an example, Figure 10-1 shows that when 20 physical CPUs are available, we effectively receive a portion of the CPU application processing power—sometimes a shockingly low portion! There are many reasons for the loss of application processing power. The most obvious is that adding more CPUs in a system requires the operating system to spend more time ensuring they are all being used as effectively as possible. Other reasons include Oracle issues and application issues. But before we get into why Oracle database servers don't scale linearly, let's consider how we can use scalability models when forecasting.

How Scalability Is Used in Forecasting

Scalability gives our forecast models an additional dose of reality. Queuing theory-based models assume that when given a CPU, the entire CPU's power is available for user-related work. This is not true, in part because a portion of that CPU's resources must be used to manage that CPU. Thus, we have the concept of effective CPU power in contrast to physical CPU power, as noted in the previous section.

To infuse that additional dose of reality into our forecast models, the physical CPUs are scaled down to effective CPUs before being placed into our forecast models. For example, if the scalability model shows that our database server's 10 physical CPUs actually supply 7 effective CPUs of power, the key is to place 7 CPUs, not 10 CPUs, into the forecast model. If a forecast predicts 12 effective CPUs are required to meet service levels, those 12 effective CPUs are placed back into the scalability model and transformed into perhaps 16 physical CPUs.

Before delving too deep into scalability issues, theory, and models, it's important not to lose sight of why scalability is important and how to practically apply scalability. Example 10-1 focuses on how to use scalability in a real-life situation.

Example 10-1. Using Scalability When Forecasting

Joseph is a capacity planner responsible for ensuring the main production database has adequate capacity to meet service levels. Joseph wants to know how many CPUs are required to bring response time out of the elbow of the curve so that queuing has virtually no response time effect.

The main production server contains 12 CPUs, and at peak processing (10 a.m. to 12 p.m. each Friday), the CPU utilization is 83% and 12.32 SQL statement executions occur each second (ex/s).

The relationship between the physical and effective CPUs was derived based on the super-serial scalability model (detailed later in this chapter). If you look closely at Table 10-1, you can see how Joseph determined the 12 CPU server delivers only 8.78 CPUs of effective, or real, power.

Table 10-1. *Relationship Between Physical and Effective CPUs Based on the Super-Serial Model* ($\sigma = 0.033$, $\lambda = 0.001$)

Physical CPUs	Effective CPUs	Utilization[1]	Response Time[1]
1	1.00	729%	−0.09
2	1.94	376%	−0.05
3	2.81	259%	−0.04
4	3.64	200%	−0.05
5	4.41	165%	−0.07
6	5.15	142%	−0.12
7	5.84	125%	−0.22
8	6.49	112%	−0.53
9	7.11	103%	−3.03
10	7.69	95%	1.74
11	8.25	88%	0.92
12	8.78	83%	0.74
13	9.28	79%	0.66
14	9.76	75%	0.63
15	10.21	71%	0.61
16	10.65	68%	0.60
17	11.06	66%	0.60
18	11.46	64%	0.59
19	11.84	62%	0.59
20	12.20	60%	0.59

[1]*Utilization and response times are based on effective CPUs, not physical CPUs.*

Before Joseph can derive the response time, he must establish the baseline—that is, the current situation at the chosen peak. The only missing value is the service time, which will be used to derive the baseline response time. To drive the point home, the following are the service time and response time calculations using both physical CPUs (12) and effective CPUs (8.78). As you can see, the results are significantly different!

Using *effective* CPUs:

$$S_t = \frac{Um}{\lambda} = \frac{0.83*8.78}{12.32} = \frac{7.29}{12.32} = 0.59\,s/ex$$

$$R_t = \frac{S_t}{1-U^m} = \frac{0.59}{1-0.83^{8.87}} = \frac{0.59}{1-0.19} = \frac{0.59}{0.81} = 0.73\,s/ex$$

Using *physical* CPUs:

$$S_t = \frac{Um}{\lambda} = \frac{0.83*12}{12.32} = \frac{9.96}{12.32} = 0.81\,s/ex$$

$$R_t = \frac{S_t}{1-U^m} = \frac{0.81}{1-0.83^{8.87}} = \frac{0.81}{1-0.19} = \frac{0.81}{0.81} = 1.00\,s/ex$$

Notice there is a significant difference in the service times, which directly impact the response times. I hope this provides some motivation to always use effective CPUs when doing serious forecasting. If Joseph were to base his decision on physical CPUs, he would likely be shocked by the poor performance, as the forecasts would be very optimistic.

Notice in Table 10-1 that at 12 physical CPUs, the observed utilization is 83%. This is the baseline and what Joseph's system exhibits during peak processing times. With a table like Table 10-1, he can view the effects of adding or removing physical CPUs. Just as important, he can determine how many physical CPUs are required to meet effective CPU requirements. Figure 10-2 shows how response time will change based on the number of effective CPUs, using the data in Table 10-1.

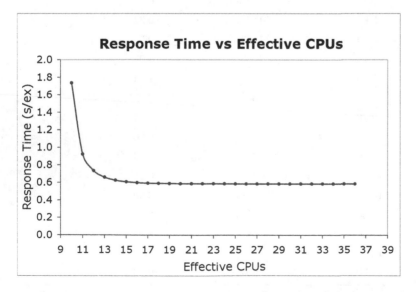

Figure 10-2. *Response time changes based on the number of effective CPUs.*

Back to the study question; Joseph needs to know how many physical CPUs are required to bring his company's current situation (83% utilization with significant queuing) out of the elbow of the curve. Looking conservatively at both Table 10-1 and Figure 10-2, the response time stabilizes beginning at around 10 effective CPUs. Reviewing Table 10-1, Joseph noticed that 10 effective CPUs will require 15 to 16 physical CPUs. Since the database server currently contains 12 CPUs, at least 3 additional CPUs would be required to bring response time out from the elbow of the curve.

What's Involved in Scalability?

Most of us in IT know in our guts that systems don't scale perfectly, no matter what the marketing literature and benchmarks claim. Besides the ever-increasing percentage of time the operating system must spend for each additional CPU, there are many other reasons why database servers don't scale linearly.

Scalability is all about seriality and parallelism. We want to minimize serialization and maximize parallelism. For example, an idle CPU is death to scalability because parallelism efforts are not able to use the idle CPU. The more processes that can run (and do application-related work) in parallel, the more scalable the system. If processes must run serially, then no matter how many CPUs a computer contains, only one CPU can be used per process, and scalability is limited.

To increase scalability, the general idea is to divide work so every CPU is involved. (The same goes for the IO subsystem.) The more a business process can be spread across multiple CPUs, the more scalable the process becomes. A perfectly scalable system will show no loss in throughput as the load on the system increases. Another way of saying this is that for every additional CPU, 100% of the additional CPU is used to do business work. As you might imagine, this is an incredibly difficult technical problem.

While those of us trained in Oracle technology tend to think of scalability as an operating system issue, this is a narrow view. Improving scalability continues to be tackled from many levels; hardware, operating systems, databases, business applications, and even businesses get involved in maximizing scalability. Here are some examples:

- Hardware manufacturers try to physically place CPUs and memory as close together as possible to reduce latency.

- Operating systems allow multiple processes to run simultaneously by attempting to break down a process into smaller components and schedule the resulting pieces on as many CPUs as possible.

- The Oracle database maximizes scalability in many ways:

  - Allows each Oracle session to have its own process (that is, a dedicated server process)

  - Divides up common work into the background processes

  - Continues to add parallelism features

  - Uses very fast mechanisms to minimize the resources and time required when memory must be accessed serially (for example, latching)

  - Allows multiple physical machines to work as a single database system

- Application developers architect their batch processes to break out and run as multiple processes.

- Businesses get involved by deploying the same application to each division.

So as you can see, scalability is not just an operating system or a CPU challenge. It affects all areas of computing, and therefore all areas of computing can get involved in maximizing scalability.

In fact, the next time someone says, "That Oracle system is a resource hog," you should say, "Yes, isn't that fantastic!" It would be a shame for users to be waiting for their work to complete when there is unused capacity available.

While sharing resources is a good thing, sharing takes effort. This effort is in the form of coordination and communication, which is essentially synchronization. No matter how many CPUs there are, at some point, resources can be utilized only serially. The more coordination and communication, the more scalability is limited. This is why even with advanced parallelism capabilities—parallel queries, parallel loading, advanced SQL execution plans, row-level locking, multiple similar latches (for example, multiple shared pool latches), and Oracle's clustering technology[1]—diminishing returns are very real and will never, ever go away. Every time communication and coordination are increased, scalability is being limited.

I find it interesting that even nontechnical people inherently know about scalability. For example, when technology is pushed as far as it can go and no more scalability is to be found, the business naturally begins to parallelize. Politics are not the only reason that large divisions or departments run the exact same application, perhaps on the same machine type, and with the same software! The businessman knows that if there isn't a computer big enough for the entire company, then perhaps there is a computer big enough to handle a division. It seems like there is always a way to increase scalability if you really need to and it's worth the cost.

You will hear and read about systems scaling to more than 1,000 CPUs. Remember that the hardware, the operating system, the database (if there is one), and the application all contribute to both increasing and limiting scalability. It's important to understand what is meant by *scaling*. Saying a system can continue to operate with thousands of CPUs does not tell us much about the degree or the amount scalability. So, sure it's possible for some systems to scale over 1,000 CPUs, but you won't see a *traditional* production Oracle database running on that system! There will be exceptions, but the hardware, the operating system, the database, and the application will all need to be involved to reach this level of useful and practical scalability.

SCALABILITY VS. QUEUING

Scalability is not the same as queuing. Given enough arrivals, queuing will occur even with perfect scalability.

For example, suppose the operating system divides a process into 100 pieces of work, yet there are only 24 CPUs. As a result, there will be 76 pieces of work queued. In this situation, scalability (that is, the ability to parallelize) is not the issue. The issue is the combination of the arrival rate, the service time, and the number of servers is causing the pieces of work to queue. However, if there were 128 CPUs, then 28 CPUs would be idle because the operating system was unable to divide the processes into 128 pieces of work. In this situation, scalability is limiting throughput. So remember that while scalability and queuing are related, they are distinct.

---

1. Just in case you are wondering, I am not implying my support or nonsupport for Oracle clustering technology (currently marketed as Real Application Clusters, or RAC). Besides the technical issues (RAC brings many), there are also the financial issues.

Speedup and Scaleup

When the word *scalability* is casually used, it is referring to one or both of the terms *speedup* and *scaleup*. By understanding speedup and scaleup, you will gain a deeper understanding of the distinct ways in which scalability is limited, as well as the basic scalability improvement alternatives.

Speedup is about getting a fixed amount of work done faster by taking advantage of additional processors. For example, if twice as many CPUs were added to the system and the process ran twice as fast, speedup would be linear. While linear speedup is possible with only a few processors, as the number of processors increases, it becomes very difficult for the process speed to linearly speed up (that is, finish sooner). At some point, work must be serially performed. The Amdahl scalability model presented in the "Scalability Models" section later in this chapter is based on intrinsic speedup limitations.

Using Oracle as an example, latching is employed to ensure certain tasks are synchronized and occur serially. So at some point, process execution will occur serially and therefore speedup cannot be linear forever. Nearly all processes have some amount of seriality that must occur. For example, a payroll batch process will have many steps that must occur in a specific order, and some steps may be dependent on multiple previous steps completing. At some point, the number of processors will exceed the amount of possible payroll processing parallelism, and the next payroll processing step will have to wait. When this waiting occurs, speedup is no longer linear.

While using faster CPUs can speed up a process (that is, it will complete sooner), the term *speedup* is not about using faster CPUs.

Scaleup is about achieving increased throughput as the load increases. For example, scaleup is linear if when the application load is doubled, the throughput is doubled. A more specific linear scaleup example would be if the number of order-entry clerks were doubled, then the number of orders processed per hour were also doubled. The smaller the individual task, the more likely scaleup can continue linearly, because all available resources (for example, CPUs) can be used.

Each of the four scalability models presented in this book, in their pure form, is directed toward speedup. The giveaway is that each has a *seriality* parameter. As you'll see when we discuss the models, we use various methods to mathematically transform a speedup-focused model into a scaleup-focused model. This is one reason why these models are commonly called *scalability models*. While not always distinguishing between speedup and scaleup can make talking about scalability easier, it does reduce the potency of discussions and can muddy the clear distinction that exists between these two concepts.

As you have probably already noticed, the interactions and effects of speedup and scaleup on real Oracle systems are somewhat fuzzy. For example, Oracle's parallel query option helps from a speedup perspective—as additional processors (CPUs or IO devices) are made available, a given query can complete sooner, because more operations can be done in parallel. But at some point, Oracle's parallel query execution plan will decide to have parts of the query performed serially. From a scaleup perspective, even when not using Oracle's parallel query capability, scaling up the number of online users to twice the original number, resulting in twice the number of queries, will not decrease query execution time. This is because each Oracle query can be associated with a single server process (dedicated server process configuration). However, at some point, scaleup will become nonlinear, and queries will need to queue until another processor is available.

When increasing application performance, one solution is to focus on speedup. For example, consider a simple Oracle data import. Suppose the import contains data for four users and is taking four hours to complete. A common solution is to break up the import by user and run all four processes simultaneously, hoping the process will complete in little more than a single hour. The goal here is speedup, as we want to decrease the duration of the process.

Another performance tuning solution is to better balance the existing workload. In this situation, we are essentially reducing, or throttling back, the workload with the intention of increasing the throughput. While this may seem strange, both the quadratic and super-serial scalability models clearly show that throughput can increase when the workload is decreased.

Our essential forecasting and Erlang C mathematics forecasting do not account for speedup or scaleup limitations, and therefore assume they are both linear . . . forever. We know this is not true. Modeling speedup and scaleup will increase our forecast precision.

Which Forecast Models Are Affected by Scalability?

The general rule is that any forecast model that has a number of CPUs (for example, m) as a parameter is affected by scalability. Consider linear regression modeling. Regression analysis is typically used to answer questions like, "How many orders an hour can this system process?" These types of questions have a fixed number of CPUs, and we are not forecasting response time. Therefore, any operating system scalability impact related to the current number of CPUs has already been taken into account.

Even with regression analysis forecasting, the scalability impact related to the Oracle database software and the order-entry system can be an issue. But experience has shown that once application-locking issues have been resolved at lower volumes, they don't tend to raise their ugly heads at higher volumes (of course, there are exceptions). And database software-related issues tend to follow the classic queuing theory response time curve pretty well. So, when using regression analysis, if you stay away from the "danger zone" where queuing lives, scalability (or the lack of it) should not be a significant issue.

If small Linux or Windows servers are being used, because of their inherent current scalability limitations, the only way to scale up to increase processing power is to add more nodes, and hope the scalability effect of those extra nodes will provide a net financial and performance gain.

The essential queuing mathematics, Erlang C-based queuing mathematics, and ratio modeling are affected by scalability. In the next section, I'll explain the most widely used scalability models and how to use them.

Scalability Models

Just as there are many forecasting models, there are many scalability models. Four scalability models are considered the classics: Amdahl, geometric, quadratic, and super-serial. They are each different and provide insights into how scalability affects real-life systems. In this section, the focus is on each of these four models. In the next section, I will show you how to more practically use the models.

You'll notice that when discussing scalability, m is not used to refer to a server. Because scalability traditionally refers to CPUs, more commonly called processors, p is used. So don't be surprised when you see p representing a processor, a server, or a CPU.

Amdahl Scaling

Amdahl scaling is arguably the most widely used database server scalability model. That said, it is also generally agreed to be somewhat optimistic because it does not consider the fact that eventually adding more CPUs or increasing the load will decrease throughput. The optimistic result could be, for example, that Amdahl scaling may transform ten physical CPUs into nine effective CPUs, when a more realistic effective number may be eight.

The Amdahl scalability model is named after its inventor, Mr. Gene Myron Amdahl. Mr. Amdahl's parents immigrated to the United States from Norway, and in 1922, he was born in the beautiful state of South Dakota. He served in the U.S. Navy during World War II, and then went on to study physics at South Dakota State University and the University of Wisconsin, where he completed his doctorate in 1952. He started working for IBM in 1952. He left IBM for the last time in 1970 (he left once before) to form Amdahl Corporation in Silicon Valley (Sunnyvale, California), where high-tech dreams are made. He then competed directly with IBM. He worked closely at times with Fujitsu, who sometimes financially invested in his ventures. He left Amdahl in 1979, and since then has been involved in various other high-tech ventures. He is most well known for Amdahl's law.

Amdahl's law is used to find the maximum expected improvement to an overall system when a part of the system is parallelized. Because a system is limited to how much work can be parallelized, there is a limit to the number of physical processors that can be effectively used.

The Amdahl capacity model is defined as:

$$A(p) = \frac{p}{1+\sigma(p-1)}$$

where p is the physical number of CPUs and sigma (σ) is the seriality parameter.

The seriality parameter has a range from zero (linear) to one (no scalability). The more parallelization a system can support, the smaller the seriality parameter. In other words, 0% seriality means 100% parallelism, which is linear scalability. The more a system can parallelize work, the closer the effective CPU number is to the physical CPU number.

Table 10-2 shows Amdahl's law being used to contrast physical CPUs to effective CPUs.

Table 10-2. *Using Amdahl's Law to Contrast Physical CPUs with Effective CPUs (σ= 0.060)*

Physical CPUs (*p*)	Effective CPUs, *A(p)*	CPU Power Lost, *p-A(p)*	% CPU Power Lost
1	1.00	0.00	0.00%
2	1.89	0.11	5.66%
3	2.68	0.32	10.71%
4	3.39	0.61	15.25%
5	4.03	0.97	19.35%
6	4.62	1.38	23.08%
7	5.15	1.85	26.47%
8	5.63	2.37	29.58%
9	6.08	2.92	32.43%
10	6.49	3.51	35.06%
11	6.88	4.13	37.50%
12	7.23	4.77	39.76%
13	7.56	5.44	41.86%
14	7.87	6.13	43.82%
15	8.15	6.85	45.65%
16	8.42	7.58	47.37%
17	8.67	8.33	48.98%
18	8.91	9.09	50.50%

Looking at Table 10-2,[2] you can see how Amdahl's law models the scalability effect. The seriality parameter is set to 0.060 and is not overly pessimistic or overly optimistic. Yet it is shocking to see the diminishing effect of adding CPUs to a system. As you can see in Table 10-2, if a forecast model calls for six CPUs, then nine physical CPUs will be required. Put another way, a nine CPU server has only six CPUs of effective CPU power.

The seriality parameter has a massive impact on the model and must be chosen wisely. Take a look at Figure 10-3, which shows the effects of various seriality parameters. The top linear line has a seriality parameter of 0—it ain't gonna happen. The more realistic parameters are 0.02, 0.04, 0.06, 0.08, and 0.10. While the various lines may look very close together, notice that they flatten relatively quickly. When the line becomes relatively flat, this means that a high number of physical CPUs is required to get just a little more effective power. So while the lines may look close together, the impact of the seriality parameter on physical to effective CPUs is significant. Later in this chapter, in the "Methods to Determine Scalability" section, I'll present ways to determine reasonable parameter settings.

■**Tip** While you will need to determine what seriality parameter matches your environment (because every system is different), for Unix environments (not Linux), 0.010 is extremely optimistic and 0.075 is very pessimistic.

2. OraPub has scalability worksheets already created. You can find them at www.orapub.com/tools.

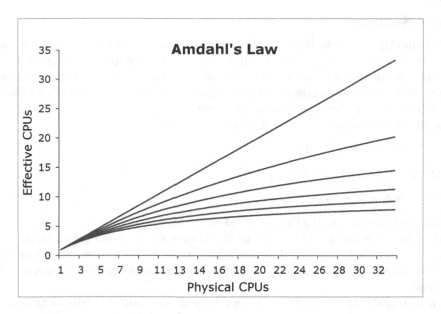

Figure 10-3. *Using Amdahl's law with different seriality parameters: from the top curve and going down, 0.0 (linear), 0.02, 0.04, 0.06, 0.08, and 0.10*

Another interesting observation about Amdahl's law is that there is a limit as to the number of effective CPUs possible. In other words, *regardless* of the number of physical CPUs, there is a limit to how much effective power the box can deliver—any box! Table 10-2 shows that once the number of physical CPUs reaches 18, you're netting about 50% of each CPU's power because of scalability issues. This can also be seen graphically by looking closely at Figure 10-3. According to Amdahl's law, the maximum effective CPU power possible is one divided by the seriality parameter. For example, if the seriality parameter is 0.060, the maximum effective CPU power is 1 / 0.060, or 16.7 CPUs. Even if the box has 64 CPUs or 128 CPUs, according to Amdahl's law, the box can deliver only 16.7 CPUs of power.

So why purchase a 64 CPU box if it can effectively deliver only 16.7 CPUs of power? The answer is that the operating system, Oracle, utilities, and the application add parallelism capabilities that *may* allow scaling beyond Amdahl's law. As mentioned earlier in this chapter, Oracle has many features created specifically to increase parallelism and allow more CPUs to be effectively used. And as I also pointed out earlier, while these types of features increase scalability, they require communication and coordination (that is, synchronization), which use a portion of the power of each additional CPU. So the diminishing returns effect will still be very real.

Regardless of the seriality parameter, scalability losses don't become significant until after there are 5 to 8 CPUs. Said another way, from a scalability perspective, architecting an operating system that can scale up to 4 CPUs is relatively easy. But when systems have 24, 32, 64, and 128 CPUs, they must employ advanced algorithms, memory architectures, and communication methods to beat Amdahl's law.

Geometric Scaling

The thinking behind geometric scaling is that CPU effectiveness diminishes exponentially. Said another way, the first CPU gives you a full fraction of power (for example, 0.86^1), the second CPU gives a fraction squared of power (for example, 0.86^2), the third CPU gives a fraction cubed (for example, 0.86^3), and so on. The fractional power parameter is called the *multiprogramming (MP) factor*, which relates to the parallelism of the system.

Mathematically, the geometric scaling formula is as follows:

$$G(p) = \Phi^0 + \Phi^1 + \Phi^2 + \Phi^3 + \cdots + \Phi^{p-1}$$

which is algebraically equivalent to this:

$$G(p) = 1 + \Phi + \Phi^2 + \Phi^3 + \cdots + \Phi^{p-1}$$

where p is the number of physical CPUs, and phi (Φ) is the MP factor.

The MP factor is the opposite of the Amdahl model's seriality parameter. If the seriality parameter is 0.25, then the MP factor is 0.75. When comparing the two models, the MP factor is commonly assumed to be one minus the seriality parameter (unless the MP factor is specifically mentioned).

Just as with Amdahl's law, according to geometric scaling, regardless of the number of CPUs, there is a limit to the amount of effective power. Because the MP factor is equivalent to one minus the seriality parameter, the maximum power geometric scaling will allow is one divided by one minus the MP factor. Mathematically, this is shown as follows:

$$G(\infty) \approx \frac{1}{(1 - \Phi)}$$

You can see this asymptotic effect for both Amdahl and geometric scaling by looking closely at Figure 10-1, shown earlier in the chapter.

Although the geometric scaling model is not used as much as the Amdahl or super-serial models, you shouldn't just dismiss it. Every production Oracle database system is unique, and you may find that your system follows a geometric scaling model very well.

Quadratic Scaling

No matter what the marketing department says, we know that if more and more CPUs are added to a system, eventually the associated overhead will cause performance to actually *decrease* with each additional CPU. Said another way, the scalability power loss continues, and eventually this power loss adds up to overtake the benefits of the additional power. This can be clearly seen in the example of using the quadratic scalability model shown in Figure 10-4 (as well as in Figure 10-1, earlier in the chapter). Neither Amdahl's law nor geometric scalability account for this harsh reality of diminishing returns. So from this perspective (and this is just one perspective), quadratic scaling is more realistic.

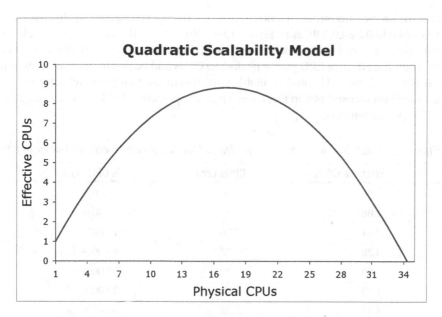

Figure 10-4. *Quadratic scalability model with an overhead factor of 0.030*

Quadratic scaling is based on the number of CPUs and also what is called the *overhead factor*. Just as with the Amdahl model's seriality factor, the overhead factor is between zero and one. Here is the quadratic scaling formula as a quadratic equation:

$$Q(p) = -gp^2 + gp + p$$

where *p* is the number of physical CPUs, and *g* is the overhead factor. The quadratic scaling formula is usually shown in this form:

$$Q(p) = p - gp(p-1)$$

While both Amdahl and geometric scaling reach a maximum number of effective CPU power and stay there (for example, $A(p) = 1 / \sigma$), quadratic scaling reaches a theoretical CPU power peak and then quickly starts eating away at the effective CPU power. The effective CPU peak function is as follows:

$$P_{max} = \left[\frac{1+g}{2g} \right]$$

The graph shown in Figure 10-4 is based on an overhead factor of 0.030. The maximum theoretical CPU power occurs at 17 physical CPUs. Here's the math:

$$P_{max} = \left[\frac{1+g}{2g} \right] = \left[\frac{1+0.030}{2*0.030} \right] = \left[\frac{1.030}{0.060} \right] = \left[17.167 \right] = 17$$

If you look closely at Figure 10-4, you can see the peak of the curve is at 17 physical CPUs, which correspond to about only 8.5 effective CPUs!

Table 10-3 shows the interesting effects of scalability based on quadratic scaling with an overhead factor of 0.060 (not 0.030, as in Figure 10-4). Notice how the effective CPUs climb rapidly (1 to 4), but then start to diminish (4 to 6) until there is no additional effective CPU gain (8 to 10). Then the effective CPU power peaks at 9 CPUs and begins to decrease (10) until finally there is effectively no CPU power available (18)! Also notice that the percentage of CPU power lost is a constant increase (4% in this case). Once the percentage of lost power hits 100%, no effective CPU power remains!

Table 10-3. *Effects of Scalability Based on the Quadratic Model with an Overhead Factor of 0.060*

Phys CPUs	Effective CPUs	CPUs Lost	% CPUs Lost
1	1.00	0.00	0.00%
2	1.88	0.12	6.00%
3	2.64	0.36	12.00%
4	3.28	0.72	18.00%
5	3.80	1.20	24.00%
6	4.20	1.80	30.00%
7	4.48	2.52	36.00%
8	4.64	3.36	42.00%
9	4.68	4.32	48.00%
10	4.60	5.40	54.00%
11	4.40	6.60	60.00%
12	4.08	7.92	66.00%
13	3.64	9.36	72.00%
14	3.08	10.92	78.00%
15	2.40	12.60	84.00%
16	1.60	14.40	90.00%
17	0.68	16.32	96.00%
18	−0.36	18.36	102.00%

Super-Serial Scaling

The super-serial scalability model (also called the super-seriality model) was developed by Neil Gunther. With the inclusion of an additional parameter (a coefficient), the super-serial model embodies characteristics of both Amdahl's law and quadratic scaling. The additional coefficient and quadratic characteristics give the super-serial model the potential to better represent scalability in an Oracle environment compared with the other scalability models presented in this chapter. Figure 10-5 shows an example of using the super-serial model.

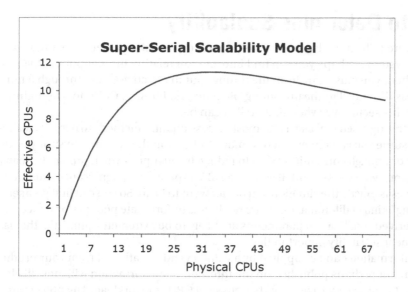

Figure 10-5. *The super-serial model with both parameters set to 0.03*

The super-serial model is defined as follows:

$$C(p) = \frac{p}{1 + \sigma\left[(p-1) + \lambda p(p-1)\right]}$$

where p is the physical number of CPUs, sigma (σ) is a measure of contention (for example, waiting for a latch or a lock), and lambda (λ) is a measure of coherency in the system (for example, issues with synchronizing a CPUs cache with another CPUs cache and Oracle cache misses).[3] If you play with the two parameters, you'll notice the sigma parameter more directly controls the initial scaleup portion of the curve, and the lambda parameter more directly controls the downward slope of the curve.

The way the super-serial function is typically written doesn't make it easy to see how this function embodies a quadratic equation. However, it can be algebraically manipulated to highlight this quadratic aspect.

Through Oracle's wait interface, Oracle contention (for example, latch wait) and coherency (for example, buffer busy wait) timing can be gathered. This provides an opportunity to derive the model's parameters. However, before realistic model parameters can be derived, significant contention must exist in the Oracle system. This presents a problem. Our goal is usually to predict when contention will be significant, and we would certainly prefer that to be in the future, not now! To get good parameter values, data must be collected at least up to the point of diminishing returns. We hope this situation does not occur in a production Oracle system. You also need to be prepared to perform some basic numeric transformations from load and throughput to physical CPU and effective CPUs, as described in the next section.

Even with the challenges of determining scalability parameters (which are not unique to the super-serial model), once the parameters are discovered, the super-serial model will most likely provide the best real-system fit compared with the other models discussed here.

---

3. For more information related to the super-serial model parameters, search the Internet for "scalability super serial."

Methods to Determine Scalability

It is exceedingly rare to be provided with robust scalability model parameters that represent your production system. Perhaps you can find information relating throughput to physical CPUs, but even then, you must transform the throughput to effective CPUs (through a normalization process described in the upcoming "Benchmark: Physical CPUs-to-Throughput Data" section). If this seems overwhelming, well, it can be.

It can be frustrating when you learn that most discussions and methods to derive scalability parameters assume you can either add or remove CPUs from the system (physically or by software control) or enough contention exists to reduce throughput (which probably means the users are unhappy with the system). If you are a DBA, experiencing significant contention for shared resources is exactly the situation you do *not* want to be in. So you can find yourself in a "chicken-and-egg" kind of dilemma. If you are not in this unfortunate poor performance situation, then the derived serialization parameters are likely to be extremely optimistic; that is, espousing near linear scalability opportunities.

Scalability information can be supplied by a willing vendor, gathered from your production Oracle system, or perhaps published on the Internet. The information will most likely relate throughput (think vertical axis) to either physical CPUs or workload. The presentation can be in either tabular format or a graph. It is rare to be provided with a clear relationship between physical CPUs and effective CPUs. It just makes it too easy for anyone to quickly draw comparisons between vendors without the help of a nontechnical commission-based vendor sales representative. But there are exceptions, especially if you have a good relationship with your hardware vendor.

Once you have scalability information, you will need to fit the information to the best scalability model and determine its associated parameters. This is not as difficult as it may seem.

In the next few sections, I will step you through how to effectively use supplied and gathered information to find a realistic scalability model and its associated parameters.

Physical-to-Effective CPU Data

Although you might be given a table or a graph relating physical CPUs to effective CPUs, this is unusual (as it allows a simple and direct scalability comparison between vendors). If you do have access to such a table or a graph, your job of determining the best-fit scalability model and its related parameters is greatly simplified.

If scalability data was provided by your hardware vendor, realize that the data was probably gathered from a specially optimized system for scalability testing, and therefore that data should be considered optimistic until proven otherwise.

Table 10-4 is an example of a table that can be used to find the best-fit scalability model based on vendor-supplied scalability figures.[4] All three scalability models (I chose not to include geometric scaling to simplify the example.) have their scalability parameter initially set to a value of 0.03, and the super-serial model's lambda value is 0.03. By changing the scalability parameters and examining the modeled values versus the vendor-supplied values, you can identify the best model.

---

4. I tried to get real vendor data for this book, but the vendors I asked became surprisingly quiet—or perhaps that's not so surprising.

Table 10-4. *Finding the Best-Fit Scalability Model Based on Vendor-Supplied Data*

Physical CPUs	Modeled Effective CPUs			Vendor-Supplied Effective CPUs	Model Absolute Value Accumulated Error		
	Amdahl	Super	Quadratic		Amdahl	Super	Quadratic
1	1.00	1.00	1.00	1.0	0.00	0.00	0.00
2	1.94	1.94	1.94	2.0	0.06	0.06	0.06
3	2.83	2.82	2.82	3.0	0.20	0.21	0.21
4	3.67	3.63	3.64	3.9	0.38	0.44	0.42
5	4.46	4.39	4.40	4.7	0.59	0.72	0.70
6	5.22	5.10	5.10	5.5	0.86	1.11	1.09
7	5.93	5.75	5.74	6.2	1.13	1.56	1.55
...	...	...	...	...	...	...	...
24	14.20	10.97	7.44	12.2	14.65	14.98	34.90
...	...	...	...	...	...	...	...

Numerical analysis is helpful, especially when verbally conveying information. But when you're trying to convince people of a best-fit line, there is nothing like a graph. Figure 10-6 graphs the data shown in Table 10-4 *after* the scalability model parameters were altered in an attempt to find the best fit with the vendor-supplied data. One way to find the best-fit graph is to change the various scalability parameters while watching the graph change.

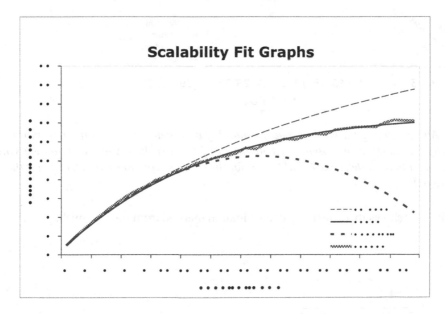

Figure 10-6. *The graph of the three scalability models and the vendor-supplied values from Table 10-4. By changing the scalability parameters (which has not yet occurred), the best-fit line can be discovered.*

To find the best scalability model fit, I always consider both the numeric data and the visual graph. I start by changing the various model parameters, minimizing the average error and standard deviation. The Microsoft Excel Goal Seek (mentioned in Chapter 5 and shown in Figure 5-36) and Solver[5] tools can be very handy! However, one problem with completely automating the process is that all data points tend to be considered, but you may never attempt to scale out that far. For example, Figures 10-6 and 10-7 show the scalability effect up to 36 CPUs. You may be interested in scaling only up to 24 CPUs. In this case, you would try to match the scalability models up to 24 CPUs, not the entire 36 CPUs.

Once scalability contention sets in, the scalability models and the vendor-supplied data rarely match, creating a significant residual (that is, model error, as explained in Chapter 9). The numeric best fit can obviously not look like the best fit. But the initial numeric approach is a good way to get a pretty good first fit. Then begin changing the parameters while carefully watching the graph. Repeating this process, you'll eventually discover the best fit for each scalability model. Figure 10-7 shows the visual results of the initial numeric process.

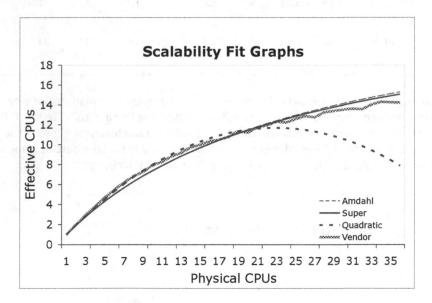

Figure 10-7. *After changing the various model scalability parameters, the best-fit model parameters for 24 physical CPUs were chosen based on numeric fit. The scalabilty model parameters are 0.0386 for the Amdahl model, 0.0386 and 0.0007 for the super-serial model, and 0.0223 for the quadratic model.*

Example 10-2 shows this scalability determination method from start to finish.

---

5. Microsoft Excel Solver is essentially a more advanced Goal Seek tool. While Solver is more complicated and there is a learning curve, its capabilities extend far beyond Goal Seek's equality seeking capabilities.

Example 10-2. Vendor-Based Scaling

Samuel is a DBA responsible for ensuring the main production database has enough capacity until the next budget cycle, which is nine months away. Each month, Sam revalidates his forecast models and then forecasts based on growth trends and business growth information. The main production database resides on a 12 CPU server, and utilization peaks at around 65%. In nine months, the workload is expected to double, from 6.11 executions per second (ex/s) to 12.22 ex/s. Samuel needs to know how many additional CPUs will be required (if any) to keep CPU utilization at 70%. Samuel was given scalability information from his hardware vendor. This is the same information shown in Table 10-4.

To begin, Samuel created a spreadsheet like the one shown in Table 10-4 with the Amdahl, super-serial, and quadratic scaling models. He performed both numeric and visual analyses to find the best-fit model. His analyses showed all three scalability models matched the vendor-supplied data up to about 12 to 13 physical CPUs, but then they significantly diverged. As you can see in Figure 10-8, the super-serial model produced by the far the best scalability match. The scalability model parameters are 0.0300 (Amdahl), 0.0300 and 0.0135 (super-serial), and 0.0250 (quadratic).

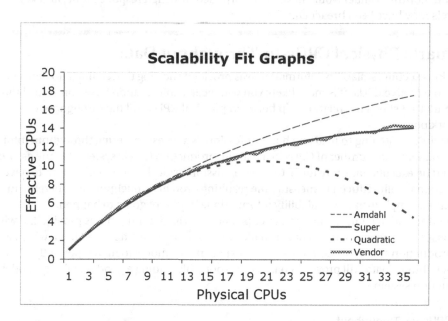

Figure 10-8. *The result of matching sample vendor-supplied scalability with various scalability models. Notice that all the models match the vendor data very well until around 13 physical CPUs. The scalability parameters are 0.0300 for Amdahl, 0.0300 and 0.0135 for super-serial, and 0.0250 for quadratic.*

Based on the super-serial scalability model, the vendor data, and the 12 CPU database server, the server is effectively providing 8.67 CPUs of power. Using the essential forecasting mathematics, 8.67 effective CPUs, an arrival rate of 6.11 ex/s, and a peak CPU utilization of 65%, Samuel calculated the missing CPU service time:

$$S = \frac{Um}{\lambda} = \frac{0.45 * 8.67}{6.11} = \frac{3.90}{6.11} = 0.64\,s/ex$$

In nine months, the arrival rate is expected to double, pushing 12.22 ex/s into the database server. Based on this expected arrival rate increase, a service time of 0.64 s/ex, and the CPU utilization at 70%, Samuel calculated the number of effective CPUs required:

$$m = \frac{S\lambda}{U} = \frac{0.64 * 12.22}{0.70} = \frac{7.82}{0.70} = 11.17$$

The forecast calls for 11.17 effective CPUs. Using the same scalability table and figure (see Figure 10-8) he used to determine the effective CPU power based on the number of physical CPUs, Samuel determined the number of physical CPUs based on the number of effective CPUs. To provide 11.17 effective CPUs of power, by referencing Figure 10-8, Samuel found he needs 19 physical CPUs.

Samuel recommended that his company budget for 19 CPUs, thereby providing about 11 effective CPUs worth of power. Obviously, scalability is very significant for this database server. About 40% of the physical CPU power is lost due to scalability. If scalability were not considered, in nine months, Samuel would have been surprised by a high response time, and key service levels may have been breached.

Benchmark: Physical CPUs-to-Throughput Data

In the previous section, scalability information was provided showing the relationship between physical and effective CPUs. It is more likely you will receive information based on some kind of benchmark that shows the relationship between physical CPUs and the throughput of some defined workload mix.

It's certainly frustrating to read and hear professionals suggest gathering throughput information by changing the number of CPUs in a real-life production Oracle system. Let me assure you, it would be exceptionally rare for IT to allow a mission-critical production system to have its CPUs systematically reduced to measure the resulting drop in throughput (and increase in response time!) simply to gather scalability information. That's not going to happen.

When information relating the number of physical CPUs to throughput is provided, it will surely be based on a benchmark. All benchmarks are based on a specified workload, which is not your production system's workload, so don't expect the numbers to match perfectly. However, the benchmark data will provide a basis for responsibly finding a good scalability model for a production system.

Physical CPUs vs. Throughput

Throughput is how much work actually occurs within a period of time and is expressed in terms of work per unit of time. Throughput, X, is a function of the number of physical CPUs, p, and is therefore commonly shown as $X(p)$. Without contention, the relationship between physical CPUs and throughput is linear. When the load begins to increase, so does throughput. But at some point, the load induces significant contention, and throughput begins to decrease. Figure 10-9 is an example of throughput and load before and during contention. This pattern occurs with all real Oracle production systems.

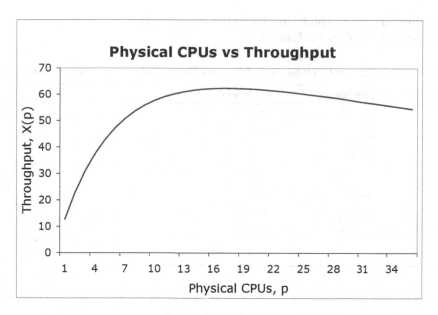

Figure 10-9. *The relationship between physical CPUs and throughput before and during significant contention. Without contention, the relationshp is linear.*

Normalizing Throughput Based on Physical CPUs

As Figure 10-9 shows, while the number of physical CPUs is known, the number of effective CPUs is *not* known. We must transform the throughput relationship to an effective CPU relationship. You probably noticed Figure 10-9 looks similar to the scalability graph in Figure 10-5. This is because the relationship between physical CPUs and effective CPUs is equivalent to the relationship between physical CPUs and throughput. Here is the mathematical representation:

$$X(p) \approx C(p)$$

where *C(p)* is a scalability function or model, such as Amdahl's law.

To establish the relationship between physical and effective CPUs, we must first establish a relationship between throughput and effective CPUs. This can be accomplished by normalizing throughput data in relation to physical CPUs, which is actually very easy to do. Here is the equation:

$$C(p) = \frac{X(p)}{X(1)}$$

where $X(1)$ is the throughput with one CPU, $X(p)$ is the throughput at p CPUs, and $C(p)$ is the effective CPU power.

For example, based on the throughput data in Table 10-5, if the number of physical CPUs, p, equals 2, then:

$$C(2) = \frac{X(2)}{X(1)} = \frac{22.7}{12.5} = 1.8$$

For each physical CPU data point, just follow this pattern. Partial results are listed in Table 10-5 and graphically shown in Figure 10-10.

Table 10-5. *Calculating Effective CPUs Based on Physical CPUs and Throughput (Figure 10-9 Data)*

Physical CPUs	Throughput	Effective CPUs
p	$X(p)$	$C(p)$
1	12.53	1.00
2	22.66	1.81
3	30.86	2.46
4	37.51	2.99
5	42.91	3.42
6	47.28	3.77
. . .	. . .	. . .

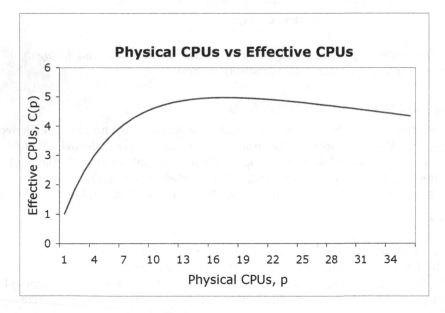

Figure 10-10. *The results of calculating the effective CPUs based on throughput and physical CPUs*

Once the throughput has been normalized, you can use the resulting table (for example, Table 10-5) and the graph (for example, Figure 10-10) to determine the number of effective CPUs based on the number of physical CPUs (or vice versa).

But suppose the benchmark tested (or most likely, *published*) data for only 1 to 12 physical CPUs, but you need data up to 32 CPUs. That's not a problem. Just as we have done previously in this chapter, simply match the available data to the best scalability model to determine the relationship between physical and effective CPUs, and you're all set! Now you can determine the number of effective CPUs related to 32 physical CPUs. Looking at Figure 10-10, you can see that 32 physical CPUs provide effectively only 4.5 CPUs of power!

Real System: Load and Throughput Data

In this chapter, I've demonstrated that a suitable scalability model can be determined when the relationship between physical and effective CPUs is known or the relationship between throughput and physical CPUs is known. This section focuses on determining realistic scalability models (and parameters) when the load and throughput are known.

It would seem obvious that the best scalability model parameters would come from real Oracle systems. While this is true and the quest a noble one, it is extremely difficult and laden with problems. But before I dig into the challenges, a clear distinction between load and throughput must be established.

Load vs. Throughput

Read this slowly: the load, N, is the number of workload category occurrences creating work for the system—for example, 91 OLTP users. Throughput, X, is how much work actually occurs within a period of time and is expressed in terms of work per unit of time—for example, 114,000 Oracle SQL statement executions per minute. Just as with the number of effective CPUs, $C(p)$, throughput, X, is also a function of the load, N, and thereby commonly shown as $X(N)$.

Without contention and scalability issues, the relationship between load and throughput is linear. For example, suppose there is no queuing and there is plenty of parallelism. In this case, nothing stops throughput from increasing at the same rate as the load. But when there is contention or a lack of parallelism of any kind, throughput will not increase as fast as the load increases. In fact, at some point, the throughput will actually begin to decrease as the load continues to increase. You may have worked on a system where the load increased so much that the work users could accomplish decreased. This relationship is shown in Figure 10-11.

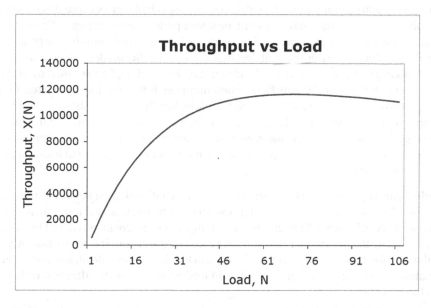

Figure 10-11. *As the load increases, if contention or the lack of parallelism exists, throughput will eventually not scale linearly (that is, throughput will not increase at the same rate as the load). If the load continues to increase, at some point, throughput will begin to decrease.*

Interesting, though probably not surprising, is that the relationship between load and throughput is reflected in the relationship between physical and effective CPUs (see Figure 10-1 and Figures 10-3 through 10-8). This is why the relationship between physical and effective CPUs can be established by knowing the relationship between load and throughput. But as I mentioned earlier, there are significant challenges in establishing the relationship between load and throughput.

The Challenges

The following are the primary challenges that must be faced when attempting to determine scalability based on a real production Oracle system using load and throughput:

Load and throughput representations: Both values must be a fantastic general representation of the system. Benchmarks can make determining scalability using load and throughput seem so simple because there is a straightforward and well-defined load, such as 1,500 scripts running simultaneously. But Oracle workloads are rarely this simple. If a system is dominated by OLTP activity, then perhaps the load can be represented by the number of Oracle sessions. However, most production systems contain a mix of OLTP and batch activity. When this occurs, the number of sessions is no longer a good general load representation. You will probably need to experiment using different load and throughput sources. Be prepared for the possibility that you may not be able to find suitable sources.

The need for a contention-laden system: When gathering load and throughput data, some of the gathering must occur when throughput is being affected by scalability issues; otherwise, the nonlinear part of the scalability curve cannot be determined with any degree of confidence. Gathering throughput-affected data becomes a challenge because this typically does not occur unless the system is experiencing severe performance problems. So you will need to wait until the system is experiencing severe performance problems before good data can be gathered. But the very purpose of developing the scalability model is to be proactive and not let poor performance occur! It's the classic "chicken-and-egg" situation. A subtle yet important fact is that the throughput-killing contention needs to be scalability-related. Concurrency issues directly affect parallelism and therefore directly affect scalability. In Oracle, concurrency issues manifest as latching, waiting for buffers in Oracle's cache, and row and table locking. If throughput is decreasing, yet Oracle concurrency issues are not significantly increasing, then a decrease in throughput may be the result of a high arrival rate and not because of scalability issues.

The math: Assuming good data has been gathered, the challenge then becomes a mathematical one. The load and throughput relationship must be normalized and transformed into a physical and effective CPU relationship. A number of steps are involved, but the results are truly amazing. But remember that the data must be good, and it is very unlikely you will be able to collect satisfactory data. If you want to follow this path, do an Internet search for "scalability super serial fit," and you should find an article or two that will walk you through the process.

I don't want to discourage you from attempting to derive scalability based on your real Oracle system, but I do want to paint a realistic picture. If you choose this path, give yourself plenty of time, be prepared for the possibility of not being able to establish a realistic scalability function, and be ready to perform some numerical normalization and transformations. If you do establish a realistic scalability model based on your real production system, you should be very proud.

Summary

While scalability can be defined in many ways and from many different perspectives, from a performance-modeling perspective, it is a function that represents the relationship between workload and throughput. Through creative mathematics, this function can be transformed into representing the relationship between physical CPUs and effective CPUs.

Scalability is especially important when forecasting changes in the number of CPUs or IO devices. Queuing theory does not embrace the realities of scalability, so if we do not create a scalability model and combine that with our forecasting model, our forecasts can be overly optimistic and less precise.

There are many ways to model scalability. In this chapter, I presented four ways to model scalability. The trick is finding the best scalability model fit (which implies finding the best parameters) and appropriately using the scalability model to your advantage. It sounds all so simple, but the realities of production Oracle systems, marketing-focused benchmarks, and vendors wary of easily comparing their systems to their competition make gathering scalability information a challenge.

Aside from forecasting, I find it intriguing and very interesting to observe how hardware vendors, operating system vendors, database vendors, application vendors, and even businesses continue to find ways to increase parallelism, thereby reducing the throughput-limiting scalability effects. Because in our hearts, even if we are not technically focused, we know that increasing parallelism can increase throughput. And increasing throughput can ultimately mean increased profits for the business IT was created to serve in the first place!

Index

Get the eBook for only $10!

Now you can take the weightless companion with you anywhere, anytime. Your purchase of this book entitles you to 3 electronic versions for only $10.

This Apress title will prove so indispensible that you'll want to carry it with you everywhere, which is why we are offering the eBook in 3 formats for only $10 if you have already purchased the print book.

Convenient and fully searchable, the PDF version enables you to easily find and copy code—or perform examples by quickly toggling between instructions and applications. The MOBI format is ideal for your Kindle, while the ePUB can be utilized on a variety of mobile devices.

Go to www.apress.com/promo/tendollars to purchase your companion eBook.

⟨ IOUG ⟩
independent oracle users group

For the Complete Technology & Database Professional

IOUG represents the **voice of Oracle technology and database professionals** - empowering you to be **more productive** in your business and career by **delivering education,** sharing **best practices** and providing technology direction and **networking opportunities.**

Context, Not Just Content

IOUG is dedicated to helping our members become an #IOUGenius by staying on the cutting-edge of Oracle technologies and industry issues through practical content, user-focused education, and invaluable networking and leadership opportunities:

- *SELECT Journal* is our quarterly publication that provides in-depth, peer-reviewed articles on industry news and best practices in Oracle technology

- Our #IOUGenius blog highlights a featured weekly topic and provides **content driven by Oracle professionals and the IOUG community**

- Special Interest Groups provide you the chance to collaborate with peers on the specific issues that matter to you and even take on leadership roles outside of your organization

- COLLABORATE is our once-a-year opportunity to connect with the members of not one, but three, Oracle users groups (IOUG, OAUG and Quest) as well as with the top names and faces in the Oracle community.

Who we are...

... **more than 20,000** database professionals, developers, application and infrastructure architects, business intelligence specialists and IT managers

... **a community of users** that share experiences and knowledge on issues and technologies that matter to you and your organization

Interested? Join IOUG's community of Oracle technology and database professionals at www.ioug.org/Join.

Independent Oracle Users Group | phone: (312) 245-1579 | email: membership@ioug.org
330 N. Wabash Ave., Suite 2000, Chicago, IL 60611

Printed in the United States
By Bookmasters